# THE RELIGION FACTOR

# THE RELIGION FACTOR

*An Introduction to How Religion Matters*

WILLIAM SCOTT GREEN
AND JACOB NEUSNER
*editors*

Westminster John Knox Press
Louisville, Kentucky

© 1996 Westminster John Knox Press

Interior photographs and illustrations courtesy of Art Resource of New York from Giraudon and Foto Marburg, France.

*Book design by Jennifer K. Cox*

*Cover design by Kevin Darst*

*First edition*

Published by Westminster John Knox Press
Louisville, Kentucky

This book is printed on acid-free paper that meets the American National Standards Institute Z39.48 standard. ∞

PRINTED IN THE UNITED STATES OF AMERICA

96 97 98 99 00 01 02 03 04 05 — 10 9 8 7 6 5 4 3 2 1

**Library of Congress Cataloging-in-Publication Data**

The religion factor : an introduction to how religion matters /
    William Scott Green and Jacob Neusner, editors — 1st ed.
        p.    cm.
    Includes bibliographical references and index.
    ISBN 0-664-25688-0 (alk. paper)
    1. Religion.  2. United States—Religion.  I. Green, William
Scott.  II. Neusner, Jacob, date.
BL48.R42   1996
200—dc20                                              96-21466

# CONTENTS

**Part 2. Religion in the Political Realm**

**Part 3. On Living Justly with Others:
Gender, Family, and the Ethic of Care**

**Part 4. Religion and the Imagination**

**Part 5. Religion and Death**

# ACKNOWLEDGMENTS

Both editors express thanks to their universities for ongoing support. That support not only takes a material form but also provides a context for their work in the world of the academy. The academy is the only place in which people ask about not religions but religion; it is the locus for generalization, the center where people gather in search of the governing rules for the very particular phenomena that religions set forth. In the other-than-academic centers of learning, whether religious or ethnic, people lay great stress on specific religions but rarely compare one religion with another or propose to generalize from religions about the character of religion. Both editors of this book find themselves in academic departments of Religious Studies in which specialists in various religions seek to learn, and to teach, about religion as exemplified by religions. Each university's department undertakes its special work, with the University of Rochester attracting some of the best undergraduates America has to offer and the University of South Florida undertaking the urgent tasks assigned to a full-service university on the urban frontier. The fact that in such remarkably different universities the study of religion flourishes as it does attests to the power of the subject and its everyday urgency.

Jacob Neusner further enjoys the advantage of teaching not only at a vast state university but also at a tiny liberal arts college. The Department of Religion at Bard College forms an intellectual community engaged in everyday conversation about important matters. The department has undertaken to compile, under Neusner's editorship, the Pilgrim Library of World Religions, initially planned as five volumes on how principal religions address common human questions. Bard's Department of Religion includes experts on Christianity, Islam, Judaism, Hinduism, and Buddhism, and in addition to their specific chapters, William Green provides the introduction and conclusion of each volume. So the partnership represented by this book, involving the departments of Religious Studies at the University of Rochester and the University of South Florida and Bard College, will continue.

As visiting professor of religion at Bard College, Jacob Neusner receives a research grant and expresses thanks to the president and to the dean of the faculty of Bard College, Dr. Leon Botstein and Dr. Stuart Levine, respectively, for their support and cordial interest in his research. He organized and undertook his share of the editing of this book principally at the University of South Florida, which has afforded an ideal situation in which to conduct a scholarly life. He expresses thanks not only for the advantage of a Distinguished Research Professorship, which must be the best job in the world for a scholar, but also for a substantial research expense fund, ample research time, and some stimulating and cordial colleagues. The University of South Florida, like the other institutions among the ten universities that comprise the Florida State University System, exemplifies the high standards of professionalism that prevail in publicly sponsored higher education in the United States and provide the model that privately sponsored, elite universities would do well to emulate. Here there are rules; achievement counts; and presidents, provosts, and deans honor and respect the university's principal mission: scholarship, scholarship alone—both in the classroom and in publication.

For William Green, the Department of Religion and Classics at the University of Rochester constitutes a working environment of persistent intellectual collegiality, stimulation, and support. The collegiality of Edward Wierenga, Douglas Brooks, Emil Homerin, Joseph Brennan, Curt Cadorette, and Anne Merideth in religion, and Deborah Lyons, Kathryn Argetsinger, and Dan Beaumont in Greek, Latin, and Arabic makes learning and teaching not only possible, but meaningful.

William Scott Green
University of Rochester

Jacob Neusner
University of South Florida and Bard College

# CONTRIBUTORS

Diane Apostolos-Cappadona, *Georgetown University*

Malcolm David Eckel, *Boston University*

John L. Esposito, *Georgetown University*

Sam Gill, *University of Colorado*

Andrew M. Greeley, *University of Chicago and University of Arizona*

William Scott Green, *University of Rochester*

Peter J. Haas, *Vanderbilt University*

Danny L. Jorgensen, *University of South Florida*

Martin E. Marty, *University of Chicago*

Bonnie J. Miller-McLemore, *Vanderbilt University*

Mozella G. Mitchell, *University of South Florida*

Jacob Neusner, *University of South Florida and Bard College*

Michael Novak, *American Enterprise Institute*

Stephen G. Post, *Case Western Reserve University*

Susan Brooks Thistlethwaite, *Chicago Theological Seminary*

John Updike

Robert Wuthnow, *Princeton University*

# INTRODUCTION

Religion makes an important difference in the lives of nations, peoples, communities, and individuals. In this book we ask, How does religion matter in the everyday lives of ordinary people and in the present-tense affairs of the communities in which we live? The emphasis is on our own country, the United States. Religion—so we maintain—makes a vast difference in the social order, and for most Americans it forms a primary fact of life. But how, in concrete terms, are we to identify the difference religion makes? The contributors to this volume provide answers to that question. Some of the writers approve of their findings, others do not approve; but all care passionately about religion and devote their lives to the study of the difference religion has made and still makes today.

If religion matters a great deal, then is religion a good thing? The answers prove surprising. Whereas some authors take a positive view of the difference religion makes, others do not concur. Both perspectives on the way in which religion shapes everyday life, personal and social, demand a hearing. But our main task here requires not judgment or evaluation of whether or not religion is a good thing but rather a set of instances in which religion plays a major role in ordinary affairs. Readers will find in these pages useful examples of how religion matters, from which they may frame for themselves a range of answers beyond those given here.

In these pages, all of us ask of our subjects, So what? Perhaps no question provokes, annoys, and unnerves students and scholars alike more than this one. But it is the key question in learning about any subject, including religion: If I know this, what else do I know? In terms set forth here, the contributors ask, So what? What difference does it make? Are you telling us something new, something insightful, something important? Why should we have a stake in what we are learning? And the main question that "So what?" provokes in response is this: If I know what you say, what else do I know, and how better do I understand things, and what further learning or insight should I then seek? Since these chapters about how religion matters in various perspectives on society, in diverse dimensions of personal life, speak to people who are studying about religion, let us turn from the subject to the circumstance: the study of religion and why "So what?" demands an answer.

This book is a companion to *World Religions in America* and tells the other half of the story that began there.[1] In that book, experts on the main religions of the world today answered three questions: What is this particular religion? How does it find a home in America? and In what ways has America changed, and been changed by, this religion? The strength of that work flows from the passion of its writers—scholars who care deeply about their subjects. With great power, each participant sets forth facts, the doctrines, communities, and normative practices of the range of religions practiced in America, the abstractions of their place in the American social order. That is one part of the task. Here we tell the other part of the story, which concerns the ways in which various religions matter in concrete and immediate terms, framed not as "Christianity teaches . . ." and "Islam maintains . . ." but rather as "Christians struggle with these problems" or "Muslims work out their place in the social order in those ways." It is a book not of large pictures and generalizations but of cases and instances. We cannot hope to portray all the ways in the world in which religion matters, so we focus on concrete examples—largely but not exclusively from contemporary America—that show how religion works in the everyday world that we all know and share. From the facts that answer theoretical questions we move to the human meaning of religion.

Other subjects do not demand that people ask, "So what?" In sciences and some social sciences—the problem-solving ones—the "So what?" usually is evident in a well-crafted experiment that makes plain in its problem and procedures how it is giving a new, better, or definitive answer to an established question or how it is posing a new question on the basis of new information. But religion straddles the border between the social sciences and the humanities, and much that we learn about religion comes to us in the media of humanistic learning: texts and artifacts that are the products of culture and have been around for a long time. When we speak of sacrifice, we do not go out and buy a lamb and kill it and flick the blood on an altar. We read the book of Leviticus and learn about the rite of sacrifice in the arid language of a book about it. So when we want to know about religion, we usually get our learning from books rather than from direct observation of how things are in real life. And we can readily lose sight of the fact that in everyday life religion is a matter of not description but of confrontation and engagement.

Thus the "So what?" of our work is not always so plain. What we study when we learn about religion—the texts and artifacts in art, literature, classics, philosophy and theology, music, religion, and, occasionally, history and anthropology—takes on a life of its own. We examine the things people have made because they are religious, but often we do not work our way back from the result of religion—the way in which the making of these things reveals why religion matters to that person or group—to the experienced reality of religion, whether personal or social. We focus on the facts without remembering the human reality that they represent and convey. Picture it this way: it is as though, in genetics, we might trace genes that cause a particular trait but take no interest in how that learning could help us understand matters and even improve them.

But our frequent neglect of the human reality of religion is not the only reason for our conviction that learning about religion requires us to learn how religion matters. There is also the matter of difference: the otherness of all religions but our own, if we have one, or of religion in its entirety if we do not. Someone else's religion may seem remote from our own experience. Much that we learn about religion focuses on abstract questions: belief, ritual, history, theory. But religion makes a difference in the here and now, which the theory and history can illuminate. If we learn how to see the religions of others as efforts to work out a human dilemma or confront a critical social issue, another's religion takes on a shared humanity, a common sensibility. The details of a particular religion, bizarre and exotic to us as they may seem, point to what we, too, address. Our capacity for empathy, for seeing the common humanity in the other, accords us the power to make sense of what seems to be nonsense. And that is the reward we seek in pursing the question of how religion matters. From the answers given by other religions, we work our way back to the questions that confront us all.

Some fields of learning lose sight of the human value of what is learned. With that loss we abandon the possibility that learning can make a difference. To choose just one current example, a leading academic journal recently published an article titled "Can Classics Die?" that chronicled the depressing decline and efforts at survival of the study of the classics, a subject that once seemed central to all humanistic learning.[2] In other fields, such as

English and history, the number of student majors has declined by half. Professors who cannot answer the urgent questions students bring to class make themselves irrelevant. Professors of English who cannot say what literature is or is not, professors of history with no story to tell, only opinions taken out of today's world and imposed in judgment on times past, have lost their students because they have lost sight of their subjects and of why people should want to learn those subjects. In urgently pursuing the issue of how religion matters, we mean to focus attention on the main point: learning, yes, but for the purpose of understanding. We do not want the study of religion to lose touch with its subject in the way in which the studies of literature and history and the classics have lost their way.

Therefore, we mean to build a bridge between the study of religion as a matter of theory and the confrontation of the reality of religion in the social order and in the unfolding of human lives. Religion matters because it infuses the life of a community that takes its shape around religious briefs and practices; because it defines the right and wrong, the meaning and the goal, of personal lives; and because in the public life of this country, religious convictions spill over into people's aspirations for political action. Whether on the Left, with its conviction that support for the weak and the poor forms God's highest demand of us, or on the Right, with its belief that the unborn child has the right to life, religion can be the primary source of political activity as well as personal opinion. Out of religion come definitions of virtue, ethical behavior, and right ways of thinking. Out of religion emerge visions of the good and just society. From religion people derive the strength to live through disappointment, suffering, and sorrow and the purpose to form lives of hope and renewal.

No author of these chapters maintains that religion brings about only what is good and constructive in the world. The headlines in the daily newspaper would mark us as naive and silly if we thought so. But we all concur that religion matters a great deal, and in spelling out some of the many ways in which religion makes a difference in practical matters of everyday intimacy, we hope to open up areas for further reflection on the here and now of religion. In a field in which the there and then of texts, history, and theory predominate, introducing important learning about the workaday world and the immediate present can only restore and renew our work.

We do not advocate religion or religiosity. We do believe, however, that religion makes an enormous difference in the world. The chapters in this volume are neither naive nor romantic about religion, and they paint a picture of religion that is not uniformly complimentary or positive. Their descriptive concreteness and specificity help us see religion's capacity for partisanship and pettiness as well as its power to uplift and transform. The chapters also show us that—in contemporary America, at least—religion does not always dominate the lives of its practitioners. Rather, religion often is in competition with other sets of values and duties and can create as much tension as it can resolve. Indeed, in some cases we will see religion seemingly at odds with itself, as different components of a religious tradition appear to make conflicting claims on its adherents.

## WHAT YOU WILL LEARN IN THIS BOOK

The book begins with what is personal and individual, set forth in six chapters on "Religion and Identity." They demonstrate, each in a different way, what religion can contribute to a person's self-understanding, to one's basic orientation and sense of persistence and continuity from day to day. Andrew Greeley describes the interplay of religion and ethnicity among the Irish and Italians in America and shows how difficult it is to separate the ethnic from the religious. Martin Marty focuses on the Gulf War and the Civil War, examining the conflicting demands of religion and nation, which are particularly acute when patriotism is perceived as a religious virtue.

Jacob Neusner offers a different perspective on the relationship of religion and ethnicity, using Judaism as an example. Jews form an ethnic group, and some Jews constitute a religious community. The paramount status accorded to Jewish ethnicity in America requires us to consider the ways in which there is, in addition to ethnic Jewishness, religious Judaism. Every religious community that is comprised of people of a common ethnic and cultural origin, whether national like Armenian Christians or worldwide like Catholic Christians, will understand the problem of finding the line between elements that directly reflect an ethnic background, such as certain foods, and religious convictions. So Neusner raises the question of Jewish "identity" by displaying the profoundly religious character of the Judaic category "Israel." His use of classical Judaic sources demonstrates that this question has persisted in the Jewish religion and shows how the classical sources continue to matter.

Greeley, Marty, and Neusner all deal with religions and questions reasonably familiar to most Americans. By contrast, Sam Gill draws us into the world of the Australian Arrarnta and their exceedingly interesting religion, in which a person's identity is, in part, determined by the mother's physical location when she discovered she was pregnant. Gill shows that "every Arrarnta person's identity is connected with a complex of interconnected ideas: country, *Alcheringa,* storytrack, and aspect of nature" and that, among the Arrarnta, identity is part of the explanation of the natural world. Then, lest we think that the attachment of identity to nature is a feature of faraway religions, Danny Jorgensen supplies a rich description of neopaganism in contemporary America and, using the example of an individual named Donna, shows how the "sacred reality" of witchcraft shapes both community and identity.

Finally, we turn to how religion matters for African Americans, the remarkable contribution religious beliefs and institutions have made to the African-American quest for dignity, equality, and inner conviction. Mozella Mitchell describes how religion helped Howard Thurman transcend the experience of racism and oppression to become the visionary founder of the Church for the Fellowship of All Peoples. The religious basis of Thurman's identity ultimately led him to see beyond a particular tradition and to develop an institution that he hoped would transcend tradition, nation, and ideology.

In Part 2 we move from the personal to the political. This section shows how religion can inform and drive political and economic behavior. Michael Novak argues that "religion is not outside life, or above it, but within it, at the heart of everyday activities," and he devotes the bulk of his chapter to an analysis of the papal document *Centesimus Annus* and its judgment about the centrality of creativity and community in the creation of economic growth. Novak suggests that attitudes toward nature that emerge from the biblical tradition inform the Western use of nature to increase wealth, and he argues that political economy—including business ethics—is not and cannot be immune from religion.

Robert Wuthnow also suggests that religious values can and do shape political behavior, and he uses a case study to make his point. In his description of the religious career of a young woman named Annalee, he shows how religious people become politically active. He suggests that five components combine to bring religious values into the political realm: social support, a sense of threat, leadership, religious belief, and communication. His article shows why religion and politics cannot, in principle, be kept separate. That point is underscored dramatically by John Esposito in an analysis of the interrelationship of religion and politics in Islam, with special attention to Egypt.

Part 3, "On Living Justly with Others: Gender, Family, and the Ethic of Care," carries us to matters of right and wrong, good and evil. Here we pass from the "is" to the "ought." The section addresses the issue of how religion structures our relationships and sense of obligation to those with whom we live in community, including our families. Persisting human community is unthinkable without family, and family is unthinkable without a theory of gender to guide the relationships between men and women. Susan Brooks Thistlethwaite suggests that "powerful religious symbols" are "organized by sex difference" and that the gender roles constructed and promulgated by religions have been less than beneficial to the ideal of equality for men and women. She concludes, "The origins of modern religions in the social and political turmoil of the axial age are translated today in the arrangement of human society according to hierarchical power relations of men over women, both in the public sphere of economics and politics and the private sphere of home and marriage."

Continuing in this vein, Bonnie Miller-McLemore shows that mainline Protestantism has been ambivalent on the question of the family. Her chronicle of her own efforts to balance her religious understanding with the demands of modern family life graphically illustrates what she terms the "age-old, still unresolved tensions between ideals of equality and ideals of male responsibility and between the claims of faith and the claims of family."

If religion has the capacity to thwart the development of equitable gender relations, it also has the power to provide a sure guide to the care of other human beings. Peter Haas examines the interplay between religion and ethics by showing how, in Judaism, an ethical decision is made on religious grounds. The case he considers entails a family's wish not to prevent the death their ill mother desires for herself, and he describes in detail the roles precedent and rabbinic authority play in the Judaic ethical process. Again, as in Miller-McLemore's article on family, part of the ethical problem is the balancing of different and apparently contradictory religious claims. The task of rabbinic authority is to show that the claims work together toward a common purpose. In the next chapter, Stephen Post takes up the theme introduced by Haas and sketches the different roles religion has played and can play in the realm of medicine. Again, he demonstrates that religious principles can both advance and derail happiness.

Parts 4 and 5 take up the issues of "Religion and the Imagination" and "Religion and Death." Religion informs the everyday world not only through the formal activities of organized religion but also through the creation of powerful structures that both inspire and shape the imagination. Diane Apostolos-Cappadona examines how religion "makes space" in her treatment of religion and sacred space. She returns to the theme of identity and shows how sacred space contributes to identity's formation. John Updike illumines religion's role in the formation of the Western literary tradition. He allows us to peer over the shoulder of America's premier writer as he reflects on the power of religion to define culture.

Finally, there is the matter of death. Nearly all the themes of the earlier pieces emerge in a fresh way in Malcolm David Eckel's description of the Buddhist way of death. The key to his essay is the way Buddhist living is the preparation for Buddhist dying, the way religious theories of death inform concrete behavior in life.

The book concludes with William Scott Green's essay on religious difference. Green suggests that the United States Constitution's commitment to freedom of religion is at the foundation of the widespread American belief in the value of a pluralistic society. He suggests ways in which a biblical model of difference has shaped Western ideas about diversity.

## WHAT IS AT STAKE?

The question "So what?" has a special relevance to religion because of the widespread assumption that religion deals with fantasy and belief rather than reality and knowledge. This book disproves such notions. It shows the vitality of religion—both constructive and destructive—in the thoughts, actions, and decisions of everyday life. As the study of religion has grown in American universities, it has experienced a strong tendency to treat religion systematically, in terms of histories, doctrines, texts, and artifacts. All these are important, and without them we would be poorer analysts of the living traditions than we are. But the living tradition—or religion lived—also is part of our study, and we hope this work can help lived religion find its proper way into, and its place in, the discourse of the study of religion. Surely our textual studies can benefit—all are important, but any study may benefit from the companionship of studies and descriptions of the concrete.

What is at stake in this book for the world beyond the classroom? A focus on the concrete is not merely an academic matter. It affects the broader public as well. In the spring semester of 1995, under the direction of William Scott Green and Nancy Woodhull, the latter a founding editor of *USA Today*, thirty-seven senior religion majors classified every reference to religion—from story to allusion—in seven national newspapers for one month (February 6 to March 5). The papers were the *Seattle Times*, the *Los Angeles Times*, the *Dallas Morning News*, the *Atlanta Journal and Constitu-*

*tion*, the *Washington Post*, the *New York Times*, and the *Chicago Tribune*. By tracking the images of religion that appear in the press day by day, the study achieved a unique national perspective on the public perception of religion in America. The results of the study were stunning and help explain the rationale for this book.

First, in the newspapers examined, religion was everywhere and nowhere. Religion was mentioned nearly two and a half times more often than it was the focus of a story on its own. The news media assume that religion is an essential part of the background of the news, and stories refer to religion frequently. But the media have trouble telling religion's story.

Second, stories about religion very often miss the point. Just 25 percent of all news stories, and only 21 percent of those on the religion page, were about beliefs and values, the core of the religions themselves. Other themes were political and legal issues (37%), illegality (19%), and internal organization (17%). Overall, these figures suggest that the media tend to apply the news criteria of politics to stories about religion.

Third, when the media do focus on the beliefs, values, and practices of a religion, the stories are often inaccurate and misleading.

The news media are not hostile to religion, but reporters are uncertain about how to cover it. Ironically, the First Amendment itself may make us gunshy of religion. Because religion is not studied in most public schools, Americans assume that religion is merely and only a matter of private opinion, rather than public conversation. Because we never learn how to think or talk with our neighbors about religious differences—in stark contrast to politics and economics—we suppose religion is primarily about feelings. We thereby unwittingly ignore or trivialize what is central in many of our neighbors' lives. The American public reflects those assumptions and treats religion as faith, not fact. But faith is a very visible fact of American life. To nurture our pluralism, we need to know why and how the beliefs and values of religious people translate into behavior. To do so, we need to see religion in practice as well as in theory, and we need to include in our study the places in which religion matters.

## NOTES

1. *World Religions in America: An Introduction* (Louisville, Ky.: Westminster/John Knox Press, 1994) was a Library Guild Selection of Methodist Church Libraries for 1994 and a Jewish Book Club Selection for July 1995.

2. "Can Classics Die?" *Lingua Franca* (September–October 1995): 61–66.

# PART 1

---

# RELIGION AND IDENTITY

# 1

## ANDREW M. GREELEY

# Religion and Ethnicity

### INTRODUCTION

Identifying with a group with whom one shares (or is thought to share) a common origin, common experiences, common memories, common beliefs, and common values is a means of self-definition and social location in a complex society. It answers in part the questions of who one is and where one comes from and whom one can trust in a social environment that is both puzzling and problematic. This identification can be based on religion, nationality, country of origin, race, and even geography. Often it is based on a combination of these factors.

Normally the word *ethnicity* is used as an umbrella term under which these various forms of identification—and the social structures and cultures that emerge from or accompany identification—can be grouped. The simple term *ethnic,* however, contains so many complicated and ambivalent connotations and so much moral and ideological weight that one must use it with caution. For some it may mean nothing more than good pasta, while for others it may mean deep-seated grievances that can tear a society apart. Whether ethnic identification is good or not is beside the point. In any large modern society there will be ethnicity. The pertinent question is, Under what circumstances can ethnic tensions be resolved by peaceful adjustment and compromise, and under what circumstances will such tensions become destructive to a society?

# THE EXAMPLE OF
# ITALIAN AMERICANS

Most Italians who came to America during the last great wave of European migration at the end of the nineteenth and the beginning of the twentieth century were hardly aware that they were Italians. The new Italian state had only just emerged. The immigrants thought of themselves as Sicilians, Calabresi, Baresi, Neapolitans, Modenesi, or Genovesi. They were quite conscious of the differences among these groups (and some of them still are), and they settled in neighborhoods where many, if not most, of their neighbors were from the same region and even from the same village. But these distinctions were too subtle for the American host society, which disliked and feared the immigrants from southern Europe. The National Commission on Immigration (often called the Dillingham Commission after the name of the congressman from New York who chaired it) wrote them all off as Italians, and indeed, as a people with a natural propensity to crime, an "innate criminal type."

Thus defined as *Italians,* the immigrants responded with the type of historic claim made by all immigrant groups to America, that they were "Italian Americans" and proud of it. They also discovered that this self-definition, linked for most of them with a parallel identification with the Roman Catholic Church, provided a base for political power, a support community, financial and commercial resources, and a culture to be proud of. Was Michelangelo an innate criminal? they asked rhetorically of the nativists who despised them.

Identification as Italian Americans also justified and reinforced the preservation of a subculture that emphasized family—and in particular, intense family relationships—more than did the host society. Research that my colleagues and I have done on family life in Italy and America demonstrates that family relationships among Italian Americans are similar to those among Italians and that these patterns are unaffected by education or age or generation in America.

Despite the continuation of anti-Italian prejudices and stereotypes (reinforced by the *Godfather* films), Italian Americans have become phenomenally successful. Their college attendance rate (for young people of college age) passed the national average in the 1940s and continues to be well above the average. Of the immigrant groups, only the Irish and the Jews surpass the Italians in income, occupational prestige, or educational attainment—and the Italians are close behind the Irish.

Some things have changed. While Italian American words and phrases (often colorful) persist, as do the appropriate gestures and facial expressions, the third and fourth generations (grandchildren and great-grandchildren of the immigrants) rarely are fluent in the Italian language. Not particularly devout Catholics in southern Italy, Italian Americans have become more "religious" in America, in part because the local parish (often with an Italian-speaking priest) became a center of immigrant community social life in a way the church was not in the old country and in part because of the influence of Catholic parochial schools, which Italians saw (as did other urban immigrants, both before and after them) as a path to upward mobility.

American society continues to be ambivalent about Italian Americans. The "godfather" stereotype persists, as does the assumption that Italians are becoming (and eventually will become) just as "American" as everyone else.

The organized-crime stereotype does not merit refutation, but it is nonetheless a major obstacle for Italians seeking national political office. The assimilation assumption is equally ridiculous, as the steady output of books and films about Italian family life should have made evident even in the absence of the empirical data that are now available from studies of Italians in Italy and Italians in America. Even intermarriage with members of other cultures (usually Catholic and most often Irish) has failed to diminish the powerful and appealing family subculture that the immigrants brought with them.

The question then arises whether pressure ought to be brought on Italian Americans to become like "everyone else." Or should the rest of American society become complacent over the alleged decline of the Italian-American subculture? Would it be a better America if Italian foods and Italian restaurants slowly diminished and then disappeared from our country? Would the cultural life of America be improved if the special visions of Italian-American filmmakers such as Martin Scorsese and Francis Ford Coppola were not replaced in the next generation? Would the nation be better off if there were no more movies like *My Cousin Vinnie* or *Moonstruck?*

And if Italian Americans are to be pressured into giving up their subculture, why should the pressures stop there? Logically, African Americans, Asian Americans, and Jews should be pressured to give up their subcultures too. While Italians are certainly not designated beneficiaries of the multiculturalist emphasis in the America of the 1990s, one nonetheless may wonder why some groups are chosen for such benefits and others are excluded, why some kinds of diversity are celebrated and others are ignored or dismissed as unimportant or irrelevant.

## THE AMERICAN ABILITY
## TO COPE WITH DIVERSITY

Despite the fact that Americans have traditionally resented and feared foreigners (and the outcry against undocumented aliens in the last decades of the twentieth century is merely the most recent example of nativist xenophobia), the success of immigrants in America and the preservation of their subcultures have not torn American society apart. Rather, one could make the strong case that immigrant groups such as the Italians have enriched the country and that their contributions could be both cherished and celebrated.

The pertinent question should be, How have the American polity and social structure been able to integrate, with a minimum of conflict, new immigrant groups with their distinctive subcultures in the midst of a persistent latent hostility to immigrants? Little attention has been devoted to this question even by the country's finest scholars, mostly because of the nativist assumption in the upper levels of the academy that "white ethnic" diversity is "going away." This assumption, combined with stereotypes about the "white ethnics," is refuted by massive empirical evidence, which nonetheless has had no impact on the scholarly elite that often is worried about multiculturalism.

At least three factors seem to be at work in America's success at coping with ethnic diversity, of whatever variety:

1. The United States has historically required only allegiance to the Constitution as a criterion of citizenship. The ability to speak English became a requirement only at the beginning of this century. Whatever nativist bigotry might demand, the country does not require that new citizens give up any element of their own heritage.

2. The prosperity of the United States has made it possible for all immigrant groups (except African Americans who were not voluntary immigrants) to become successful in America in a relatively short period of time and for their children to exceed the success of the native-born Americans. When there is more than enough prosperity to go around, interethnic conflict often becomes unnecessary.

3. There is no history of bitter conflict among the larger white ethnic groups as there is among, let us say, the various Balkan nationalities in their native lands. The Italians and the Irish have never oppressed or murdered each other in the old countries. Indeed, in many parts of Italy there is strong devotion to Irish saints who brought Christianity back to the peninsula after the first waves of

"barbarian" invaders (San Donatu in Florence, for example). While it is true that conflict over political and economic turf exists in the American urban context, hardly ever (save among criminal gangs during Prohibition) has this conflict become murderous. While the Poles have reason to resent Germans and the Irish to resent the English, these resentments, even in the old countries, have rarely produced mass violence.

The United States therefore has been fortunate (some might say lucky) in its ability to cope with diversity. The balance, based as it is on the assumption of equal opportunity, may be a delicate one. It remains to be seen whether the imposition of racial quotas and the assumption that some groups are more worthy of respect than others in the final decades of the twentieth century will destroy the national consensus that holds nativism in check. Punitive legislation against Mexican immigrants suggests that the consensus is under assault.

In contrast, the Italians, who were condemned by the country's elites and who never had a quota in their favor, are not likely to feel anything more than mild resentment against quotas and multiculturalism, if only because reverse discrimination against them is unlikely to affect many Italian Americans. In times of serious economic hardship, however, reverse discrimination might have a much more serious negative impact on American pluralism.

## THE EXAMPLE OF THE IRISH

The story of the Irish is much like that of the Italians, though three aspects of the Irish immigrant story merit consideration:

the influence of Irish Americans on political problems in Ireland;
the popularity of being Irish, despite the persistent negative stereotype of the group;
the religious differences between Irish Catholics and Irish Protestants.

### The Irish and the American Political Scene

Irish Americans provided decisive financial and political support to the cause of Irish independence in the late nineteenth and early twentieth centuries. Faced with powerful anti-Irish bigotry, Irish Americans were convinced that only when Ireland took its "rightful place" among the nations would Irish Americans be respected. This argument turned out to be mistaken. Anti-Irish bigotry continued long after the establishment of the Irish Free State in 1922. However, it is doubtful that the final expulsion of the English from the twenty-six counties of the Free State would have occurred if it had not been for Irish-American money and political pressure. In this respect the Irish were like other American ethnic groups, such as the Jews and the Greeks and the Poles, in their attempts to influence events in their land of origin.

After the establishment of the Free State (which became Eire and then the Republic of Ireland, and eventually, simply Ireland), most Irish Americans lost interest in the politics of Ireland. Some Irish money went to the support of the Irish Republican Army (IRA) in ensuing years, but despite efforts of the Irish and British governments to scapegoat Irish Americans for the violence in the separated six counties, in truth only a few Irish Americans were aware of the complexities in Northern Ireland, and fewer still contributed money to continuation of the conflict. However, when the IRA announced a cease-fire in 1994, a number of prominent Irish Americans were involved in the prelude to the end of the fighting, most notably Senator Edward Kennedy and his sister Jean Kennedy Smith, then the ambassador of the United States to Ireland. The beginning of peace negotiations also increased interest in Ireland among many Irish Americans.

### The Irish Identity

In the journals and the cartoons of the nineteenth century (and especially in the popular cartoons of Thomas Nast), the Irish were depicted as savage, apelike brutes with clubs in one hand and a large container of alcohol in the other, or as slovenly and stupid maids (the names Brigid and Nora became negative stereotypes). "Irish Catholic" is still an epithet among some members of the country's intellectual and cultural elite, mostly because of a residue of anti-Catholic bigotry, which has not been extirpated. Research findings about the enormous success of and persistent political liberalism among Irish Catholics are still dismissed out of hand.

In fact, however, being Irish is extraordinarily popular in the United States. According to work done by Professor Michael Hout, approximately four million Irish have immigrated to the United States. By natural increase, there should be approximately fourteen million people who identify as Irish. In fact, forty million so identified themselves in the United States Census. Using the somewhat stricter definition of primary ethnic identification in the NORC surveys, the number would fall to almost twenty-five million Americans who identify themselves as Irish. Hout offers no explanation for the difference between fourteen million and the higher numbers, save that perhaps in intermarriages there is a tendency to identify with the Irish. Just as a drop of "Negro blood" was enough to make one a "Negro" in the Jim Crow South, so perhaps a single Irish grandparent or great-grandparent is enough to give one the right to claim to be Irish in contemporary America. Unpopular with the elites, the Irish seem very popular with the rest of America.

### Irish Catholics and Irish Protestants

While the United States Census, in a notable repression of freedom of legitimate academic inquiry, refuses to ask a religious question, survey results show that approximately half the Americans who describe their national background as Irish also describe their religion as Protestant. So surprising does this finding seem to many that an African-American scholar once wrote to me rejecting it on the grounds that he couldn't image an American Protestant admitting that he was Irish. In fact, he seemed to have forgotten about George Wallace, Richard Nixon, Jimmy Carter, and, more recently, Bill Clinton.

Irish Protestants live disproportionately in rural areas and in the South, especially in the rural South. Most of them are descendants of families that came to America before 1850, and they are Baptists, not Presbyterians as we might assume. Their educational and occupational achievements are relatively low, the result probably of their southern and rural backgrounds.

Who are they? Apparently they are a mix of various groups—Scotch-Irish Presbyterians who migrated from Ulster before and immediately after the Revolutionary War to escape the taxes they were required to pay to the established church and to improve their financial situation; Celtic Irish who had converted to Protestantism during the Penal times; and Irish Catholic day laborers who came to America—especially to the South—in the years before the famine, seeking land of their own. This last group of "bog Irish" were Irish-speaking and only loosely affiliated with the Catholic Church. In the absence of priests, they drifted away from Catholicism within a generation or two.

Despite the differences of background, religion, and public notoriety, there are some similarities between Irish Catholics and Protestants. For example, both display high levels of emotional well-being and a propensity to choose occupations in government service.

The phenomenon of two different branches of the American Irish illustrates strikingly a phenomenon that exists in many ethnic groups—timing.

The date of immigration to America has a profound effect on different waves of immigrants. Both the condition of the sending society and the condition of the host society can have a considerable impact on the development of an American ethnic group.

On balance, the United States has been able to absorb so many different ethnic groups because the hyphen in the hyphenated American is, in fact, an equal sign, a way, perhaps, of recalling the land left behind and honoring the culture brought along but also, and more important, a way of proclaiming one's Americanism.

Ethnic identification is also an option in American society that is more available to some than to others. In theory, no one is constrained to be an "ethnic." Moreover, the degree of intensity of ethnic identification is thought to be a matter of personal choice. In practice, however, it is not always that simple. It is relatively simple if one wishes to proclaim that one is no longer Welsh or Welsh-American but simply American. It is more difficult for one to announce that one has ceased to be Italian-American; still more difficult to deny that one is identified as Jewish; and most difficult of all to reject African- or Asian-American[1] identification.

## RELIGION AND ETHNICITY

Clearly, religion is an important part of ethnic identification. Members of many ethnic groups are bound together even more tenaciously by the fact that they share a common religion. In some groups, particularly the Orthodox, the church becomes the center of community life with an intensity that is even more vigorous than that of the East European Catholic "nationality" parishes. Whether "Jewishness" is determined by being part of a religion or an ethnic group is a matter of much debate within the Jewish community. Some deny that being Jewish is a matter of religion at all. Others assert that if it is not religious, it is nothing. To many outsiders, it seems to be both.

The issue is, To what extent can religion be separated from nationality? For instance, are Albanian Orthodox Albanian because they are Orthodox or Orthodox because they are Albanian? Is their religion shaped by their ethnic background and their national pride? Would they still identify themselves as Albanian if there were no Albanian Orthodox Church? Similar questions could be addressed to Irish and Italian and Polish Catholics, to German Lutherans, to Scottish and Dutch Calvinists.

The answer is not as easy as the question. Most devout folk would choose religion as their primary identifying factor if they were forced to make a choice, but even the particular form their religion takes is—in part, at least—shaped by the national heritage to which they owe some (even unconscious) affiliation. Often religion represents, as it does in Northern Ireland, for example, one of many factors—economic, social, cultural, historical—that constitute the memories of shared experiences that shape an ethnic heritage. The religious differences between or among ethnic groups may be less theological than historical (as is surely the case in Northern Ireland), but that does not make such differences any less religious either in the minds of those within a group or in the obvious sense that different groups have different "stories" of what life means. (Catholics in Northern Ireland are perhaps somewhat more dour than their coreligionists in the Republic—and not without reason. But they are nowhere near as dour as their Presbyterian neighbors.)

It should also be remembered that in practice Catholicism is an extremely flexible religion and can adjust with greater or lesser ease to almost any culture in which it finds itself. If Irish and Polish styles of Catholicism are different in the United States, the reason is that, while both groups are devout, their religious practices differ greatly in the old countries.

In theory, then, it is difficult, if not impossible, to separate religion from ethnicity. In practice, any attempts to do so are doomed to be self-deceptive, if not dangerous—as when church planners try to merge Mexican and Italian parishes.

## ETHNICITY ELSEWHERE

American ethnicity is a complex, albeit relatively peaceful, phenomenon. Despite the tensions, let us say, between blacks and whites in American cities, the violence between them is not at all like that between Catholics and Protestants in Northern Ireland or Serbs and Croats in the Balkans. Outside the United States, ethnicity or nationalism tends to be much more dangerous. Of the fifty million people who have died in armed conflict since the end of the Second World War, most have perished in "ethnic" conflicts—in Rwanda, Burundi, India, Pakistan, Bangladesh, Angola, Mozambique, Indonesia, Algeria, and the former Yugoslavia, for example. In some cases the combatants are of the same religion (Catholicism in Rwanda and Burundi; Islam in Pakistan, Bangladesh, and Algeria). In other situations they have the same skin color or the same, or very similar, historical experiences. In many cases (Bosnia or Indonesia, for example) the groups that suddenly begin killing one another have lived together in relative peace for decades. In what was once Yugoslavia, the killings went on apparently with the sanction of the churches that are an important part of the ethnic identity of the various southern Slavic peoples. In most places where ethnic genocide has taken place, an outsider would find it difficult to distinguish between the conflicting groups. Not many Americans would be able to tell the difference between an Ibo and a Yoruba in Nigeria, any more than a Nigerian could, without considerable experience, distinguish between a "Prot" and a "Teague" in Northern Ireland. It is the neighbor who is almost the brother that we are most likely to kill.

Americans were astonished that when the socialist empire folded, so many of the old nationalist conflicts in Eastern Europe erupted again. In fact, with the exceptions of the Balkans and the Caucasus, post-socialist Europe has remained peaceful to the mid-1990s. The British, French, Italians, Spaniards, Swedes, and Germans seem finally to have resolved conflicts that date back to the time of Charlemagne. War among these countries is almost unthinkable and has been replaced by polite wrangling within the bureaucracy of the European Union. If the Quebecois should someday separate from the rest of Canada, the separation may be messy and ill-tempered, but it will hardly be violent, much less genocidal. Even in the so-called Commonwealth of Independent States (the former Soviet Union), ethnic conflict is mostly occasional (again, with the exception of the Caucasus). The triumph of reason over the old hatreds is by no means complete, as the violence within the so-called United Kingdom reminds us. Yet there seem to be reasons for hope that at least in the European and North Atlantic worlds, diversity can exist without generating violence. In Africa and Asia, there is much less reason to be sanguine.

## CONCLUSION

It is not helpful, however, to decry the resurgence of tribalism around the world. The very word *tribalism* has come to mean the offense of those who belong to different tribes from our own. American foreign policy, made by men and women who themselves have often been deracinated by their education in elite graduate schools, has all too often been based on the premise that tribalism is yielding to the "universalism" of the "modern world." This is a dangerous fallacy for anyone who must deal with tribes other than one's own to believe. Because humankind is the product of its own past, and because it tends to identify in some way or other with particular places (what else would one expect of a reflective primate?) and with those with whom it perceives itself as sharing history, territory, and beliefs, there will always be ethnic diversity. The question is not whether the species can afford ethnicity as the globe becomes one marketplace and one polity. Ethnic identification is not an option.

The question is, rather, how diversity can be tolerated and perhaps, eventually, even enjoyed without humans feeling justified by such differences in killing one another. Surely one conclusion that we must come to is that the worst of the world's political criminals are those who stir up ancient ethnic hatreds as a means to political power, especially when these demagogues happen to be the leaders of religion.

## NOTE

1. Such politically correct terms as *Asian* or *African* or *Hispanic* or *Native American* subsume substantial diversity. Most Hispanics, to say nothing of Asians, would identify with the nation of origin (or in the case of Puerto Ricans, commonwealth of origin).

## STUDY QUESTIONS

1. What are two benefits that come with identification with a group? Can you think of others not mentioned by Greeley?

2. Why, according to Greeley, is the term *ethnic* complicated and ambivalent? Do you agree with his explanation? Why? Why not? Can you think of other reasons that a term like this carries such ambiguous connotations?

3. What are at least four benefits of identifying the self with an ethnic group, for example, with Italian Americans? Do you see similar benefits through identification with your own ethnic tradition? Explain your answer.

4. Name at least two difficulties that may arise by associating the self with an ethnic group. Again, use Italian Americans as your example. Have you had similar difficulties from within your own ethnic tradition? Explain your answer.

5. What are three factors at work in the American success in coping with ethnic diversity?

6. Name at least three places outside America where ethnicity is a far more volatile issue. Why do you think that such divisions exist?

7. Give two reasons it is difficult, if not impossible, to separate religion from ethnicity.

# 2

## MARTIN E. MARTY

# Religion and Nationality

Religion, at least in the modern world, cannot get along without coming to terms with nations, nationality, and nationalism.

Nations, at least in the modern world, welcome the support of religious groups. When nations oppose religion, they sometimes develop forms of nationalism that also look and act like religions.

Look at old films of Adolf Hitler preaching hate at a Nuremberg, Germany, rally; watch films of the ceremonies marking the death and entombment of Chairman Mao Tse-tung of China. You will there see the anti-Christian Nazis and the antireligious Communists trying to satisfy needs that religion usually has met.

Religious people need symbols, such as the menorah, the cross, the lotus, and the crescent. The totalitarian nationalist, for whom the nation offers and demands everything, will offer substitutes: the swastika, the hammer and sickle. Religious leaders tell stories in the form of myths. These are not ordinary stories; they are extraordinary ways of making "truths" stick in the mind. Nationalists also create myths. Religions employ rites and ceremonies. Likewise, ruthless nationalists provide ways of marking birth, adolescence, marriage, crises, and death. If they fail to do this, they will lose their power.

Religions produce martyrs, people who will sacrifice their lives for a cause rather than deny their faith. What about nationalism? It asks and demands that millions die for its causes, and tens, if not hundreds, of millions have "made the ultimate sacrifice" in this century—for their tribe and, more often, their nation.

Religions help people know who they are. Believers are or become "the people of Israel," "the people of God," "the faithful." They use language that helps tell others who they are and informs them whom they can trust. So with nationality: to be a Bosnian, an Ulsterman, an American, is a mark of identity, often a stronger one than any that religions can provide. Tell me that you are a Methodist and I may not know much about you. Tell me that you are an Algerian and I may know much more.

If nations, nationalities, and nationalisms can act like religions, they also welcome support of religious groups and are very demanding when they do not receive it. If we look at a recent incident, the Persian Gulf War, and then at the American Civil War—a more remote conflict with longer-lasting effects—we will learn how entangled religion and nationality are. We will also see that they cannot seem to get along without each other, however much minorities on each side of the divide may try to keep religion and nationality separate.

## THE PERSIAN GULF WAR

### Scene One: Religious Leaders and the Persian Gulf War

At 3 A.M., Baghdad time, on January 17, 1991, United Nations troops, led by Americans, started dropping bombs on and firing missiles at the capital of Saddam Hussein's Iraq. Americans who for some time had not paid much attention to being American, to being nationalist, watched the war on television. Suddenly, most of them found that while they were interested in the technology of what came to be called Desert Storm, they also measured the return of impulses in their hearts that many did not know were there. They flocked to churches to pray for their troops because so many congregations had servicemen and -women on the scene and because they all cared, whether or not they knew the people at risk. Whether or not they prayed, many Americans felt surges of patriotic instinct that some had predicted would never return after America's defeat in the Vietnam War two decades earlier. Now their pulses raced, their hearts beat; ex–couch potatoes leaned forward on their couches and cheered as SCUD missiles presumably hit their targets. Most Americans backed their president, George Bush, and made instant heroes of Generals Colin Powell and and Norman Schwarzkopf, constant figures on the television screen. There were rallies and parades of support. One saw flags on doorposts. American nationalism was "in"; dissent was "out."

The day before the war, American citizens had felt free, often on religious grounds, to question the use of military force against Saddam Hussein, though everyone agreed he was an evil tyrant and a threat to peace. Then war came. The next day such citizens found their patriotism and good sense questioned if they had the nerve to speak up against the United States and its allies' use of such force instead of negotiation to prevent war and yet achieve some positive goals.

Religious leaders especially felt the force of sudden change when the nation, nationality, and nationalism stirred people. From August 7, 1990, when President Bush dispatched troops and weaponry to the Persian Gulf area, until hours before the 3 A.M. raids began, most of the responsible clerical leadership was urging the government and the United Nations to negotiate, to talk, to use embargoes, not to threaten the lives of innocent civilians who were trapped by the follies of the Iraqi leader. They knew that Iraqi nationality was an accident of people's birth and not the result of dedicated choice or belief. Hussein later tried to extend his cause by issuing a call for Islamic holy war, but few in the Muslim world followed this call.

From August until January, major denominational and interreligious organizations, Protestant, Catholic, and Jewish, kept calling for alternatives to drawing the United States into war. It became a truism to say that if you had the title *bishop* in front of your name, you were calling on the nation you loved to be patient. Most Catholic, Lutheran, Episcopalian, and United Methodist bishops joined rabbis and moderators, denominational task forces and councils and assemblies, who urged America, Remain peaceful!

President Bush, an active Episcopalian Christian and commander in chief of the U.S. armed forces, heard all their testimony. But he also knew that not all members of the faith groups were of one mind. He knew he could find spiritual counsel from sources other than these leaders. The president called the White House evangelist Billy Graham and television pastor Robert Schuller for counsel and prayer. The rules of the White House and pastoral games demand privacy, so no one revealed what was talked about. Whatever it was, within hours the president unleashed the military forces, as if the bishops and churches and rabbinical councils had not uttered a word against such a prospect.

His decision was immensely popular. Oil interests were at stake. Hussein had been an aggressor, and all the world knew it. Not only was the Iraqi leader hateable, he was hated. Not only did the Iraqi leader's call for a holy war fade; some of *us*, Americans of many faiths or no faith, began to think of our cause as the holy one.

The religious leaders who had opposed the war grumbled and mumbled, but most of them went along with the new policy. They had chaplains of their faith on the scene; they were not heartless about the American troops. Many of them had served in World War II, in the Korean War, and maybe even in Vietnam. They knew how important civilian support is, and protesting seemed unwise and even dangerous.

Soon the war ended. The troops came home, and the believers joined the welcoming crowds and lined up for parades. Many of them had "welcome home" ceremonies and felt reinforced in their nationality and nationalism. The president, according to the polls, was as popular as any had been in decades.

The nationalist glow did not last. A year later Bush was defeated in an election, and Saddam Hussein remained in power. The Persian Gulf War was becoming forgettable, and American nationalist fever seemed to go as it came.

There were aftermaths, however.

### Scene Two: The Religious Conscience, the Nation's Demands

To dwell longer on the aftermath of the war may lead to the notion that our topic is "Religion and War" and not "Religion and Nationality." But the case for connecting religion and nationality becomes most clear when one thinks about war and tells stories about it. War brings out the instincts and reasons that reinforce nationality and go into the making of nationalism. So here is another story.[1]

Chaplain Garland L. Robertson in 1968 volunteered to fight in Vietnam. "In order to be a good Christian, you had to be a good citizen. To be a good citizen, you did what your country asked," he has said. He was awarded a Distinguished Flying Cross in 1970. But Robertson later had second thoughts about the war. He entered a seminary, earned a doctorate in ethics, became a pastor, and in 1982 combined love of church and love of nation by signing up as an air force chaplain. His record in service was almost perfect, and people commended him for leadership. One day, as America was moving toward war in the Persian Gulf, Robertson heard that Vice President Dan Quayle had said to the troops ready in Saudi Arabia, "The American people are behind you."

Were they? Robertson thought not, and he said so in a letter printed in the Abilene, Texas, *Reporter News* two weeks before the missiles and the bombs headed for Baghdad. In the letter, good military man Robertson said he knew troops would respond if the president asked. But "the need to use military force" in this case, he thought, was still "an open issue—one which the citizens of this country will not allow to be decided in the vacuum of sectarian perception."

The citizens of the country! Nationality and nationalism would inspire them to back the troops. But, Robertson reported, troops were coming to him as chaplain "for help in settling a conflict between their moral beliefs and the country's policy." Their chaplain spoke up for them—and soon found how the mix of religion and nationalism could cause reaction. Abilene is a city with two hundred churches, many of them filled with military people and retirees. The Robertson phone and those of his superiors at the base were hot for days after the letter appeared, as angry nationalists questioned the chaplain's patriotism and wanted his neck and hide. No matter how well his superiors had been rating Robertson, they now entered very negative comments into his record and tried to doom him. The higher-ups pushed him lower down into a windowless room and offered retirement. But he loves his nation and the people he serves and said so. He was then honorably discharged, but he *was* discharged, losing his family pensions and, in the eyes of many, his good name.

"The most pressing issue," the chaplain later summarized, "is, Are we ministers of the church or ministers of the state?" The angry Abilene churchgoers had no answer ready. Robertson says, "If you're consistent with the teachings of your church, there will always be tensions between being a minister and being an officer."

Not only officers and chaplains and other military figures feel such tension; not only clergy and other leaders in religions feel it. Religion makes one set of demands and nationality makes another. Often each can be supportive of the other's. Chaplain Robertson knows that. But he also knows that when the passions of war, the belief in patriotism, and fear for the nation or pride in the nation take over, "church" and religion usually come in second—or last.

The Gulf War was not long enough, its effects were not sufficiently long-lasting, the emotions it evoked were not deep enough, the issues were not sufficiently profound for it to have a long-term effect on religion and nationality. To learn how nationality gets formed and tested and how religion relates to it, we need an even more revealing case study. Because this book is being read chiefly in the United States, we will take another American instance. Though it happened long ago, the Civil War is by far the most searing and bonding event since the nation was shaped in 1776 and 1787. A close-up of that event will help sort out and force the issues of "religion and nationality," because that war's effects still shape America and those who live here.

## THE CIVIL WAR

### A Close-up from Civil War Novels, Songs, and Reports

Stephen Crane was not present at the Civil War battle of Chancellorsville, Virginia, May 1–3, 1863—he was not born until 1871—but it is believed that Chancellorsville was the incident about which the novelist wrote thirty years later. His story, the classic *The Red Badge of Courage,* was fictional, but thousands of veterans said it captured perfectly the way that troops of one nation—momentarily two nations after the South's secession, the Union and the Confederacy—experienced up close what national and religious leaders miles away treated very differently. Here is one snapshot; it finds the young "hero" at the side of a tall, wounded soldier who is dying, and who then dies:

> Under foot there were a few ghastly forms motionless. They lay twisted in fantastic contortions. Arms were bent and heads were turned in incredible ways. It seemed that the dead men must have fallen from some great height to get into such positions. They looked to be dumped out upon the ground from the sky. . . .
>
> In the lane was a blood-stained crowd streaming to the rear. The wounded men were cursing, groaning, and wailing. In the air, always, was a mighty swell of sound that it seemed could sway the earth. With the courageous words of the artillery and the spiteful sentences of the musketry mingled red cheers. And from this region of noises came the steady current of the maimed.
>
> One of the wounded men had a shoeful of blood. He hopped like a schoolboy in a game. He was laughing hysterically. . . .
>
> At times [the new young solder] regarded the wounded soldiers in an envious way. He conceived persons with torn bodies to be peculiarly happy. He wished that he, too, had a wound, a red badge of courage.
>
> The spectral soldier was at his side like a stalking reproach. . . . As he went on, he seemed always looking for a place, like one who goes to choose a grave. . . . The tall soldier held out his gory hand. There was a curious red and black combination of new blood and old blood upon it. . . .
>
> Suddenly, [the tall soldier's] form stiffened and straightened. Then it was shaken by a prolonged ague. He stared into space. To the two watchers there was a curious and profound dignity in the firm lines of his awful face.
>
> He was invaded by a creeping strangeness that slowly enveloped him. For a moment the tremor of his legs caused him to dance a sort of hideous hornpipe. His arms beat wildly about his head in expression of implike enthusiasm.
>
> His tall figure stretched itself to its full height. There was a slight rending sound. Then it began to swing forward, slow and straight, in the manner of a falling tree. A swift muscular contortion made the left shoulder strike the ground first.
>
> The body seemed to bounce a little way from the earth. "God!" said the tattered soldier. . . .

The youth had watched, spellbound, this ceremony at the place of meeting. His face had been twisted into an expression of every agony he had imagined for his friend.

He now sprang to his feet and, going closer, gazed upon the pastelike face. The mouth was open and the teeth showed in a laugh.

As the flap of the blue jacket fell away from the body, he could see that the side looked as if it had been chewed by wolves.

The youth turned, with sudden, livid rage, toward the battlefield. He shook his fist. He seemed about to deliver a philippic.

"Hell—"

The red sun was pasted in the sky like a wafer.[2]

A century after Crane wrote, most of us routinely see so many deaths on television, in fictional programs or in images from the Balkans or North Africa, or elsewhere, that some of the shock value of the novel's scene may be lessened. Still, picture yourself being the tall soldier, dying for the Union as his nation, and the young one, looking on, looked into: "Hell—" Now, multiply the scene 360,000 times for the Union and about the same number of times for the Confederacy, for that is how many died in the four years of war. Add to that the 275,175 wounded on the Union side and something like that for their enemies; being wounded was often less merciful than being killed. Picture being the widow of a soldier on either side, or one of the returning winners and losers who saw their homes devastated and their fortunes gone. Picture what "nationality" means in time of war crisis.

An interruption: I, who tell these stories and write this, am not a pacifist. Though a peacemonger, negotiator, preferrer of embargoes to missiles, I know there are times when the call of nation and nationality to use arms may have to be responded to. I do not picture Chaplain Robertson writing his Abilene letter or myself not answering the call when a Hitler threatens a race, a continent, a world. We shall look at positive sides of nationalism. The purpose of this ghastly telling is to highlight elements that go into support of the nation and its causes—in this case, elements from the Civil War, some of whose causes evoke positive moral response even today—and to show nationalism's power to act like religion and draw support of the religious.

Back to the plot.

### The Larger Picture:
### The Civil War and Two Nationalisms

A year or two before Crane's tall soldier and new young soldier experienced their agonies, but after thousands of others had, Julia Ward Howe visited an encampment of the Army of the Potomac and was impressed. She was not a natural-born hawk, not a militarist. She was a religious liberal and a Boston reformer of considerable common sense. But to support the cause, she reached for religious, even biblical, imagery and turned her national sentiments into the themes of a cosmic war. She sat comfortably at a desk in the Willard Hotel in the capital city of Washington, not miles from the encampment but light-years away from the Chancellorsville battlefield and others like it, and wrote the most sung, most stirring, best-loved hymn to religion and nationality in American history. Keep Stephen Crane's soldiers in mind, and think or sing with Howe:

> Mine eyes have seen the glory of the coming of the Lord:
> He is trampling out the vintage where the grapes of wrath are stored;
> He hath loosed the fateful lightning of his terrible swift sword:
> His truth is marching on.

> I have seen Him in the watch-fires of a hundred circling camps;
> They have builded Him an altar in the evening dews and damps;
> I can read His righteous sentence by the dim and flaring lamps:
> His day is marching on.

> I have read a fiery gospel writ in burnished rows of steel:
> As ye deal with my contemners, so with you my grace shall deal;
> Let the Hero, born of woman, crush the serpent with his heel,
> Since God is marching on.

> He has sounded forth the trumpet that shall never call retreat;
> He is sifting out the hearts of men before His judgment seat:
> Oh, be swift, my soul to answer Him! be jubilant, my feet!
> Our God is marching on.

> In the beauty of the lilies Christ was born across the sea,
> With a glory in his bosom that transfigures you and me:
> As he died to make men holy, let us die to make men free,
> While God is marching on.

The churchgoers of Abilene have often sung those words. So have Jewish war veterans, who never are called to sing about "Christ" at synagogue and would never do so. But at the Veterans of Foreign Wars or American Legion posts, the call of nation comes first for many. High school choruses, some of whose members have to protest when religious themes come up in their choral numbers, never get criticized for singing "The Battle Hymn of the Republic." If someone did challenge the singing of such songs and the chorus resisted the challenges, anyone who chose not to sing would likely face community criticism.

Take it apart. This hymn is about armies and a nation, the American Union, but "the glory" takes "the coming of the Lord" at the end of history and places it in the encampments near the Potomac. A scriptural angel (from Revelation 14) asks the faithful who await the coming to gather the grapes for God's winepress. The chorus, "Glory, Glory, Hallelujah," also comes from the last book of the Christian Bible but now is sung by non-Christians in support of their nation. "The terrible swift sword" is God's avenger in Revelation 19; the angel was a figure that Protestant commentators long used against Catholicism. Now it was to work against the Confederacy, the new would-be nation to the south of the Willard Hotel and the Potomac encampments. And the trumpets of Revelation became the bugles of the Union, Julia Ward Howe's nation.

Religion, including religion connected with nationality, is not only sung. It is spoken, preached, and written about. The preachers on both sides in this event that illustrates how nationalism forges American identity were busy.

In the South, it was the preachers who led everyone else in defending slavery, which in the eye of the public—if not of all the historians—was the main moral issue, if not the sole cause, of the "War between the States." (When the two nationalisms were or still were felt to be at stake, even to call the conflict the Civil War was to tread on sacred and dangerous turf.) God, the southern preachers were sure, wanted them to use the "terrible swift sword" against the abolitionists, the emancipators, the hated Union in the North that wanted to impose its will on the southern ways. God wanted the South to secede, said the preachers, to break off and form a new nation, "baptized in blood," around holy causes such as the defense of slavery and a way of life.

The foremost historian of the religion of the "Lost Cause," Charles Reagan Wilson, conveniently summarizes the heritage with its relics, artifacts, traditions, rituals, and religious trimmings:

> The Confederate experience led southerners to see their historical past in transcendent, cosmic terms. Southerners came to believe that God had not abandoned them but instead had chastised them, in preparation for a greater destiny in the future. . . . [The myth of the Lost Cause] became the basis for what anthropologists would see as a functioning religion. It was not a formal religion; no First Cause of the Lost Cause ever existed. But it was the focus for a complex of religious phenomena.
>
> The Lost Cause had icons, including pervasive images of Robert E. Lee, Jefferson Davis, and Stonewall Jackson—the Lost Cause Trinity. The Confederate heroes were portrayed as saints, prophets, and martyrs. Their images were found in schools and on the stained glass windows in selected churches. Southerners had their sacred artifacts, such as the Confederate

battle flag, the song "Dixie,"and the ubiquitous Confederate monuments. There were distinctively southern rituals, such as Confederate Memorial Day, the dedication of Confederate monuments, the funerals of Confederate veterans, the reunions of living veterans. These ritual events were the focus for prayers, sermons, and speeches recalling the Cause and the failed Confederacy. . . .

The Protestant churches were crucial in keeping alive a religious interpretation of the Lost Cause. The Baptists, Methodists, and Presbyterians remained regionally organized after the Civil War, and their ministers pledged an active role in nurturing the idea that the South's past had continuing spiritual significance. The Episcopalians were even more prominently involved as leaders of southern society. . . . Two key theological concepts were at the heart of the religious interpretation of the Confederate experience—southerners were a Chosen People but they were also a Tragic People. They had been destined to crusade with honor for a cause they saw as right, but they had been destined to lose and suffer.[3]

In the South, according to historians, the religious leaders were the main promoters of troop morale, and there were great religious revivals among the armed supporters of what became the Lost Cause. Some estimates say that between one hundred thousand and two hundred thousand troops on both sides "got religion" during their time of service. Not only does nationalism "use" religion, the causes of nationality may enhance it.

The Union had the advantage of having won, so the Union myth more easily became the American myth. If, as Charles Reagan Wilson said, the South had to "lose and suffer," the North, said the Union's preachers, had to "suffer and win." And its poets said that Americans were once again—the old Puritans had first taught this partly forgotten lesson—a, or even *the*, "chosen people."

The greatest American writer of the mid-nineteenth century, Herman Melville, though he later had second thoughts, was typical in his nationalism when he wrote *White Jacket* in 1850. Like most other writers on American nationality, he traced the roots to ancient Israel and then connected the old covenant with the new Israel:

Escaped from the house of bondage, Israel of old did not follow after the ways of the Egyptians. To her was given an express dispensation; to her were given new things under the sun. And we Americans are the peculiar, chosen people—the Israel of our time; we bear the ark of the liberties of the world. Seventy years ago we escaped from thrall; and besides our first birthright—embracing one continent of earth—God has given to us, for a future inheritance, the broad domains of the political pagans, that shall yet come and lie down under the shade of our ark, without bloody hands being lifted.

God has predestined, mankind expects, great things from our race; and great things we feel in our souls. The rest of the nations must soon be in our rear. . . . Long enough have we been sceptics with regard to ourselves, and doubted whether, indeed, the political Messiah had come. But he has come in *us*, if we would but give utterance to his promptings.[4]

Our example, begun with Stephen Crane and Julia Ward Howe and continued with Herman Melville, clearly is best developed in the North. If one wants to see how religion and nationality mesh in the United States, it is worth looking at some of the custodians of religion, the clergy. In this Union example, we might start at the top of the clergy. The Reverend Horace Bushnell—never heard of him?—in his prime was the premier Protestant preacher of the day, at a time when Protestants "ran the show" in America. He kept busy writing and preaching during the Civil War years. He could mount his pulpit at North Congregational Church in Hartford, Connecticut, and know that the press would pick up his words, publishers would print them, and some leaders in Washington, including, perhaps, President Abraham Lincoln, would see them. Thus Bushnell, though out of uniform, helped the Union cause.

When the Hartford Congregationalist preached about nationalism and its moral causes, he tried not to forget the kind of soldiers about whom Stephen Crane wrote—though he tended to deal with them in the plural, just as Julia Ward Howe did in the abstract when she talked about "terrible swift swords." Bushnell told his people that God was chastening, purging, disciplining, and causing his chosen nation, America, to suffer for some higher purpose. Americans had to learn that a nation needed a higher loyalty, a religious one, toward God:

> Without shedding of blood there is no . . . grace prepared. There must be reverses and losses, and times of deep concern. There must be tears in the houses, as well as blood in the fields; the fathers and mothers, the wives and dear children, coming into the woe, to fight in hard bewailings. Desolated fields, prostrations of trade, discouragements of all kinds, must be accepted with unfaltering, unsubduable [*sic*] patience.
> [Yet] we shall then have passed the ordeal of history. Our great battlefields will be hallowed by song. Our great leaders and patriots will be names consecrated by historic reverence. We shall no more be a compact, or a confederation, or a composition made up by the temporary surrender of powers, but a nation—God's own nation.[5]

Here is Bushnell in 1864, raising his voice and the temperature:

> We associate God and religion with all that we are fighting for. . . . Our cause, we love to think, is especially God's and so we are connecting all most sacred

impressions with our government itself, weaving in a woof of holy feeling among all the fibres of our constitutional polity and government. . . . The whole shaping of the fabric is Providential. God, God is in it, everywhere. . . . Every drum-beat is a hymn, the cannon thunder God, the electric silence, darting victory along the wires, is the inaudible greeting of God's favoring work and purpose.[6]

The testimony of two novelists, one reformer-hymnist, a contemporary historian, and one preacher has to suffice here, though a hundred other preachers are waiting in the wings with thousands of texts to match Bushnell's. But we are not finished dealing with the complex issues of religion and nationality as revealed by two nations that had once been one and that went to war with each other, making use of some of the same myths and symbols, rites and ceremonies, moral claims and textual backgrounds. How to find a way out of this?

Fortunately for anyone who wants to see a somewhat more positive side of the issue, there was a contemporary, Abraham Lincoln, who left behind texts that are the classics of the American experience. As commander in chief of the Union forces and as president, Lincoln always insisted that all the states were still the United States; he would not let the Confederacy go. Lincoln also identified some themes that can guide citizens who debate the issue even today.

Here is Abraham Lincoln, pondering (in a note intended for his eyes only) what was going on:

> The will of God prevails. In great contests each party claims to act in accordance with the will of God. Both *may* be and one *must* be wrong. God cannot be *for* and *against* the same thing at the same time. In the present civil war it is quite possible that God's purpose is something different from the purpose of either party—and yet the human instrumentalities, working just as they do, are of the best adaptation to effect his purpose. I am almost ready to say this is probably true—that God wills this contest, and wills that it shall not end yet.[7]

That document dates from September 1862; it was on March 4, 1865, that Lincoln went public with such sentiments in the classic "Second Inaugural Address." Reviewing the events since 1861, he said, "Both parties deprecated war; but one of them would make war rather than let the nation survive; and the other would accept war rather than let it perish." Nationality and nationhood were at stake. Then Lincoln turned to religion:

> Both [parties] read the same Bible and pray to the same God, and each invokes his aid against the other. . . . The prayers of both could not be answered; that of neither has been answered fully. The Almighty has his own purposes. . . .

> With malice toward none, with charity for all, with firmness in the right as God gives us to see the right, let us strive on to finish the work we are in, to bind up the nation's wounds.[8]

## WHAT ALL THESE STORIES MEAN
## FOR RELIGION AND NATIONALITY

For all the military illustrations, this chapter is not about conflict and war—John Esposito, when dealing with Islam in chapter 9, will address that point—but about nationality, nationhood, and nationalism. That will become clear as we draw some conclusions and set forth some notions about what religion does and how it works when issues surrounding the nation are at stake.

First, the use of Abraham Lincoln at the climax of our story suggests that right at the top (the most revered president) and at the center (the Civil War) of a nation's history, one can find occasions for reflecting on the meaning of nationality that will provide lessons for ages to come. It is easy to see that all religion collapses when superpatriots make hypernationalist claims. It is easy to see a nationalism like this becoming a religion that displaces historic faiths. When something like that happens, there are good reasons to be uneasy about "the religion of nationalism" being a form of idolatry.

The record of Abraham Lincoln shows, however, that one can be loyal, as Lincoln was all but fanatic about "the Union"; that is, a person can keep some perspective. Students of religion like to speak of the idea of seeing something "above" ordinary, day-to-day life as seeing and then honoring "the transcendent." Citizens, people in politics, those running the affairs of nation, and a rare case like that of Chaplain Robertson can try to bring an awareness of "transcendent justice" to bear on ordinary existence.

Martin Luther King, Jr., did so. He was religious in the conventional churchly sense, an African-American Baptist pastor who used biblical language with ease. King combined that with a kind of sacred rhetoric about the Declaration of Independence and the Constitution of the United States. He appealed to the nationality of Americans north and south, white and black, in order to reform the nation itself. So, clearly, some of the symbols of combined religion and nationality are positive.

A second good word for nationality: it can help tell you who you are. Nationalism may be an exaggerated, dangerous modern growth with roots in ancient Israel, medieval England, and modern Euro-America. But nationality helps people transcend—that word again, now meaning "to stand above"—their "tribes." I use the word *tribes* cautiously, because, again from ancient Israel, this time down to modern Native America, one can speak of tribes positively. They carry on traditions, including good ones; they help people transmit values, which families are too small and brief-lived to do by themselves. But they can also traffic in tribal*ism*, of the sort the world sees too much of today: God is on the side of "my" tribe, a product of race/culture/religion/ethnicity/history, and has to be against "your" side, and there is naturally nothing you can do about it. Better duck, get out of the way, or get killed.

Nations have killed more than have tribes in this century, though tribalism is catching up as a killer. But nation and nationality, because they may be mixes of ethnic, religious, racial, and cultural groups, can make it possible for people to enter world politics on different terms from simply lethal ones. Nations have to give and take, win some and lose some, compromise and negotiate. They are not at war all the time!

The tribe tells too much about who you are. The nation is less defining. It is dangerous for individuals and groups not to have a secure identity, and people will go out of their way to find the place that gives them one. The Spanish philosopher José Ortega y Gasset once said that if you do not have an identity, you will be like a drop of mist in an unformed, undefined cloud. With something like a nation and a nationality, you acquire some elements of an identity. Your life acquires more outline, form, and definition. The Irish poet W. B. Yeats said that you cannot grab the universe bare-handed. You need a glove, and the nation can serve.

Third, nations can mobilize toward good ends and will often use religious means to get there. I do not mean that nations always have to take over or take captive the religious groups in order to pursue nationalist ends. I do mean that personal faith and communal religion can motivate people to better serve national purposes. In America, the majority of hours and dollars given for charity and in volunteering are attracted through religious appeals. Without them, the nation would be vastly poorer.

Nationality, as an ingredient in nationhood, plays a part in the political and welfare intentions of a society. America does not only raise armies and fight wars. It has political institutions that are designed to "promote the general welfare." Not all citizens agree on taxing and spending policies; citizens are not *supposed* to agree 100 percent on national purposes. They are supposed to argue. But the vast majority of them buy into the notion that not all that is needed to meet the needs of the poor; to assure standards of safety in drugs and quality in foods and other products; to build roads, fight crime, and the like, can be done by private citizens, secular interest groups, and churches and synagogues. Appeals to nationality—in this case, American citizenship—can help people meet human needs.

Many symbols and myths of nationality can be used positively. The American drama, for instance, is not only one of conquering, displacing, enslaving, confining to reservations, exploiting. Abraham Lincoln liked to talk to the nation about the need to notice "the better angels of our nature" and "the mystic chords of memory." It is important for the health of a republic that its citizens remember and retell the stories of heroines and heroes, saints and pioneers, role models and self-sacrificial groups. These stories usually have to do with heroic individuals or team players in interest groups, some of them religious. But these groups belong not only to themselves; they are part of a "grand narrative" of the larger nation. When their stories are told by Walt Whitman and other poets, by Dorothy Day and other activists, by the reporters who watched the space shuttle *Challenger* go down, even by the people who arrange ceremonies to help citizens deal with grief after such events, they can motivate people whose lives might otherwise lack purpose.

Nationality can represent "public life," where people transcend their private and interest-group existence. In public people "bump into each other," bring their colorfulness and conflict into open view, where it can be enjoyed in one case and dealt with in another. Many of these "bumpings" will have a kind of religious cast to them: Memorial Day, mournings after assassinations or disasters, celebrations after Olympic victories or Desert Storms or signings of treaties are all examples. So are acts of national repentance and declarations of new intentions.

The balance sheet, then, shows that nationalism can be a rival religion or can take over religions; that nationality gone wrong can lead to aggressive wars and self-justifications. It has been demonstrated that people can lose their heads more readily over the flag than over the crescent or cross or star; that it is easier, more inflaming, and more endangering to persecute the dissenter in the nation than to excommunicate the heretic in religion. We could go on with many sentences that include "that it is," and still it is possible for us to see positive sides to nationality and ways to "transcend" the worst and participate in the best, or at least to work for the relative goods.

This means one is saying about nationality the kind of thing one must say about religion: it is a mixed bag, and responsible humans have to have ways to draw the best out of it. They will sometimes succeed. Glory, glory, hallelujah for that.

## NOTES

1. See Eric Schmitt, "Military Chaplain Fights a Battle over Loyalties," *New York Times*, December 21, 1993, A8.

2. Stephen Crane, *The Red Badge of Courage*, in *Prose and Poetry*, ed. J. C. Levenson (New York: The Library of America, 1984), 115, 129–30, 133–37.

3. Charles Reagan Wilson, "The Southern Civil Religion, 1920–1980," in Rowland A. Sherrill, ed., *Religion and the Life of the Nation: American Recoveries* (Urbana: University of Illinois Press, 1990), 65–66.

4. Quoted in one of the best resources on our subject, Ernest Tuveson, *Redeemer Nation* (Chicago: University of Chicago Press, 1968), 156–57.

5. "A Discourse Delivered on the Sunday after the Disaster of Bull Run, in the North Church," and an excerpt from a Bushnell book, both quoted in James H. Moorhead, *American Apocalypse: Yankee Protestants and the Civil War, 1860–1869* (New Haven, Conn.: Yale University Press, 1978), 140–41. This is the best source on religion and the Civil War.

6. Horace Bushnell, *Popular Government by Divine Right* (Hartford, Conn.: L. E. Hunt, 1864), 12, 15.

7. Quoted by Cushing Strout, *The New Heavens and New Earth: Political Religion in America* (New York: Harper & Row, 1974), 197.

8. Reprinted in Winthrop Hudson, *Nationalism and Religion in America* (New York: Harper & Row, 1970), 85–86.

## STUDY QUESTIONS

1. What are three ways in which religions resemble nationality? Give examples of your answers.

2. Garland Robertson said about the Gulf War, "The most pressing issue is, 'Are we ministers of the church or ministers of the state?'" What did he mean by this statement? Give at least two examples from the Gulf War to support your answer.

3. Horace Bushnell was considered a "custodian of religion" during the Civil War. Read the excerpts of his sermons on pages 25–26. What words suggest to you that religion and nationalism are closely related?

4. What are at least three ways in which nationality, like religion, works toward a "good end"? Do you agree with Marty's assessment? Why? Why not?

5. What are three ways in which nationalism can be a rival to religion or "take over" religion? Can you give examples of such rivalry in today's society?

# 3

## JACOB NEUSNER

---

# Being Israel:
# Religion and Ethnicity in Judaism

Religion defines how groups of people see both themselves and the other, or the outsider. The power of religion to impart meaning and significance to group life shapes the news from day to day, whether the news comes from the Near East, South Asia, Latin America, Europe, or here at home, in North America. Much of the international conflict in the world today takes place between nations that also form religious communities: Muslim against Christian against Judaist (practitioners of Judaism), Hindu against Muslim, Hindu against Buddhist, and so on across the globe.

But these examples of the power of religion to define the limits of "our crowd" and to set apart "you people," the other, or the outsider, pertain to negative events and large and impersonal forces. Here at home, religion tells us who we are in personal ways, making individuals into a group and making the group a great deal more than the sum of its members. When some high school kids form a club, the club is the members. When they come together by reason of their shared faith, they march into eternity together. And they may well be the same people who formed the club.

All of us join many clubs, define the crowd we run with in a variety of ways. Religion is commonly one of them. and when it is, it changes everything. When I was in high school, I happily floated from one circle of friends to another: my homeroom, the school paper, the literary magazine. I worked in my father's newspaper office and printing plant every afternoon and on weekends, so I had friends down at the paper. Each of these groups took shape around shared activities. We were a "we" because we put out the school paper or because we did a job together.

But there was one group that took shape because we shared not an activity but a belief. The Jewish students in my class formed another group, not because we had to but because we wanted to. We were welcome to join anything we wanted; there was little anti-Semitism in our lives. But because we were not only Jewish by ethnic identification but Judaic by religious practice and belief, we identified with one another, enjoyed one another's company, did Judaic things together, such as going to our temple's youth group or attending synagogue services together (temple is for Reform Judaism, synagogue for Conservative and Orthodox Judaism). The boys all had entered the status of bar mitzvah, responsible adults in Judaism. The boys and the girls alike all had been confirmed at our local Reform or Conservative congregations.

The religion, Judaism, brought us together and told us what—among other things—we were. The prayers that we recited (and still recite) called us "Israel," meaning not the State of Israel, the Jewish state across the seas, but that holy people, the people of Israel, of whom the Hebrew Scriptures spoke. In West Hartford, Connecticut, in 1947, we were that same family, the children of Abraham and Sarah, Isaac and Rebekah, Jacob and Leah and Rachel, about whom we read in Genesis. Our past brought us to Sinai, where we accepted the Torah and said, "We shall do and we shall obey." We were sad because of the destruction of Jerusalem by the Babylonians in 586 B.C. and by the Romans in A.D. 70. We remembered the tragedy of the expulsion of "our ancestors" in 1492 by the Spanish, when Spain became fully Christian again, and we were deeply distressed by the murder of over five million Jews in Europe by the Germans during World War II, which we read about after the war in the headlines of the *Hartford Courant*.

## RELIGION AND
## METAPHORS OF BELONGING

So our religion, Judaism, made us members of a family, endowed us with a history, formed relationships between us and a long-ago past, made us part of a group that extended far beyond the borders even of our own state, Connecticut. When we think about how religion creates communities, defines nations, shapes people's view of who they are and who the other is, we not only address warfare in Europe or strife in India or Ireland or the State of Israel; we take up the single most powerful and most decisive defining force in the social world of nations and peoples today.

In the setting of William H. Hall High School in West Hartford, Connecticut, we were Israel; in that place and moment we stood for, we embodied, the very same people to whom the Hebrew Scriptures of ancient

Israel (the Old Testament) are addressed. Because we believed that, for here and now, we are "the Jews" or "Israel," we saw ourselves as a group. What brought us together was not work we did together but our faith. What this means, in concrete terms, is that our religion told us we were part of a group of people whom we had never seen and never would see. It gave us ancestors not in our family albums, made us care about people long dead and about what happened to them, and, above all, told us that "we," of the past and the present and the future, dead, alive, and unborn, all form a group.

Judaism did not make us into a clique or a club or an in-group (or outcasts, for that matter). That group—that "Israel" which in our own circumstance we formed—was explained to us in various terms. It was a family, but not a family like other families, related by nature. It was a nation, but not a nation like France or America or the State of Israel. It was a "holy people," the like of which no one ever knew. Religion at that time and ever since has told me who I am by explaining that I am part of a group, that family or nation or people. It tells me who that "we" is that forms the group with me, and it also indicates who the many people are who do not belong to that group: who "you" are.

Now, when religion tells people who they are, it always speaks of a world beyond the one people see and know in the here and now. When, to explain who they are, several people or families who live in a village call themselves "villagers" or "people who live in such and such a village," they speak of the simple, palpable facts of their everyday life. Growing up in West Hartford and thinking of myself as a part of that little town (as it was in those days), I did not need to believe in more than I could see every day: the library, the town hall, my high school, Farmington Avenue, Asylum Avenue, Albany Avenue—these formed the geography of my town and the outer limits of my world. But being told by my religion that I was something else required me to consider myself part of a social group that was both tangible—there were others who believed in Judaism and went to the local temples or synagogues—and intangible.

Take the case of Judaism, for example. When we called ourselves Israel and meant by that the same group of which the Hebrew Scriptures, or Old Testament, speak, we claimed for ourselves a standing and a status that the simple facts of daily life did not, and could not, validate. We Jews imagine ourselves to be something that the world does not define in an ordinary, this-worldly way. We compare ourselves to some other social group and allege that we are like that group or continue it or embody it in the here and now. By the statement "We are Israel" or "We are the Jewish people," meaning that people of which scripture speaks, we are alleging, "We are like that Israel of old," of which the scriptures speak. The same is so when Christian residents of a given locale call themselves "the church" or "the body of Christ." Then they speak of what is not seen though very real. In each of these cases, the claim that "we" are "Israel" or "we" are "the body of Christ" forms an instance of how a religion defines a metaphor to explain the character and standing of a social entity. These two instances, "Israel" and "church," therefore supply familiar examples of how religions create social groups and explain to those groups what and who they are—and also, therefore, who is an outsider to that group.

That is why, when we speak of such large abstractions as society or people or nation—for instance, when we use the word *family* to mean a social entity or aggregate of persons beyond the one in which we grow up and to which we bear blood relationships (e.g., calling a friend or a political ally a "brother")—we move onward from the concrete to the abstract. Religions transform human relationships from the natural to the enchanted. I can give a concrete example of how religion may create a family beyond the natural one by quoting from the Mishnah:

A. [If he has to choose between seeking] what he has lost and what his father has lost,

B. his own takes precedence.

C. . . . what he has lost and what his master has lost,

D. his own takes precedence.

E. . . . what his father has lost and what his master has lost, that of his master takes precedence.

G. For his father brought him into this world.

H. But his master, who taught him wisdom, will bring him into the life of the world to come.

I. But if his father is a sage, that of his father takes precedence.

Mishnah Tractate Baba Mesia 2:11

Here is a very explicit statement that there is a father besides the natural father—in the case of Judaism, the teacher or sage. And the reason for this relationship is given: while the parents bring the child into this life, the master brings the child into the life of the world to come. Now, we know that the master is not really the father. But in religion, the ordinary is transformed into the extraordinary, and in the case before us, a family other than the natural one is brought into being by an act of imagination and faith. That is how reflection and imagination in general terms about the commonalities of specific things form an exercise in thinking about "the social order" in concrete terms.

What this means in the concrete example of how Jews turn themselves into that holy Israel of which scripture speaks now has to be spelled out. So we ask, How, exactly, does Judaism define that social entity, Israel, of which it speaks? At issue is not a nation-state, the State of Israel, but a supernatural and holy community. For Judaism, Israel is the locus of the kingdom of God, since to Israel the Torah is given. "Israel" is a supernatural category, for Israel consists of all those who are born in Israel, except for those who deny the principles of the faith. The categories are defined in terms of belief: affirming a given doctrine, denying another. That fact bears in its wake the implication that Israel as a social entity, encompassing all of its members, is defined by reference to matters of correct doctrine. All "Israelites"—persons who hold the correct opinion—then constitute Israel. Here is an Israel that, at first glance, is defined not in relationships but intransitively and intrinsically. What this means is that Israel is not a social entity at all like other social entities but an entity that finds definition, as to genus and not species, elsewhere.

## DEFINING ISRAEL

A.  All Israelites have a share in the world to come,

B.  as it is said, "Your people also shall be all righteous, they shall inherit the land forever; the branch of my planting, the work of my hands, that I may be glorified" (Isa. 60:21).

C.  And these are the ones who have no portion in the world to come:

D.  He who says, the resurrection of the dead is a teaching which does not derive from the Torah, and the Torah does not come from Heaven; and an Epicurean.

Mishnah Tractate Sanhedrin 10.1

The passage alleges that Isaiah's statement "Your people shall all be righteous . . . shall possess the land" means that all Israelites inherit the world to come. So Israel is defined inclusively: to be Israel is to have a share in the world to come. Israel, then, is a social entity that is made up of those who share a common conviction, and that Israel therefore bears on otherworldly destiny. An "Israel" is a social group that endows its individual members with life in the world to come; an "Israel(ite)" is one who enjoys the world to come. But no definition of a group ends up saying everybody is in. Part of defining—the important part—spells out who is excluded. Excluded from this Israel are Israel(ite)s who, within the established criteria of social identification, exclude themselves. A critical belief of the Judaism represented here is that the dead are raised to life at the end of days; the resurrection, this Judaism maintains, is a teaching of the Torah. It follows, of course, that the Torah must be understood as a gift of God that "comes from Heaven." An Epicurean in this context is someone who holds that this world is all that there is. The power to define by relationships does not run out, however, since in this supernatural context we speak of an Israel that is unique; we still know who is "Israel" because we are told who is "not-Israel": specific nonbelievers or sinners.

The consequent questions are, How has this supernatural social entity come into being? And how do outsiders gain a place within it? The answer to the first question defines matters for the second. The answer is, Israel becomes Israel through the Torah. It must follow that an ethnic definition is set aside in favor of one that invokes faith, covenant, obedience. These may form a cover for ethnic chauvinism, unless Gentiles may enter on equal terms with Israel. And that is made explicit. That Israel becomes Israel or Sinai through accepting the Torah is formulated in the following language:

A.  "The Lord spoke to Moses saying, Speak to the Israelite people and say to them, I am the Lord your God":

B.  R. Simeon b. Yohai says, "That is in line with what is said elsewhere: 'I am the Lord your God [who brought you out of the land of Egypt, out of the house of bondage]' (Ex. 20:2).

C.  "'Am I the Lord, whose sovereignty you took upon yourself in Egypt?'

D.  "They said to him, 'Indeed.'

E.  "'Indeed you have accepted my dominion.

F.  "'They accepted my decrees: "You will have no other gods before me."'

G.  "That is what is said here: 'I am the Lord your God,' meaning, 'Am I the one whose dominion you accepted at Sinai?'

H.  "They said to him, 'Indeed.'

I.  "'Indeed you have accepted my dominion.'

J.  "'They accepted my decrees: "You shall not copy the practices of the land of Egypt where you dwelt, or of the land of Canaan to which I am taking you; nor shall you follow their laws."'"

Sifra to Ahare Mot 194:2

Commentary to Leviticus 16

But theories of divine origin of ethnic groups surely circulate broadly, so the claim that because the Torah brings Israel into being, Israel therefore forms a supernatural social entity, not an ethnic group, need not be in the statement just given. That Gentiles belong on equal terms when they accept the same Torah that makes Israel the people of God changes the ethnic into the universal. The Gentile who accepts the Torah, the covenant, the commandments, is transformed, no longer what he or she had been but now become utterly a new creation.

Accepting the Torah makes an ordinary human being into an Israelite. Then the proselyte becomes fully an Israelite. This is not a matter of mere theory. We recall how critical to the formation of Israel is genealogy, with Israel defined as wholly the descendants of the same couple, Abraham and Sarah. It must follow that if the Gentile enters Israel, it must be either as a second-class Israelite—the Gentile possessing no physical genealogy at all—or as a first-class Israelite—the Gentile deemed fully a child of Abraham and Sarah. This obviously is not matter of theory. Can the Gentile's child marry a home-born Israelite? If so, then Israel is not ethnic at all; if not, then it is. And as a matter of fact, the Gentile's daughter may marry into the priesthood:

1. A. "[If he] will give me bread to eat and clothing to wear":
   B. Aqilas the proselyte came to R. Eliezer and said to him, "Is all the gain that is coming to the proselyte going to be contained in this verse: '. . . and loves the proselyte, giving him food and clothing' (Deut. 10:18)?"
   C. He said to him, "And is something for which the old man [Jacob] beseeched going to be such a small thing in your view, namely, '. . . will give me bread to eat and clothing to wear'? [God] comes and hands it over to [a proselyte] on a reed [and the proselyte does not have to beg for it]."
   D. He came to R. Joshua, who commenced by saying words to appease him: "'Bread' refers to Torah, as it is said, 'Come, eat my bread' (Prov. 9:5). 'Clothing' refers to the cloak of a disciple of sages.
   E. "When a person has the merit of studying the Torah, he has the merit of carrying out a religious duty. [So the proselyte receives a great deal when he gets bread and clothing, namely, entry into the estate of disciples].
   F. "And not only so, but his daughters may be chosen for marriage into the priesthood, so that their sons' sons will offer burnt offerings on the altar. [So the proselyte may also look forward to entry into the priests' caste.]"

Genesis Rabbah 70:5

It follows that the Gentile is no longer a Gentile upon entering Israel, and this can only mean that Israel forms not an ethnic category but a supernatural one.

In American and Canadian society, people often think of the Jews as an ethnic group, comparable to Italians or blacks or Chinese, rather than as a religious group, comparable to Catholics or Protestants. As a matter of simple fact, some Jews do not practice Judaism but are regarded, and regard themselves, as Jews; the groups that they form are rightly classified as ethnic only. But other Jews—a great many, as a matter of fact—do practice Judaism in one or another of its systems, whether Reform or Orthodox or Conservative or Reconstructionist. These, too, are ethnic Jews, but they also are religious and therefore "Judaists,"or practitioners of Judaism. And the passages of the holy books of Judaism that we have examined show that Judaism is a religion and not an ethnic identification. As we see, one could not enter the Israel of these holy books through ethnic-territorial assimilation, for example, by marrying a Jew and following Jewish customs and ceremonies. One entered Israel only through an act that we must call "religious conversion," but when one did (or does), that person would become fully and completely Israel, as though his or her ancestors had stood at Sinai. The reason, of course, is that by accepting the Torah, the convert personally takes up a position at Sinai.

If Judaism is a religion, not an ethnic identification, then what does Judaism mean by "Israel," referring not to the State of Israel but to a supernatural community, a "kingdom of priests and a holy people"? Israel, for rabbinic Judaism, forms the counterpart and opposite of Adam. Adam in Eden, in sinning, stands for humanity when it disobeys God. Israel in the Land of Israel in ancient times stands for Adam in Eden, Israel having received the land as Adam did Eden, as a gift from God, and having lost the land as Adam lost Eden, by reason of disobedience. So from the viewpoint of Judaism, humanity knows two stories, one of Adam in Eden, the other of Israel in the Land of Israel. These stories form counterparts to each other. But they also mirror each other, for the Torah intervenes. Let us start with the comparison of Adam in Eden and Israel in the Land of Israel, demonstrating that Israel's history in the land is comparable to Adam's history in Eden:

2. A. R. Abbahu in the name of R. Yosé bar Haninah: "It is written, 'But they are like a man [Adam], they have transgressed the covenant' (Hos. 6:7).

   B. "'They are like a man,' specifically, like the first man. [We shall now compare the story of the first man in Eden with the story of Israel in its land.]

C. "'In the case of the first man, I brought him into the garden of Eden, I commanded him, he violated my commandment, I judged him to be sent away and driven out, but I mourned for him, saying, "How . . ."'" [which begins the book of Lamentations, hence stands for a lament, but which, as we just saw, also is written with the consonants that also yield, 'Where are you'].

D. "'I brought him into the garden of Eden,' as it is written, 'And the Lord God took the man and put him into the garden of Eden' (Gen. 2:15).

E. "'I commanded him,' as it is written, 'And the Lord God commanded . . .' (Gen. 2:16).

F. "'And he violated my commandment,' as it is written, 'Did you eat from the tree concerning which I commanded you' (Gen. 3:11).

G. "'I judged him to be sent away,' as it is written, 'And the Lord God sent him from the garden of Eden' (Gen. 3:23).

H. "'And I judged him to be driven out,' 'And he drove out the man' (Gen. 3:24).

I. "'But I mourned for him, saying, "How. . . ."'' 'And he said to him, "Where are you"'' (Gen. 3:9), and the word for 'where are you' is written, 'How. . . .'

J. "'So too in the case of his descendants, [God continues to speak,] I brought them into the Lord of Israel, I commanded them, they violated my commandment, I judged them to be sent out and driven away but I mourned for them, saying, "How. . . ."''

K. "'I brought them into the Land of Israel.' 'And I brought you into the land of Carmel' (Jer. 2:7).

L. "'I commanded them.' 'And you, command the children of Israel' (Ex. 27:20). 'Command the children of Israel' (Lev. 24:2).

M. "'They violated my commandment.' 'And all Israel have violated your Torah' (Dan. 9:11).

N. "'I judged them to be sent out.' 'Send them away, out of my sight, and let them go forth' (Jer. 15:1).

O. "'. . . driven away.' 'From my house I shall drive them' (Hos. 9:15).

P. "'But I mourned for them, saying, "How. . . ."'' 'How has the city sat solitary, that was full of people' (Lam. 1:1)."

Genesis Rabbah 19:9

In this passage we see how a verse of scripture is used to make a point, and the point throughout is the same: that we can compare each step in the downward spiral of Adam with each step in the downward spiral of Israel.

But there is an important difference between Adam and Israel. Israel and Adam are counterparts but opposites. What Adam did not succeed in accomplishing, Israel realized in abundance: obedience to the Torah. Adam and Israel are comparable but not wholly alike. They are the same and not the same, because Israel has the Torah, which presents Israel with the possibility of escaping from the situation of guilt and alienation from God in which Adam is trapped. True, Israel's history in the land is the counterpart of Adam's history in Eden; with the destruction of Jerusalem in 586 B.C., Israel was driven out of Eden. But Israel can come back.

The difference between the situation of Adam and the situation of Israel finds its definition in the Torah. The Torah forms the antidote to Adam's sin. But then Israel has to regain the land—that is, Eden—by the act of reconciliation with God that takes place through voluntary obedience to the covenant, the Torah, the commandments. Then Israel overcomes the situation of Adam; the Torah provides the occasion, but only Israel supplies the actuality. At this point, in this context, we have to ask ourselves how any aspect of this language speaks of an "ethnic identity." Forming the counterpart to Adam defines Israel in much the same way that the Last Adam is defined as counterpart and opposite to the first one, and the Last Adam is no more a this-worldly and secular figure than Israel is ethnic. How the category *ethnic* fits into the present context is not at all clear. That "Israel is God's people" forms no more ethnic a statement than that Adam stands for humanity. Israel and Adam form species of the same genus, and what differentiates between them is the Torah.

God left the world in stages because of Adam's and Adam's descendants' actions, and God returned to the world in stages because of Abraham's and Abraham's descendants' actions. So Israel forms the medium by which God comes down to earth. This is stated in the following terms: God entered the world on account of Israel, and God departed from the world because of Israel's actions; the center of God's presence was the Temple in its time but the presence abandoned the Temple in due course:

A.    There were ten descents that the Presence of God made into the world.

B.    One into the Garden of Eden, as it says, *And they heard the sound of God walking in the garden* (Gen. 3:5).

C.    One in the generation of the tower of Babylon, as it is said, *And the Lord came down to see the city and the tower* (Gen. 11:5).

D.    One in Sodom: *I shall now go down and see whether it is in accord with the cry that has come to me* (Gen. 18:21).

E.   One in Egypt: *I shall go down and save them from the hand of the Egyptians* (Ex. 3:8).

F.   One at the sea: *He bowed the heavens also and came down* (2 Sam. 22:10).

G.   One at Sinai: *And the Lord came down onto Mount Sinai* (Ex. 19:20).

H.   One in the pillar of cloud: *And the Lord came down in a pillar* (Num. 11:25).

I.   One in the Temple: *This gate will be closed and will not be open for the Lord, God of Israel, has come in through it* (Ezek. 44:2).

J.   And one is destined to take place in the time of Gog and Magog: *And his feet shall stand that day on the Mount of Olives* (Zech. 14:4).

Fathers according to Rabbi Nathan 34:8.1

Here we see an entirely supernatural issue. When we speak of Jesus Christ, God incarnate, we invoke a category that is no more "biographical" or historical than Israel is ethnic. In the formulation at hand, the category *ethnic* proves to be simply out of place, monumentally irrelevant to the frame of reference and the language of discourse. Israel evokes a variety of comparable categories in Christianity, at some points serving as the counterpart to the mystical body of Christ—the church—at other points as the counterpart to Jesus Christ, the opposite of Adam, and still elsewhere taking up still other tasks in the theological enterprise.

## CONCLUSION

The way in which Judaism represents its "Israel," meaning the holy people, is a concrete example of how religion defines the social order. When it comes to creating social groups, religion gives concrete definition to what lies beyond immediate experience, as much as to what is formed of concrete encounter. Religion has the power of transforming cells of like-minded persons into believers and believers into a church, the saved, holy people, a supernatural family, or (as is most common) even a social entity that is altogether unique. Religion has the power of turning into a thing we can use to define and identify what is, in fact, ineffable abstraction, intangible relationship, process beyond palpable perception. Religion takes the concrete and turns it into something general and encompassing, just as the word *power* changes a blow or the word *love*, a kiss, into something both abstract and universal. And that is assuredly the fact, whether religion addresses God in heaven or speaks of humanity in the home, street, and town; whether it identifies a building as holy, defines a properly performed gesture as sanctifying, or declares two or three individuals to form a society, a holy entity—for instance, the embodiment here and now of God's people or God's own person or body.

In all, in religious groups—not just the local church or mosque or synagogue but the body of Christ, the Nation of Islam, or Israel the holy people—we deal with people who come together from time to time—hence, temporarily—but who see themselves as forming a lasting society. Religion transforms individuals and families into a corporate body, imputing relationships other than those natural to location or family genealogy. That is the power of religion: to name and treat as real the otherwise random confluence, in belief and behavior, of isolated groups of people; to persuade those families that they form part of something larger than their limited aggregations, even though no one in those families has ever seen, or can ever encompass in a single vision, the entirety of that something more, that entire nation, mystical body, entity unto itself. In simple terms, religions speak of social entities made up of their devotees. These they turn from concrete entity in the here and now into abstractions merely represented in the here and now. The social group is transformed from what the world sees to what the eye of faith perceives, becoming, in the case of a Judaism, an "Israel," and in the case of a Christianity, "the mystical body of Christ" or "the church," That transformation, by faith, not only defines reality "out there" but turns out to make history; it even explained to some teenagers in West Hartford, Connecticut, forty years ago, who they were and who everybody else was. And for us all, from then to now, that same Judaism has explained much about the world we know—and try to change for the better.

## STUDY QUESTIONS

1. According to Neusner, what is the function of religion in general? What are four specific functions of religion, for example, in Judaism? Do you think that these functions are specific to Judaism? Why? Why not?

2. What does it mean for Neusner's high school community to say, "We are Israel?" Be specific.

3. What are two intangible characteristics of being part of a religion? How does the Mishnah Tractate Baba Mesia 2.1 on page 35 demonstrate your answer?

4. What text allows "Israel to become Israel"? Can a Gentile be on equal terms within Israel if he or she accepts the Torah? Discuss why. How is this notion of "conversion" similar or different from your own tradition?

5. What is the major distinction between ethnic Jews and religious Jews? Can you point to particular examples of such a distinction?

6. Give three concrete ways in which Judaism represents Israel.

# 4

## SAM GILL

---

# Linking Human Beings to Nature: Australian Arrarnta Religion

In his book *A Brief History of Time*, physicist Stephen Hawking tells a story about attending a conference on cosmology organized by the Jesuits in the Vatican.[1] At the conference, Hawking proposed that, according to his understanding that space-time is infinite and has no boundaries, there was no beginning, no moment of creation, for the universe. At the conclusion of the conference, the attendees were granted an audience with the pope. Thinking about the scientific ideas he had proposed, Hawking describes his bemusement when the pope told the conference members it was all right to study the evolution of the universe after the big bang but they should not inquire into the big bang itself because, being the moment of creation, it was the work of God. Throughout his book, Hawking sees the domain of religious explanation shrink as his scientific theories advance. This antagonism between science and religion is all too familiar.

One thing religions do is explain the natural world. But today, with fellows like Stephen Hawking peering into the very processes of the creation of the universe, how can we possibly understand this function of religion? With religious officials such as the pope (if Hawking recounts the pope's comments correctly) limiting the work of God to the moment of creation and, seemingly, limiting the religious to the work of God, what is there for religions to explain? In the view shared by a pope and a physicist, is not religious explanation merely that which is pre- or nonscientific? Will religious explanation not fall as science rises?

To put science and religion in opposition in this way is misleading and naive. First, it shortchanges the work of both science and religion. Second, it fails to understand what an explanation really is. The word *explain* means "to make understandable," that is, to make meaningful. Anything, including nature, can be made meaningful in a number of ways. Although different ways of explaining—in this case, science and religion—may focus on the same subject—in this case, nature—the explanations each gives need not be compared or placed in conflict with each other. Religions can and often do explain nature in ways that are important for human beings to live meaningful lives.

To show how religions explain what we think of as the natural world, I present in this chapter an extended discussion of the Arrarnta, an Aboriginal people living in the great red desert in central Australia. The Arrarnta are a large group who share language, a kinship system, a way of life, and a vast area of land.

Try to imagine yourself among the Arrarnta. What is the sequence of images that moves through your mind? First, you likely picture the island continent of Australia and where it is on the globe relative to the other continents, especially to the place where you are as you read this. If you are in North America, you will think of Australia as "down under," that is, in the Southern Hemisphere, and as "antipodal," that is, on the other side of the globe. Having that image of Australia, you then try to focus on the center of Australia by searching your memory for images from books, films, and maybe personal experience of this vast desert region.

Having acquired this image, you turn to the term *Arrarnta*. Likely you do not know anything about these people. But knowing that they are Australian Aborigines helps. Now you can picture yourself in this location among broad-faced, dark black, nearly naked people. Perhaps you associate the image of these people with others around the world—Africans and Native Americans—and feel remorse at their destruction, curiosity at their seemingly exotic nature, or maybe even disgust or pity at what appears to you as their primitiveness. As you imagine yourself among the Arrarnta, you may see men hunting kangaroos using spears and boomerangs and women gathering grubs and roots. If you have read a little about Australian Aborigines, you may recall that these hunter-gatherers live pretty much as their ancestors lived, as they have lived for perhaps forty thousand years. That is a long legacy.

To imagine yourself among the Arrarnta, or even in Australia, you had to have a conception of the world as a globe, the earth. Then, through a process of modifying this image of the world, you located Australia and, finally, the Arrarnta. In your view, the modern Western view, the world is comprised of diverse lands and peoples. And seeing the earth as a globe implies that the earth is but one small body in a universe filled with planets, solar systems, stars, and galaxies.

There is likely also a temporal aspect to your image of the Arrarnta. Seeing them as people whose way of sustaining life has changed little over the centuries, you may think about them using such terms as *archaic, ancient, primitive, traditional,* all of which place the Arrarnta in the past compared to you and those around you, who live in the contemporary, modern world. If you think of the Arrarnta in these temporal terms, you share the views of many important scholars in the late nineteenth and early twentieth centuries. The Australian Aborigines were of great interest to scholars during this time because they believed the Aborigines represented an early stage in the development of human culture. To study the Arrarnta was, in this view, like time travel back through millennia.

## THE ARRARNTA IDENTITY:
## COMBINING TIME AND PLACE

The Arrarnta view of their world is very different, at least until the very recent introduction of Western-style educational programs for Arrarnta people. They do not think of their world in terms of these spatial and temporal maps and images at all. The Arrarnta identify themselves and their world in several ways. They have personal names, but they are rarely called by these because personal names are considered an intimate part of the self. The Arrarnta think of themselves primarily in terms of "country." Though this is a very complicated notion, one aspect of it is not completely unfamiliar to us. When we meet new people, we often ask them where they live or where they are from. In North America we often identify people in terms of the region or area where they live or where they grew up. We refer to people as "southerners," "easterners," "New Yorkers," "Canadians," and so on. We even refer to the president of the United States by the place where he lives, the White House. The Arrarnta version of this kind of geographical identity is primary. But it gets more interesting.

An Arrarnta person receives his or her country identity from the place where the person's mother is when she first realizes she is pregnant. Feeling this new life within her body, she looks to the area about her to identify what country it is. But she does not identify it in terms of a mental map of the region, divided into sections or provinces. Rather, she recognizes a feature in the landscape that is the living reminder of events told in religious stories and enacted in rites. The stories tell of heroic figures who arose from the land and walked across it, creating through their actions its distinctive features. These are the ancestors or relatives of the present-day Arrarnta. Natural, topographic landforms are identifiable with the actions or appearances of these heroic figures. The heroes both are these natural forms and are in these natural forms.

It is important now to discuss the term *nature.* When I say that Arrarnta religion explains the natural world, I do not mean that the Arrarnta have a conception of nature that resembles ours. Though the term *nature,* as used during the last several centuries, has meant a great many things in Western cultures, minimally it has referred broadly to the physical world that has not been constructed or created by human existence. Further, insofar as the natural sciences focus their attention on the explanation of nature, there is the implication that nature exists and functions according to uniform, universal principles.

Explanations like these are irrelevant and completely useless to the Arrarnta.

## *ALTJIRA:* A WAY TO UNDERSTAND THE NATURE OF THE WORLD

When we think of origins, likely we think of events of long ago, of the beginning, of ancient history. We place these origins at the beginning of a time line that runs to the present and promises to extend indefinitely into the future.

But the Arrarnta's concepts differ markedly from ours. The Arrarnta are not interested in origination in the sense of cosmic creation. They tell stories of their ancestors that explain the meaning and origin of elements of their world.

Nor does time, for Arrarnta people, resemble our concept. In fact, time is not all that important. The Arrarnta live in a world of seasons and cycles that repeat endlessly. There are no mechanical clocks or calendars numbering the hours, days, and years. They have terms only for the first several numbers. There are no permanent buildings or monuments by which to mark the linear passage of time. An Arrarnta encampment leaves no trace on the landscape within a year or two of its abandonment. The Arrarnta do not write or have books, so they keep their histories in their living memories. While time is reckoned, and there is a sense of time passing as people grow older and as generation succeeds generation, there is no sense of either the ticking seconds of time or the long linear march of time.

We have constant reminders of how the world is changing rapidly around us. Think of such obvious things as changing clothing styles, cars identified by year, the aging of houses and buildings and personal possessions. Think about how recent decades—the 1960s, 1970s, 1980s—are identified with distinctive characteristics. Everywhere we turn we are reminded of change. Yet change is scarcely an aspect of Arrarnta experience.

Arrarnta experience might best be characterized as *abiding*. The Arrarnta identify the time of their heroic ancestors as ancient or far past. But what might they mean by this distant past? Their active memories are of people and human events that span no more than several generations. The era of the ancestors simply precedes these memories. It is a time that parallels the present but precedes it by several generations. Far more important than when the events in the stories occurred is that the stories tell about what is abiding. The Arrarnta call the era of their ancestors *Altjira*, which refers more to the ancestors and their actions, considered abiding events, than to a period of time. The term is often translated by the English term *Dreamtime*, which is clearly misleading.

*Altjira* refers less to a time than it does to an understanding of the nature of the world. *Altjira* refers to the events that explain the existence of "country," but it is not as much an explanation simply of how it came to be as it is the set of stories an Arrarnta person possesses by which he or she can negotiate and manipulate his or her relationship to other Arrarnta and to what we would call "the natural world."

*Altjira* stories depict journeys across the landscape of beings who are identified with some aspect of the natural world, for example, a wildcat (*tjilpa*), witchetty grub (*udnirringita*), or hakea flower (*unjiamba*). In ritual, these stories are told through song and dance dramas. When sung, the stories are sometimes described as "songlines," that is, song sequences that tell the story that crosses the land. I like to think of the event sequences as "storytracks." These storytracks are representations of the journeys of the *Altjira* beings and what they did at each place they stopped.

For the Arrarnta, then, what we think of as the natural world—comprised of places in the landscape and also of all the plants, animals, and living forces in the landscape—is significant because of the actions of the ancestral beings. The stories of the *Altjira* place the events in the past, but features in the landscape connected with the story events are identified with the living force of the heroic beings, and these places are repositories of the spirit children left by the heroes, as a living part of themselves, to become human beings.

So *Altjira* is both past and present, both temporal and spatial. W.E.H. Stanner has suggested we think of *Altjira* as an "everywhen,"[2] while Tony Swain has referred to it as "abiding events."[3] Specific *Altjira* are identified at once with a track across the landscape, specific places along that track, and elements (wind, rain, lightning) and species (opossum, kangaroo, goanna) of the natural world.

The scenario is similar among these many stories. The meaningless landscape is assumed in the story to exist already. At a named, physically identifiable location, the heroic figures, the ancestors of living Arrarnta, arise from the ground. They travel across the landscape to another geographically identifiable location, where they camp. They meet other groups of people with whom rituals and stories are exchanged. Spirit children, identified with the ancestral heroes, are left in the ground at these locations. The Arrarnta believe that it is these spirit children who enter and impregnate a woman as she travels in a specific location. Finally, the heroes die and turn into a feature of the land or simply return into the earth at a given location. Wooden or stone objects called *tjurunga* (I discuss these below) are often left behind, which bear physical reminders of the adventures of these heroes.

To the Arrarnta, heroic *Altjira* beings are aspects of the natural world. They are also identified with the country determined by the itinerary those figures took in traveling across the land. In some sense, the living Arrarnta are living representations of these figures and owe their lives to the spirit children the heroes placed in the land.

So you see, every Arrarnta person's identity is connected with a complex of interconnected ideas that are more or less synonymous: country, *Altjira*, storytrack, and an aspect of nature.[4] Among the Arrarnta, there are many storytracks by which individuals identify themselves. Storytrack, or country, is a characteristic of one's identity gained at birth, and it remains with one for life. All people who are born to the same country or storytrack share a common identity. This means, for example, that every person whose mother was near a place associated with the abiding events of the wildcat will be identified as "wildcat." Every storytrack has obligations for its members, such as the performance of rites, the keeping of knowledge, the care of ritual objects (*tjurunga*), and, most important, care of the country. Every storytrack has privileges for its members, such as access to land area to hunt and gather, to travel, and to know the locations of water.

If we try to imagine how an Arrarnta would map her or his world, we might expect the Arrarnta person to picture an area divided into bounded spaces, each space distinguished by specific abiding events. But we must remember that these series of events are interconnected, forming tracks across the land, and it is the interconnection of abiding events that is essential to their coherence. Further, various storytracks or countries can include events that occur at the same physical location.

So a different kind of map seems more appropriate. Imagine a map of an area in which the general perimeter is indistinct. Across this area are sets of intersecting lines (you might think of them as distinguished by different colors), drawn to show the travels of various groups of *Altjira* beings. Points along these lines designate places where abiding events occur. The place of an abiding event in one track (country) may be the location of a different abiding event for another track. This map is distinguished by a grid of partially intersecting and overlaid tracks. In some areas one track is predominant, while in other areas another predominates. But in no area is one track exclusive. Notice how this kind of map contrasts with the ones by which we located the Arrarnta in Australia. This is the kind of map conceived by someone who lives in the area being mapped and who knows the world only to the extent of the experiences of the living people in his or her culture. From this perspective, the perimeter is blurry at best, if it even exists.

Notably, for the Arrarnta it is more appropriate to think that a person belongs to the land than that the land can belong to any person. The Arrarnta people are divided into many groups. Each group is identified as an element or species of nature (the designation of track or country). The storytracks that tell of the sequences of abiding events intersect with one another as they march across the same landscape. There is no hierarchy among these groups. Consequently, among the Arrarnta there is no war or contest over territory. There is no central governing body among the Arrarnta and no hierarchy or ranking among the groups.

## STORYTRACK

Perhaps the most important way an Arrarnta person identifies him- or herself is in the terms of the storytrack that intersects the place where his or her mother is when she discovers she is pregnant. When this woman returns to her people after the day of gathering, she tells the elders (men) the news. The elders, especially those who are also identified with the abiding events of this place, go to the place indicated by the prospective mother and look for an object called a *tjurunga*, likely a stone, that they identify with this place by means of the relationship of its physical characteristics to the abiding events of this storytrack. This personal *tjurunga* is placed in the secret storehouse of the group that identifies with this storytrack.

In the Arrarnta world, no physical objects endure for long except *tjurungas*. For each group that identifies with a common storytrack there is a permanent set of *tjurungas* other than the personal *tjurungas*. These permanent *tjurungas* are usually large, flat, oval-shaped objects made of stone or wood, on which are inscribed designs that relate the events of the storytrack. Though these objects and their designs are very secret, contemporary Arrarnta painters use the styles and motifs in their art. Arrarnta traveling through country that is not their own avoid the storehouses of *tjurungas*. Trespass can lead to severe punishment.

Are you beginning to see how Arrarnta religion explains the natural world? To us, the desert home of the Arrarnta may seem a near-featureless land. To the Arrarnta, every hill, unusual arrangement of stones, tree, cave, pool, and valley is the location of one or more abiding events. Many of these places bear the presence of the *Altjira* beings who are the ancestors of those who are identified with the series of abiding events that cross these places. These beings are identified with elements of the natural world, and their travels are strung together in storytracks crossing the land, from place of abiding event to place of abiding event. The primary way an Arrarnta individual identifies her- or himself is by the element of the natural world that names country, storytrack, *Altjira* beings, or group, all of which are virtually synonymous.

## SOCIAL ORGANIZATION
## AND THE NATURAL WORLD

Arrarnta religion is inseparable from social organization, but Arrarnta practices are more complex than we might expect. Remember that the primary way an individual identifies him- or herself is by country or storytrack. This provides the primary group identity for Arrarnta as well. But that a woman is identified as "witchetty grub" does not mean that she will be near a witchetty-grub abiding place when she discovers she is pregnant. This means, then, that the primary individual and group identity does not pass along bloodlines. In terms of our social organization this would mean that a man named Smith married to a woman named Jones could have a child who possibly would be identified as either Smith or Jones but also possibly as Brown or McIntosh or the like, depending on where the mother was when she discovered herself pregnant.

But in Arrarnta culture there are also social relationships that depend on bloodline. These go by the terms *kirda*, designating the father's side, and *kurdungurlu*, designating the mother's side. A person associates by means of a *kirda* relationship to the country of his or her father, and by means of a *kurdungurlu* relationship to his or her mother's country. These types of relationships extend to the preceding generations as well, that is, to grandparents and great-grandparents. *Kirda* and *kurdungurlu* relationships to land are complementary. These relationships also carry complementary responsibilities in the performance of the rites associated with the countries of one's parents.

This is complex, but notice how Arrarnta society is woven into an intricate web of relationships all having to do with how the natural world is made meaningful. It is impossible for the Arrarnta simply to saunter casually through the landscape. Every person must know his or her storytrack (that is, country) and those of his or her mother and father and their mothers and fathers. One must know how all these storytracks correspond with a sequence of imprints represented as physical features at specific geographic locations in the natural landscape. Though the land may seem a lifeless and life-threatening desert to us, to the Arrarnta it is filled with the vitality of the ancestors, with storytracks, with social ties, all identified with elements of the natural world.

And there are other ways in which Arrarnta religion explains nature. All of the members who identify with a common country also identify with the name of this group, an aspect of the natural world—for example, witchetty grub, wildcat, blue jay, or willy wagtail (a bird). Each group, as it exists in an extended area, is responsible for congregating annually at one of the places where one of the abiding events for this group happened. At this place they perform rites for the purpose of increasing the supply of whatever aspect of nature it is with which they identify. For instance, the witchetty-grub group will meet at a witchetty-grub site and perform rites to increase the number of witchetty grubs. The performance of these rites often correlates with the oncoming season of abundance. The witchetty-grub group then gathers the grubs and distributes them to other groups in the area. They will eat only a token amount of grubs when they are gathered, after the performance of the rites, and will abstain from eating them at all other times. Year after year, the witchetty-grub group will go to other significant witchetty-grub sites along the storytrack to perform these rites. Over a number of years of ritual performances, the entire witchetty-grub storytrack is traced. This means if a person identifies with witchetty grub, she or he does not eat grubs at all except in a ritual setting, but she or he is a member of the group responsible for the abundance of the grubs for all Arrarnta. And such is the pattern for all groups.

Thus the plants, animals, birds, and even weather phenomena such as rain and lightning are, for the Arrarnta, given meaning by Arrarnta religion far beyond their significance as contributors to practical needs. Indeed, practical needs such as the supply of food for the community are incorporated into these religious explanations of nature.

## INITIATION

While the religiously based explanations of elements of the natural world weave Arrarnta society together, there are other aspects of the religion that divide it. I suggested this when I noted earlier that a storage place for *tjurungas* is avoided by all people except the members of the group identified with these objects. The rituals and stories of "country" are secret, or considered highly privileged. Only initiated members of the group have the right to tell the stories, perform the rites, know the songs, and do the dances of their storytrack. Furthermore, there are distinctions between male and female privileges, bodies of knowledge, and performance responsibilities.

A large part of Arrarnta religion focuses on the long, physically difficult process of initiating the young into the knowledge and practices of their "country." For males, it is a process of several stages that unfolds over a number of years, beginning around age ten and perhaps not fully completing until age twenty-five or thirty. A description of these initiation rites shows the importance of the explanations of nature provided by a person's storytrack and country.

The rites for males are long and complex, but they can be summarily described as four separate actions that occur at different places and times: (1) throwing the boy in the air, (2) circumcision, (3) subincision, and (4) fire ceremony.

At the appropriate time for beginning the initiation process, the men and women meet at the center of camp. Standing close together in a group, the men take the initiate boys, one by one, and throw them repeatedly into the air and catch them. The women dance around the group of men. Next, the men paint the boys' chests and backs. The nasal septa of these boys are pierced and bored through, so the boys may begin wearing nose bones. The purpose of this rite is said to promote growth, to mark the separation of the boys from the females in their camp, and to establish special relationships between the boys and the elder men who will direct their initiation process.

Several years after this throwing rite, circumcision is performed. At a location identified with an individual boy's country or storytrack, the initiated men of the boy's *Altjira* group seize the initiate and carry him to the ceremonial ground. During much of this rite the boy is kept hidden behind a brush pile or brake, while dance dramas are performed on the ceremonial ground. The women grease and paint the initiate's body. In anticipation of teaching secret knowledge to the boy, the group subjects him to a terrifying rite. A bull roarer (a flat board whirled on the end of a string, producing a roaring sound) is sounded nearby, and the boy is told this is the voice of a spirit being who will carry him away should he reveal any of the secrets he is to learn.

For days, the boy, fasting and confused, is shown—but without satisfactory explanation—ritual objects and dance dramas of the events of the ancestors associated with the group to which he belongs. After many days, the boy is carried to the ceremonial ground. While songs that recall how the *Altjira* beings established the practice of circumcision are sung, the boy's foreskin is pulled out as far as possible and cut off. It is important that the boy not cry out from the pain of this operation. The blood from the wound is collected in a shield. The men bring out the bull roarers they used earlier to frighten the boy, to show him it was these, not the voice of a fearful spirit being, that made the frightening noise he heard. The boy's wounds are smoked to help stop the flow of blood, and the boy is isolated from the community while the wounds heal.

After five or six weeks, the boy is the subject of yet another rite of initiation: subincision. The women, who participated in the circumcision rite, are excluded from this rite. Again, dance dramas and songs reveal further secret knowledge to the initiate. The culmination of the rite occurs when the boy is seized and laid face up on the body of a man who is lying on his stomach on the ground. With the boy held in this position, the underside of the penis is stretched out, and the urethra is cut open the length of the penis with a stone knife. Blood from the subincision wound is collected in a shield and poured into the fire.

At each of these rites, the initiate receives a descriptive name that indicates to what stage he has progressed in the initiatory process.

The final rite of initiation, called the "fire ceremony," may not occur for some years after subincision. It is a part of another extensive ceremonial complex, called *Ingkura*, that is performed only once in several years for a given group. A description of this ritual complex is essential, both to understand more fully how Arrarnta religion explains nature and as context for the final male initiation rite.

*Ingkura* is a major festival that is performed only once in several years by any storytrack group. *Ingkura* lasts several months and involves all of the people identified with the host group and their families, from a large region. There are several phases to this rite.

The first phase is preparation. The *Ingkura* takes place at the site of a major abiding event in the storytrack of a group. At the ceremonial grounds on this location, a mound (called *parra*) two feet wide, thirty feet long, and a foot high is erected to represent the storytrack of the group. Once the site is determined, messengers are sent throughout the region to invite people to the festival. For several weeks, people trickle to the festival location. Much social activity, including dancing, takes place among those awaiting the beginning of *Ingkura*.

The next phase, which lasts two months or more, involves the performance of dance dramas. Men who are responsible for a particular body of knowledge gather groups to help them present this knowledge publicly in the form of a dance drama. Several different dance dramas may be performed at intervals every day and night. These dances portray the actions of the *Altjira* beings at one of the group's abiding events. They involve body painting, the use of poles and ritual objects (especially *tjurungas*), storytelling, and singing. Each drama is identified by specific geographic location within the storytrack. It is at these times that much knowledge about the storytrack is passed among the people. *Tjurungas* are carefully examined. Participating in one of these dance dramas is an honor and also gives participants the privilege of obtaining knowledge, that is, a fuller explanation of the natural world.

The *Ingkura* is hosted by a single group with a common storytrack, but because members of this group are married to members of other groups, there are people present from many different countries, many storytracks. *Ingkura* serves to perpetuate within the group the knowledge of the storytrack but also to reveal it to people of other groups. This is another example of how storytrack serves to separate and integrate Arrarnta society through explanation of the natural world.

During the *Ingkura*, the male initiates are shown some of the dance dramas, yet they fast and are often kept hidden so that they see only hints, hear only clues. Finally, in a flurry of rites performed for the initiates over several days, *Ingkura* comes to a close. The climactic rite involves placing the initiates on green branches that are set over pits of burning coals. The initiates must endure the intense heat of the coals, often in addition to intense desert heat, until the men permit them to arise, perhaps after four or five minutes. After this fire ceremony the initiates are considered fully men, yet they must still go into the bush for a few days before returning to assume their role as responsible and knowledgeable adults.

This is the religious process by which the Arrarnta explain nature. Though you may be horrified by these initiatory actions, you must also appreciate the extent, complexity, and profundity of their religious explanations. To be born to a particular country, one has much to learn. The learning unfolds gradually, in ritual, in travel, in song and dance. Even the fully initiated man has only begun to learn about the abiding events on which his whole life depends. Though it is not well documented, women have a less rigorous but no less important process of becoming adults and learning their country. Through the practice of religion throughout life, an Arrarnta will never stop learning about the natural world.

## CONCLUSION

Religious explanations of the natural world are not static, isolated bits of knowledge. These explanations provide a grid, a set of resources, and principles of relationships by which all Arrarnta people manipulate and negotiate their way through life and the world. For example, if a person wishes to travel into a particular area, she or he will examine the various storytracks with which linkages can be established. A woman's choice of whom her son should marry will doubtless take into account the prospective bride's country, because this will give the woman access, through her son's marriage, to this land. It may appear that marriages, travels, and social relationships are restricted by the rules regarding country and storytrack, but the situation must be seen the other way around. Life is made meaningful by the potential offered by these explanations of the natural world. Relationships are made by the selection, interpretation, and application of these explanatory models.

We can draw from this brief introduction to Arrarnta religion a general perspective that may be broadly useful. Note that even within Arrarnta religion, the existence of multiple storytracks suggests there are many systems for explaining the natural world. These explanations need not be consistent, and often they may be in conflict. The kangaroo storytrack differs significantly from the flying ant storytrack. Yet the Arrarnta do not exclude one of these in preference of another. There is no imposed hierarchy, no corner on truth or meaning. As a result, when storytracks cross, as they often do, knowledge is shared and it is considered a privilege to learn about the storytracks of others.

Using the Arrarnta system as an analogy, science and religion may be considered two storytracks in the landscape of our explanatory world. In this light, each is a viable and important way of explaining the natural world. Neither need be denied by the other. No wars need be fought to eliminate either or to reduce one to the other. Those who follow each track ought to be eager and to consider it honorable to learn the stories of the other. Both may be seen as providing the resources by which human beings can go about the business of making their lives meaningful.

## NOTES

1. Stephen W. Hawking, *A Brief History of Time: From the Big Bang to Black Holes* (New York: Bantam Books, 1988), 116.

2. W.E.H. Stanner, "The Dreaming," in T.A.G. Hungerford, ed., *Australian Signpost* (Melbourne: F. W. Cheshire, 1956), 51.

3. Tony Swain, *A Place for Strangers: Towards a History of Australian Aboriginal Being* (Cambridge: Cambridge University Press, 1993), 22ff.

4. This complex has often been referred to by the term *totem*, derived from the Ojibwa (Native American) language. I am not using *totem* here because scholars have shown that the term leads to misconceptions and misunderstandings.

## STUDY QUESTIONS

1. What are two reasons that make opposing science and religion both "misleading and naive"?
2. What community of persons does Gill use to explore the relation between religion and the natural world? Name several ways in which this community serves Gill's purpose.
3. If the Arrarnta do not think of their world in terms of spatial and temporal maps, describe at least three ways in which the Arrarnta identify themselves and their world. Be specific.
4. How does the Arrarnta receive his or her "country identity"? What do you see as significant about relating a sense of place to the act of birth?
5. What do the Arrarnta mean by the term *Altjira?* How does this differ from Western culture's understanding of time? How might *Altjira* be similar to Western culture's understanding of time?
6. What are three characteristics of the Arrarnta notion of storytrack? How is the storytrack significant for how Arrarnta religion explains the natural world?
7. What are three elements of Arrarnta "kinship" practice that also have religious significance? Why would Gill suggest that "religion is inseparable from kinship"?
8. Describe four rites of initiation in which the males of the Arrarnta must participate. Do you see similar religious rites of passage in other religious traditions? in your own religious tradition? Be specific.

# 5

## DANNY L. JORGENSEN

# Neopaganism in America:
# How Witchcraft Matters Today

### AN INTRIGUING INVITATION

I was not surprised when Donna asked me to participate in a pagan ritual with her and a few friends. She practices witchcraft. Her religion, also known as Wicca, or the Craft, is the most prevalent form of paganism among contemporary Euro-Americans. Practitioners borrow freely and loosely from classical paganisms, especially the nonbiblical religions of Egypt, Greece, and Rome, as well as the pre-Christian religions of Europe, Western occultism (the Hermetic-Cabalistic tradition, including astrology, alchemy, tarot, and the like), and a variety of other sources. Neopaganism more accurately describes this religious movement in America today, since it is not directly connected, historically or socially, with traditional pagan religions.[1] Donna's invitation would provide a rare opportunity to examine the most important things religions do: create and enact a sacred interpretation of reality.

My interests in Neopaganism are scholarly. As a sociologist of religion, I study what religionists think, feel, and do, approached as nonjudgmentally, respectively, and empathetically as is humanly possible. Whenever it is appropriate, I employ a unique research strategy called "participant observation," or ethnography. The aim is to observe religionists and gain direct access to their experiences, meanings, and activities, sometimes by participating with them. These research findings are presented to other scholars of religion for further examination in an effort to enhance our understanding of particular religions and, most important, of what they tell us about religion in general.

Donna's invitation presented me with an intriguing opportunity to experience Neopaganism directly while conducting scholarly research on a new, alternative religion in American today. My participant observation confirmed that Wicca, like all religions, provides believers with an ultimately meaningful, sacred interpretation of reality—the most important thing that any religion does. The sacred reality defined by religion provides believers with social values, social rules, and ethical principles for conducting their lives; practices and rituals for enacting their vision of reality; forms of organizing their collective existence; and ways of defining and identifying themselves. A description of how this works teaches us why and how Neopaganisms, especially Wicca, are religions that matter in the United States today.

## THE THEORICUS RITUAL

I entered Donna's temple anxiously anticipating the unfolding event.[2] Black cloth swooped down from the ceiling and walls, covering the only window. Black imitation fur covered the floor. With only a few candles lit the room was very dark, and it was difficult to discern what awaited me in this sacred ritual space. The air was warm, almost damp, and the smell of incense filled the room.

As my eyes began adjusting to the darkness, I noticed five banners hanging on the wall to the east. They seemed to float in universal, astral space, yet I detected that three of the banners displayed Hebrew letters, and the other two were composed of rather unusual configurations of crosses and triangles. A cubical altar was located at the center of the dark space. I vaguely discerned that it held a fan, a lamp, a cup, salt, and symbols of the four elements—earth, air, water, and fire. My mind raced to make sense of it all—it almost seemed to touch my soul—but the meaning escaped me.

As I entered the temple, the other participants filed in behind me, assuming their preappointed positions in the darkness.[3] I, representing Anubis, stood at the north, with Osiris and Isis to my left in the east. Horus was on my right to the west, and Maat stood directly across from me to the south. Osiris and Isis, as spiritual king and queen, spoke of mundane things to their son, the manifested king, Horus. Once we entered magical space, however, they were free to talk with everyone. Maat was there to speak on behalf of the candidate, Donna. I, Anubis, would act as Donna's guide in this ritual initiation to the grade of Theoricus, the grade of air.

Blending techniques borrowed from Egyptian, Hebrew, and European sources, the circle was cast, defining the temple as sacred, magical space. It was created by the power of "the word," a vibrational tone echoing through the universe. The powers were summoned through identification, by naming them. Then, with a knock, the temple was opened.

Osiris directed Maat to bring the candidate into the readied temple. A few moments later Maat reappeared, leading a hooded Donna into the room. Donna, in this vulnerable condition, stumbled around the temple, attempting to follow Maat's instructions. "Why are you here?" Osiris queried the initiate. I, like the others, listened carefully to her response. She had asked for our assistance with the initiation. We could refuse her entrance into the grade of air if, at any point, her reasons were insufficient or her preparation was judged to be incomplete.

"Like all who walk this path," Donna began, "my first step was into the earth grade. When I took that initiation," she continued, "I realized that I had not taken care of the mundane. It became my goal to obtain a bachelor's degree. To start a path that would eventually lead to a career. I come to you tonight with that degree," Donna exclaimed, handing Osiris a piece of paper. Taking it from her, he examined it carefully, then passed it around for the rest of us to see. I confirmed that it was her college diploma.

"So what do you want from us now?" Isis asked bluntly. "I wish to be admitted into the air grade," Donna replied with solemn thoughtfulness. "With help from the powers of air, I will continue in school. My goal is to obtain a Ph.D." Maat and I, Anubis, approached the candidate, standing beside her in support of the request. "So be it," proclaimed Osiris.

With Maat's assistance Donna kneeled, placing the cubical cross in her hand. Knowing what was expected from her, the candidate raised the cross in midair and took her oath, clearly articulating her intentions. Only then did Maat reach out to her, removing the hood.

Taking Donna's hand, I led her to each of the four quarters. At each location she was challenged by the elemental powers. Divesting all knowledge she had of them, she was allowed to pass each quarter. Donna identified associations made with colors, tools, letters, angels, archangels, gods, and goddesses. Then, approaching the center, she explained to Isis and Osiris the meaning of the symbols on the altar, along with that of the cubical cross.

After she had rendered satisfactory explanations, Osiris stood before the candidate. He made a majestic bow, and the candles were blown out by the powers of air. Black space was all that was left. And then, as is in the power of the word, Osiris's voice resonated through the darkness:

"Can you enlist help from the powers of air? You must have names and knowledge that identifies these forces," he prompted. As suddenly as the lights went out, a new light appeared in the west. Horus, standing there, before the candidate, asked, "Tell me, what is this I hold?" He thrust out the caduceus, the insignia of Hermes. Carefully examining it, Donna began to explain the tool. Obviously she had studied it.

Next, Osiris challenged Donna to explain the tree of life, the black and white pillars free standing in black astral space, and the cross and triangle resting on the altar. The banners on the wall had changed, replaced by three different Hebrew letters. The one cross-and-triangle banner had moved to the west wall. Yet Donna was able to explain everything. With a blessing, Osiris placed the candidate on the tree of life for one brief moment. With love and kindness, he handed her a pendant. "Now, what is this, Donna?" he inquired. "It's my shoe, my Monopoly shoe," she exclaimed with delight. "I am the shoe in Monopoly, because I must walk the board. Monopoly is the game I must play, the game we call life."

Osiris instructed Anubis to announce that Donna had entered the grade of air. After I did so, everyone joined me at the center of the temple. Lounging there, we relaxed, conversing with the initiate and telling her about our experiences and adventures with the academy. The room was warm with our happiness and love for her. Playfully, we advised Donna of the path's challenges. She responded with all the enthusiasm of the fool but the mastery of the magician, about to depart on the journey.

Eventually, Osiris announced that it was time to close the temple. Again, the power of the word was used to release the powers, with thanks and salutations. A prayer was uttered, and with a knock, the temple was closed.

## NEOPAGAN BELIEFS AND THEIR CONSEQUENCES

Donna's religious beliefs define a completely enchanted world, yet one that is very real to her and to other neopagans. The world around us, the one we experience and perceive as real, is meaningless except for how we define it. Our experiences of the world become meaningful through our symbolic interpretation of them. The mental images (ideas or concepts) contained in language specify what we hold to be real, what does and does not exist, and the sense or meaning of it all for us. What human beings take to be reality thereby is socially constructed: we create it, define it, assign it meaning, share it with one another, and sustain it by way of symbolic interaction with one another and with the larger environment. These socially constructed interpretations, formed as symbolic images, define what we *believe* (and claim to know as reality) about everything.

All beliefs—religious, political, scientific, economic, and so on—advance interpretations of reality or of certain aspects of it. Religious beliefs differ from other beliefs in that they provide comprehensive, ultimately meaningful, sacred interpretations of reality. Other beliefs, such as scientific, political, or national ideologies, may provide exhaustive interpretations of reality, and they sometimes even function like religions. Religious beliefs are unique, however, in defining reality as sacred, divine, or pertinent to ultimate concerns (gods, spirits, energies, forces) that are not, in and of themselves, natural or human.

### Characteristics

Neopagan beliefs are extremely diverse, but they share certain fundamental characteristics. All reality, animate and inanimate, according to neopaganism, is imbued and vitalized with the life force, spiritual energy or sacredness. These beliefs therefore are animistic. They also are pantheistic, meaning that deity or sacredness is in all people and all things—human beings are or may become sacred or godlike. Neopagans believe that sacredness or divinity is plural, multiple, multifaceted, and diverse: there are multiple deities, or deity is present in many different things and may take multiple forms. Their image of supernatural reality therefore is polytheistic.

Neopaganism believes that everything, all reality, is interconnected and interrelated in complex ways. Adherents believe that, in spite of its great diversity, this reality ultimately forms a unity, or wholeness. ("As above, so below," according to a famous Western occult dictum.) They maintain that inanimate things (rocks or planets) are connected to animate ones (biological life-forms); the life-worlds of plants, insects, and all forms of animals, including human beings, are interconnected and interdependent; and all of this, the earth and its inhabitants, is connected and intertwined with the great mysteries of the universe—the sacred, the life force, cosmic energy, and deity.

Wicca and most, but not all, forms of neopaganism feature some notion of a female deity, the Great Goddess. According to neopagans, she is immanent, present in everything, rather than transcendent, external to and beyond mundane reality, and in the traditional image of the Western God, she rules over everything. Emphasis on the Goddess in no way precludes the idea of a male deity. The sacred—divinity, the life force—balances polarities (opposites), the most important of which are female and male forces, energies, or spirits. Some forms of neopaganism, such as those borrowing from the pre-Christian religions of northern Europe, emphasize a male deity such as Odin instead of or in conjunction with a female one.

Neopagan goddesses and gods may take many different forms or none at all. Some believers think literally, in terms of embodied, personified deities, while others regard them strictly as figurative or metaphorical images—that is, as useful symbols but not literal descriptions of reality. The Great Mother (or Great Goddess), according to neopaganism, has three aspects—maiden, mother, and crone—reflecting various natural cycles, such as birth and death. The moon is one of her symbols. Aphrodite, Artemis, Astarte, Brigid, Ceridwen, Demeter, Diana, Hectate, Ishtar, Isis, Kore, Melusine, and Venus are a few of the names for the Great Goddess. The Horned God, the Great Mother's opposite and, frequently, her consort, is a common image of the male god. A bull or the sun typically symbolizes him. He is called Anubis, Apollo, Coeus, Evohe, Hermes, Jupiter, Mercury, Odin, Orpheus, Osiris, Pan, Thor, Thoth, Zeus, and many other names.

Neopagan reality is a completely enchanted, highly mystical one. The ordinary principles of sensory experience, observation, and Western scientific rationality do not apply. The great mythic stories of human existence, those of the Egyptians, Greeks, Romans, pre-Christian Europeans, and other nonbiblical, traditional, indigenous cultures and peoples, such as the American Indians, fascinate neopagans. Science fiction serves as a valued resource, and contemporary practitioners are adept at creating and re-creating their own mythic realities. Whether the images are literal or figurative, neopagans believe that the gods and goddesses, along with a vast assortment of ordinarily invisible forces, energies, and spirits, are real and alive. They influence and interact with human beings, and people may interact with them. Fiction becomes fact, and fact becomes fiction. The mundane world of daily life thereby is an enchanted drama, a fairy tale or a game, like Dungeons and Dragons, played out on a cosmic stage.

### Values and Ethics

Religious beliefs envision the proper, moral order of things, especially human society. They specify what is valued (good) and devalued (bad). These values identify what matters the most—the goals of the religion— and they direct believers to act in ways that will accomplish these goals. Religious values define everything that believers are expected to do. They structure all human relationships and social institutions, from marriage, family and kinship, education, economics, and politics to the most mundane, everyday life activities. Insofar as the world is not as it should be, religion exists to make it all right.

Neopagan values derive from the principle that everything is interconnected and harmoniously balanced as a whole. The big problem with the contemporary world, according to Neopaganism, is that the fundamental unity of all things has been disrupted and the world is therefore out of order. The natural environment, human relations (culture and society), and the supernatural (sacred, divine) have become disconnected, unbalanced, and inharmonious. People are estranged from one another: men from women, parents from children, and one ethnic group, nation, or culture from another. People are out of touch with the air, water, earth, plants, and other animals composing the natural environment, including our own biology. People, culture, society, and nature are not connected with the supernatural, the divinity of all things. Neopaganism's fundamental values aim to restore the essential, sacred order among all of these things. Until this happens, neopaganism maintains, all things will be unable to fulfill their true, divine potential, resulting in very negative consequences for all.

Neopaganism teaches profound respect for the planet Earth, speaking of it as "Mother Earth," one aspect of the Great Goddess. Because of this value, Neopaganism commonly is regarded as a "nature" religion. It urges believers to live in harmony with the natural environment by respecting its order and seeking to coordinate their activities with it. Human destruction of the natural environment is a violation of the sacred, a crime that produces divine sanctions such as the lack of clean air and water, adequate food supplies, and other conditions conducive to human existence on the planet. Not surprising, many neopagans embrace ecological and environmental causes and participate in related political-action groups. Unlike some environmentalists, they generally do not oppose modern science or its technologies. Scientific technology, most Neopagans believe, may be used for good or evil purposes, much like magic.

Neopaganism teaches that people are part of nature and its order, not separate from it. Through our biology we are part of nature, one of its animals, and we are interconnected and interdependent with it and its basic order. Death, for instance, is natural and inevitable. Our current existence, according to most Neopagans, merely is a phase of some cycle. At some other time we may be incarnated otherwise, or reincarnated in another form. Human sexuality also is viewed as part of nature, a natural function to be expressed. It also is part of human society, one of the ways in which we are interconnected, and it is divine and part of our sacredness too.

Neopaganism cherishes human freedom, equality, and justice as sacred values. It teaches that human beings should be free to realize their divine potential, that all people are equal to one another, and that people should treat one another respectfully and responsibly as equally sacred beings. When one category or set of people, such as a nation, ethnic group, social caste or class, or gender, dominates another and thus brings about inequality, the sacred order of things becomes unbalanced, and people consequently suffer injustice. Neopagans believe that social inequality and unbalanced human relationships produce crimes of violence—abusive relationships, rape, murder—and warfare.

Religious beliefs reinforce and justify (legitimate) the values and resulting social structures of groups in the most powerful way possible. Prescribed institutions, such as marriage or a specific political system, are advanced as part of the divine, ultimate, sacred order. These institutions consequently are much more than simply convenient ways of structuring human relationships. Any failure to conform to these institutional expectations and arrangements is much more than a crime against society. Deviance is a violation of the sacred scheme of things and an offense against the most powerful forces of the universe.

Social rules or norms that specify proper (right) and improper (wrong) actions support the values defined by a religion's beliefs. Neopaganism values human freedom very highly, resulting in a radical individualism. Believers see it as a religion of liberation, of do's rather than don'ts. The central ethical teaching is, as long as it does not harm anyone (or anything, including yourself), do what you want—"Lest ye harm none, do what you will." Except as governed by this central ethical principle, almost nothing concerning what a person chooses to eat, drink, or smoke or how a person talks, plays, works, or interacts with other people is expressly prohibited. Seeking pleasure and happiness is encouraged, as long as their pursuit is ethical. Neopaganism encourages people—women as well as men—to express and enjoy sexuality, free from male-dominated cultural imagery and social conventions, constrained only by the ethics of mutual respect, responsibility, and not doing harm.

Sanctions (rewards and punishments) for doing right or wrong always reinforce religious values and ethics. Neopaganism promises that whatever a person does, right or wrong, returns to them "three times over." Ethical activity contributes to the fundamental Neopagan values. This generally means the realization of the true, divine potential of things and, thereby, the restoration of the harmonious balance among them. Neopagans expect that ethical conduct will enable them to achieve their divine potential, thereby securing a balanced existence within the sacred order. This, in turn, holds the promise of great magical power to use and direct the forces of the universe at will, enabling believers to satisfy their needs and desires.

## NEOPAGAN PRACTICES AND RITUALS

The images of reality advanced by a religion's beliefs become real through human activity. When people use these images to interpret their experience and conduct their daily lives, they enact the reality envisioned by religious beliefs. Whether or not the beliefs are accurate reflections of the world matters little, since even grossly distorted images of reality have very real consequences for believers. If people believe something is real and act on this basis, their action will have genuine consequences for them. Human existence thereby becomes meaningful in the ways envisioned by the religion. It is through human action, especially practices and rituals, that a religion lives and influences the lives and activities of its members.

My conversations with Donna frequently focused on Neopagan practices and rituals, especially magic (also spelled *magick*, to distinguish it from illusionism). Magical practices seek to transform the way believers think about reality and thereby to bring about changes in it. Neopagans employ a wide variety of magical practices: meditation, visualization, trance, chants, charms, divination, hexes, spells, and so on. Almost anything, however, that produces a result, some change of events, is seen as magical. If thinking about yourself in terms of some aspect of the Goddess changes your self-image, this act (imagining yourself differently) is considered a magical one.

Many magical techniques, such as studying, meditating, and visualizing, aim to bring about transformations of consciousness, the ways in which people envision themselves and the world around them. Neopagans sometimes regard shifts or alterations of consciousness as the highest form of magic, since these changes are very difficult to achieve and produce the most radical results. Learning to see the world as enchanted—animated by invisible forces and spirits—commonly requires years of serious study and meditation. This achievement alters the world of daily life forever. Its consequences are not unlike being transported to an entirely different planet (reality), one inhabited by theretofore invisible energies, forces, spirits, and deities.

Neopagans also employ magic for the purpose of effecting concrete, material changes in more or less ordinary, everyday life events. I watched

Donna break up a street fight and disperse the crowd, for example, by chanting the word *police*. When I was having domestic problems, she gave me a consecrated bundle of an herb, sage, with instructions for using it magically to banish negative spirits or energies from my home. Neopagans commonly meditate while burning a consecrated candle as a magical act aimed at securing a job, money, love, or improved health. Practitioners sometimes consider this to be a form of "low magic," since they believe these practices require less demanding magical techniques and produce less extraordinary results than "high magic."

The practice of magic is a way of life for Neopagans. Every situation its practitioners encounter and everything they do may be treated magically. Magic is used regularly for making life's decisions: defining a situation, identifying possible courses of action, selecting an appropriate course of action, and acting. Neopagans find it especially useful for treating situations that they regard as problems, large and small. Shortly after I first met Donna several years ago, for example, she learned from a physician that she had cancer. Over the next few months, she employed a variety of magical techniques to discern more about the cancer, ways of treating it, and the outcome of her condition. Then she accepted surgical treatment to remove it. Donna interpreted this orthodox medical procedure as a form of magic, and she believes that her cure was magical.

Neopagan rituals are a more routinized (standardized or regularized) form of magic. The principal rituals or festivals celebrate mythic interpretations of ecological, solar cycles, based on the traditional wheel of the year—the seasons—as envisioned by European paganism. Usually called "sabbats," particularly by Wiccans, the four major rituals, or greater sabbats, are Samhain (November Eve, or Halloween, around October 30–31), Oimelc (also called Brigid, or Candlemas, around February 1–2), Beltane (May Eve, around May 1), and Lughnasadh (around August 1). The four lesser sabbats, celebrating the solstices and equinoxes, are Yule (winter solstice, around December 20–23), Eostar (spring equinox, around March 20–23), Litha (summer solstice, around June 20–23), and Mabon (fall equinox, around September 20–23).

Neopagans also gather at more or less regular intervals (sometimes called *esbats* by Wiccans), such as the full or new moon, weekly, or whenever members feel the need. They perform formal ceremonies—separate from or in conjunction with other ritual occasions—when conducting initiations, marriages (called "handfasting"), and sometimes funerals. They may conduct other rituals for a special purpose, such as treating illness, dealing with life's small and large problems, or almost any reason.

Religions usually create special, sacred places for worship and conducting rituals. Neopagans prefer to worship out-of-doors in a forest, park, farm field, or large, private backyard, although some of them have religious buildings. When they worship in a building, it typically is the home of a member. Wiccans usually do not create permanent structures for ritual purposes. Any place dedicated for sacred use is a Wiccan temple. We used a bedroom in Donna's house, one employed regularly, but not exclusively, for ritual purposes.

Whatever space is used, neopagans usually supply it with an altar. The altar frequently is a table (although it might be the ground, a rock, a tree stump, and so on), located to the north and equipped with various ritual tools or implements. The more essential items include an *athame* (knife); a chalice (cup); containers holding water, salt, and usually incense; assorted candles in different colors; and sometimes statues or pictures of deities. The altar at the north and candles located at the other cardinal points, east, south, west, outline the sacred space. Neopagans usually envision the temple as a circle of sufficient size to encompass all the participants.

Neopagans, especially Wiccans, commonly conduct rituals in the nude, a state they call "skyclad." Most believers also have special ceremonial robes and costumes, including headdresses, jewelry, and ritual implements, such as an *athame,* stave, wand, or sword. Costumes usually are handcrafted, either completely or by modifying purchased items (chorus robes are popular), and they reflect personal preferences, group identifications, and membership ranks as specified by color and other symbols. We were clothed for the Theoricus ritual. Donna instructed me to dress comfortably in particular colors corresponding to the deity I symbolized. The other participants wore loose-fitting ceremonial robes, created or customized for this rite, and several adorned themselves with colorful symbols (such as the moon and the sun) that were skillfully painted on exposed body parts, such as the face.

Ritual scripts derive from any number of sources: classic texts, current books, the innovative adaptation of textual materials, or the creative imagination of the participants. Ceremonial occasions frequently are performed from a written or known text, but none is required, and many groups improvise and conduct some rituals free-form, without a script. The ritual we performed was patterned after the "ceremony of the grade of Theoricus" as outlined in Israel Regardie's *The Golden Dawn: A Complete Course in Practical Ceremonial Magic.*[4]

Donna invited the participants to her house, a beach house on an island in a quiet suburban neighborhood to plan the ritual. After explaining what she expected, Donna turned the meeting over to Bear, an expert in ceremonial (occult) magic. He walked us line by line through the text of the ritual, explaining the esoteric language, discussing its purpose, and helping us understand what we would be doing. We spent the next three hours doing this.

We retained the essential structure of the ritual, certain key scenes, and some of the occult jargon, but we streamlined and simplified the script greatly. Bear and Donna wrote up a revised version of the personalized ritual, and we met again the next week to discuss and rehearse it further. We subsequently spent three more hours practicing together before conducting the ritual.

Pagan rituals vary considerably from group to group and ritual to ritual. Most rituals, however, have similar structures containing a discernible beginning, middle, and end.

Casting a circle usually marks the beginning of the ritual. It is a form of magic, a way of creating sacred space and securing a safe place of worship. Typically, the high priestess (or her representative) invites the participants into the circle, welcoming and blessing them. As people enter the circle, she may make the sign of a pentagram on each participant's forehead, exchange kisses on the cheek with them, and offer the Wiccan greeting, "Blessed be." The worshipers file in one by one, forming the circle by always moving clockwise to whatever point they choose to occupy. Sometimes they join hands. The participants frequently create a festive atmosphere with live or taped music and song. Neopagans approach ritual with great respect, but they seek to attain a joyful, fun, and even playful collective mood.

Next, the high priestess and whomever she has selected to assist (typically two or three other people, commonly including a high priest) move from the north to the east. They stop at each of the cardinal points to recite an invocation. It is an invitation for the gods and goddesses to join in the activities, inspiring and protecting the participants. The high priestess typically invokes the deities by pointing her unsheathed *athame* to sky and earth, tracing a pentagram in salute while reciting words of invocation, as the other participants join her. A helper may sprinkle salt water at each point around the circle while another assistant carries smoldering incense. They usually traverse the circle three times, charging it with sacred energy and power, thus completing the beginning of a ritual. The worshipers expect to remain within the sacred space unless they receive permission from the high priestess to leave. After granting such a request, she cuts them a symbolic (imaginary) doorway for exiting and returning.

The middle portion of the neopagan rituals contains various activities that are indicated by the ritual's central purpose. The ritual might be conducted for a specific reason, such as initiation, handfasting, meditation, healing, or solving some problem (perhaps by casting a spell), or it might be one of the major or minor festivals. A Yule ritual, for example, generally celebrates the longest night of the year, when darkness (death) rules and begins to change into light (life); and Beltane is a fertility rite, a celebration of life, frequently involving a maypole dance.

The ritual's activities may be planned, part of a routine, or entirely spontaneous. The worshipers commonly socialize by talking, singing, drumming, dancing, all the while enjoying the occasion. They frequently pass cakes (breads, cookies, or other foodstuffs) and wine (actual wine, fruit juices, or some other kind of beverage) and sometimes feast on additional foods, then or later. The central part of Neopagan rituals may last a short period of time—whatever time is needed to complete the principal function—or it may go on for one to four hours or more, depending in part on the purpose as well as on the inclination and mood of the participants.

The conclusion of Neopagan rituals reverses the beginning. It consists of dismissing the deities and opening the circle. Typically, the high priestess, with or without helpers, thanks the goddesses and gods and asks for their blessings while standing at the altar. Then she moves eastward to each cardinal point and releases the deities, perhaps with a banishing pentacle. Finally she opens the circle, commonly by raising her *athame* to the sky, then to earth, opening her arms, and observing that the "circle is open but unbroken." Once this is accomplished, the ritual concludes and the worshipers are free to leave.

## NEOPAGAN SOCIAL ORGANIZATIONS

The character of a religion's beliefs largely determines the social structure and organization of its members' activities. Beliefs that make exclusive claims to truth (that is, that they are the only source of truth about reality) generally produce orthodox, authoritarian versions of the faith and, in turn, formal, tightly structured organizations. Belief systems that make more pluralistic claims to truth (ones that acknowledge more than one source of truth about reality) commonly produce many different versions of the faith, none of which is regarded as absolutely definitive, and they generally result in less formal, more loosely structured organizations.

Neopaganism is extremely pluralistic. Its beliefs derive from many different, if similar, sources, and substantially new beliefs emerged when adherents mixed, combined, and rearranged existing beliefs as interpretations of present-day realities (a process called *syncretism*). Although believers sometimes claim ancient origins, the contemporary revival may be most directly credited to Gerald B. Gardner (1884–1964), a retired British civil servant. After the 1951 repeal of the Witchcraft Acts in Britain, he published two very influential books, *Witchcraft Today* (1954) and *The Meaning of Witchcraft* (1959). His version of witchcraft is known as "Gardnerian."

Other varieties of contemporary witchcraft seem either to derive from the occult environment of the 1950s, the Gardnerian tradition, or they represent more recent developments. They were imported to the United States by students of the Craft (such as Raymond Buckland, Janet and Stewart Farrar, and Doreen Valiente) and through texts, and in North America they produced further innovations. Besides traditional Wiccan Neopaganisms (those claiming continuity with the old European paganisms), popular varieties of witchcraft today include Alexandrian, a branch founded by Alex Sanders, an English contemporary of Gerald Gardner; Dianic, a general label commonly used to identify feminist and womanist forms of neopaganism that stress a goddess religion; and the Radical Faeries, one way of describing the appropriation of neopagan spirituality by gay men.

Other Neopaganisms stress elements of ancient traditions, such as the religion of the Egyptian goddess Isis, or European paganisms such as the religions of Norse and Teutonic cultures (Odinism, for example) and, especially, those of the British Isles (for instance, the Druids). While the traditional practice of voodoo, Santeria, Candomblé, and the religions of indigenous cultures (like those of Native Americans) is entirely separate from the current revival of the Craft, these religions have stimulated interest and experimentation among contemporary Wiccans and neopagans. Current practitioners also have borrowed freely from other major religious traditions (Eastern religions such as Taoism, Hinduism, and Buddhism, as well as esoteric and mystical interpretations of biblical religions, for example) and from conventional philosophies (such as existentialism), sciences (the new physics), and psychiatry and psychology, as well as the humanities (classics and mythology) and social sciences (anthropology and sociology).

Neopaganism thereby takes many different, highly complex, and eclectic forms. Conventional categories, such as a simple distinction between religion and science or among the usual types and forms of religion, do not capture it adequately. Neopaganism is closely akin to varieties of contemporary feminist spirituality as represented in the writings of Carol

Christ, Judith Plaskow, Rosemary Radford Ruether, Naomi Goldenberg, Mary Daly, Riane Eisler, Marija Gimbutas, and Erica Jong. Before about 1980, there probably were as many distinctive Neopagan organizations as Wiccan groups in the United States. Today, however, different varieties of Wiccans dominate the Neopagan movement. They freely mix different varieties of witchcraft with other forms of paganism and other contemporary religious innovations.

Some Neopagans, called "solitaries" when Wiccan, worship alone. Most, however, including many who periodically are solitary practitioners, participate in collectivities or groups. The typical group, frequently identified as a coven or circle (if Wiccan), an order, a lodge, an institute, a council or association, and, sometimes, a church, is small, usually composed of anywhere from three to twenty members (about a dozen members is considered ideal). Participants generally think of the group as a family. While some groups are exclusively male or female, most attempt to maintain a balance in the number of women and men. Most groups are composed of like-minded people with similar social characteristics (age, education, occupation) and backgrounds.

The pluralism and radical individualism of Neopaganism largely determine that the structure and organization of members' activities are loose, informal, and highly flexible. Because Neopaganism lacks standardized beliefs (orthodoxy), formal leadership positions, formal membership roles, and hierarchical (ranked) group structures are, for the most part, unnecessary. All members are viewed more or less as equals. They generally are free to believe and do what they choose, and therefore there is little need for leaders to decide what beliefs are correct or how people should behave. Authority and organizational hierarchy contradict Neopagan pluralism and individualism. Because Neopagan organizations lack much formal structure, they are extremely fragile, precarious, and highly susceptible to dissolution and disorganization. Most groups vanish in less than ten years, and very few survive the founding members without undergoing major structural transformations.

While leadership is not completely lacking within Neopagan groups, leadership functions such as directing the performance of rituals commonly are informal and frequently are shared among the members, all of whom may be priests and priestesses. Sometimes a particular person more regularly (but informally) leads group activities because no one else is willing to take responsibility, and some groups defer leadership to someone because of their special expertise (greater knowledge), without formally designating the role as authoritative.

Some Wiccans and many other Neopagans form more structured groups. They formally acknowledge a high priestess and high priest, who have more or less equal authority but different roles (the one of high priestess being, functionally at least, more prominent and important), as well as various membership ranks. Typically, the high priestess founds the coven, selects the high priest, and directs most group activities. Members who aspire to her role usually are free (and sometimes, encouraged) to form their own covens. Neopagan groups spawned in this way are connected to one another by a complex web of informal and, sometimes, formal social relationships. Other membership ranks include people being screened for initiation, initiates in training, initiated members, adepts (those who have mastered the basics), and priestesses and priests. While the current trend, especially among Wiccans, is away from hierarchical formation, some Neopagan organizations structure their groups in more elaborate hierarchies. Modeled after traditional occultism, these groups contain many degrees, or ranks, based on a person's proficiency with the group's teachings and practices.

## THE NEOPAGAN REVIVAL
## IN AMERICA

The Neopagan revival has attracted several hundred thousand Americans, most within the last fifteen years, although no one knows exactly how many believers are in the United States or elsewhere, particularly in Europe. Neopaganism claims to be a religion without converts, yet most participants come from another religion. While Neopagans do not recruit members actively, they willingly share their religion with people who express an interest. Americans typically become interested in these religions by reading books (on feminism, occultism, magic, science fiction, ecology), through information and classes provided by occult bookshops, and, especially, through contacts with believers. Conversion generally is a lengthy process, lasting a year or more until a person has acquired sufficient knowledge to be initiated as a group member.[5]

American Neopagans generally are equally divided by gender (there may be a few more women than men). Most are adults between twenty and sixty years of age, although the children of members are becoming more visible and active. They are almost exclusively white, predominantly urbanites, and working- to middle-class. Most Neopagans are high school–educated; one-half or more have some college experience or a degree, and a significant proportion (perhaps as many as one-fourth) have some kind of postgraduate training or a degree. About one-half are employed in working-class occupations (as secretaries, clerical workers, folk artists and craftspeople, cooks, mechanics, and the like), while the other half of the Neopagan population works predominantly in service and professional fields (computing, teaching, nursing, accounting, law, and business). Neopagans therefore seem to be rather ordinary Americans, contrary to popular stereotypes of witches as strange, maladjusted, mentally ill, perverted people.

## How It Matters

Like all other religions, Neopaganism symbolically defines what believers take to be reality, which is specified by certain beliefs or claims to a knowledge of the composition and order of all existence. Myths or sacred stories commonly present the neopagan vision of reality. Like all religions, it provides certain goals (values), a sense of good and bad (morality), rules of right and wrong conduct (ethical norms), and ways of enacting the envisioned reality in the form of practices and rituals. The character of these beliefs also influences the manner in which members structure and organize their activities socially.

Neopaganism selectively draws on older religious traditions and other sources of knowledge, combining distinctive themes in different and novel ways. It is one of many new alternatives to the socially dominant religions of the United States. Like the other new religions, it proposes alternative ways of thinking, feeling, and acting toward the world of the present and future. Neopaganism's reality is enchanted; pervaded and animated by the sacred life force, which is in and of all things; and harmoniously balanced by opposing forces composing a multifaceted but unified totality.

The sacred stories of Neopaganism tell how the world is and teach believers how to correct problems. Neopaganism sees the modern world as unbalanced, and it aims to treat this problem. It focuses specifically on the lack of human equality, particularly male domination, and on human destruction (desecration) of the planet. It directs believers to treat all things—one another, all life forms, the planet—with respect, harming no thing. Its practices seek to restore the natural harmony of the universe, the cosmos, through magic. Magical practices provide ways of transforming human consciousness and directing the forces of the universe through mind and will. Magical rituals empower human beings to restore the cosmic order, and they celebrate the harmonious, peaceful unity of all things.

## Its Consequences for Others

Neopaganism, like many new religious alternatives, sometimes is viewed with disdain and even hostility from the standpoint of established religions and the dominant society. Witchcraft especially provokes popular cultural images of bizarre beliefs, weird practices, or strange, perverted people. Most of us grew up with the stereotype of diabolical, devil-worshiping, baby-eating, spell-casting, pointy-hatted, broom-riding, evil-doing Halloween witch-hags. Many of us also are familiar with folktales about witches as temptingly beautiful, sexually alluring young women who consort with the devil and bewitch unsuspecting, morally pure men. These conventional images have nothing to do with the beliefs and practices of contemporary Wiccans or any other variety of Neopagans.[6] There are a few self-designated Satanists in the United States, but they are not part of the Neopagan revival.

Many Americans, however, believe that diabolical, devil-worshiping witches exist. The media regularly report on mysterious animal mutilations and sacrifices, the desecration of graves and other seemingly strange happenings in cemeteries, and assorted criminal acts, all of them attributed to witches and their craft. A surprisingly large number of Americans are willing to share stories of ritual sacrifice, infanticide, incest, rape, murder, and other crimes allegedly committed by crazed witch or pagan cults. Although not a single, solid piece of independent evidence exists to support these charges as the activities of witches or similar, so-called cults, there can be no doubt that people believe and act on such allegations.

These negative depictions of witchcraft therefore are very real, even if what they claim is completely mistaken, and they have very real, truly powerful, and sometimes appalling consequences. Youthful Americans employ them as outrageous countercultural symbols. Heavy-metal rock bands, for example, use these depictions to underscore intergenerational differences, to signify rebellion from social conventions, and to titillate the public. These symbolic images are a source of popular cultural entertainment, a huge mass media enterprise that also includes magazine stories, books, television programs, and an almost endless series of movies.

Some of the consequences of the traditional images of witchcraft and paganism are much more serious and far less frivolous or entertaining. Contemporary Wiccans and other neopagans, not unlike the practitioners of other minority religions, frequently report discrimination in the workplace and other public arenas. Gunshots were fired toward the members of a local Wiccan coven several years ago, apparently by their neighbors in an otherwise quiet, middle-class suburb. In spite of our constitutional commitment to freedom of religion, intolerance for those whose beliefs differ too much from the socially dominant traditions and customs is an extremely unfortunate but undeniable feature of American life, past and present.[7]

## Its Future

Neopaganism matters because its beliefs define images of reality that believers find to be a meaningful response to the conditions of modern societies, and its practices provide ways of treating those conditions and related problems. Neopagan social organizations also are an adaptation to modern life. It is no accident that Neopagans think of their groups as families. These groups help satisfy the members' desire for intimate, family-like relationships—the kind of groups that were the foundation of premodern societies. Although these primary groups still exist in modern societies, they have changed, and many moderns experience difficulty in realizing their needs and desires within traditional social groups, including the family.

The manner in which Neopaganism is organized socially serves the needs and desires of the members. Participants are free to choose a primary group, redefine it, or change groups as their needs and interests vary with the rapidly changing circumstances of the world today. Although most Neopagan organizations are short-lived, the demise of one group generally leads to the formation of new ones. Even more elaborate networks of friendship and other relationships also connect Neopagans. Most of the country's larger cities contain loose alliances of diverse Neopagan individuals and groups. Neopaganism's social organization thereby represents a highly functional, creative, extremely flexible adaptation to modern social life, one that is self-regenerating. It is more than sufficient to sustain an authentic and enduring religious movement of significance in the United States today.

### NOTES

1. Magical practices were an integral part of the folk religions of pre-Christian Europe. People used them to ensure an abundant harvest or otherwise to manipulate nature for human benefit, to prevent illness or treat it, to ward off evil and bad fortune, to discern future events, and to help make everyday life decisions and secure happiness. They sometimes engaged in sorcery or magical practices intended to harm their enemies. Western images of witchcraft and the popular stereotypes associated with it, however, were created by Christianity in late medieval and early modern Europe. The widespread pre-Christian image of a horned god was translated (transformed) into the Christian devil, and magical practices increasingly were defined as evil. Rival versions of Christianity employed the resulting stereotypes to label and discredit

one another, and the elite classes opportunistically used them to secure social power and control. Most of the people accused of witchcraft during the European witch-hunting craze probably were Christians. Many of them were older, unmarried women, the wise ones of the peasant village, who used folk magic to help other people.

The early Euro-American colonists imported a vast assortment of magical beliefs and practices along with all existing stereotypes of witchcraft. Folk magic functioned much like a religion, without being named or regarded as such, for a majority of Americans, most of whom thought of themselves as at least nominally Christian.

Witchcraft stereotypes consequently have little to do with the pagan practices of past or present. Similarly, there is little evidence to support the claim that the contemporary Craft is continuous historically with the "old religion" of Europe—witchcraft, a goddess-worshiping fertility cult, driven underground and suppressed by Christianity. The folk religions of pre-Christian Europe were transformed radically, along with all of the basic social institutions, by modernity (scientific rationality, industrialization, urbanization, capitalism, and nationalism).

2. The ritual we performed was a form of initiation. While this initiatory rite was unique, it exhibited many of the essential features of other neopagan and Wiccan rituals. This account of the ritual is based on my field notes and recollections of the event, as well as Donna's reflections on it as recorded in her "Book of Shadows"—a personal journal maintained by many Wiccans. This essay benefited greatly from discussions with Donna and her critical readings.

3. The people Donna selected to participate in the ritual, a total of six— three women and three men— all (except me) are members of her lodge and similar to other American neopagans. I am a white, forty-four-year-old, single (divorced) university professor. Donna is a white, single (divorced) woman, thirty-four years old, a recent college graduate and beginning graduate student. Bear is a single, white male, forty-five years old, college-educated and employed as a computer programmer. Ylime is a white, single, college-educated woman, thirty-five years old and successfully employed as a freelance journalist specializing in computer technologies and software. Rayna is a twenty-eight-year-old, married, white woman. She is completing a doctoral dissertation in anthropology at an Ivy League university and is looking for academic employment. Michael, Rayna's spouse, is twenty-six years old. He holds a master's degree in environmental science, recently graduated from law school, was admitted to the state bar, and is employed by a state environmental agency.

Donna selected each of the participants for a specific purpose, and she assigned each of us the role of a particular deity. For ritual purposes, I was to perform the role of the god Kerux, who was being envisioned as Anubis (also known as Hermes, or Thoth). Ylime was assigned the role of the goddess Isis. Bear was there to symbolize the god form of Osiris, a principal male deity. Rayna would perform the role of Maat, another form of the Great Goddess. Michael was envisioned as Horus, another image of the primary male deity.

4. Israel Regardie, *The Golden Dawn: A Complete Course in Practical Ceremonial Magic. The Original Account of the Teachings, Rites and Ceremonies of the Hermetic Order of the Golden Dawn*, 6th ed., rev. (St. Paul, Minn.: Llewellyn Publications, 1989).

5. The prior religious backgrounds of neopagans reflect the American religious landscape in general, except that Jews seem to be doubly represented. About 50 percent are former Protestants, about 25 percent are former Catholics, approximately 5 to 6 percent are former Jews, and the rest (about 20 percent) come from another or no religion.

6. These mistaken and distorted images of witchcraft had very real consequences. They resulted in the torture and murder of thousands, perhaps millions, of Europeans, especially older, single women, peasants, and ethnic and religious minorities. In the American colonies far fewer people suffered persecution or died than in the European witch craze. Even so, the consequences sometimes were tragic. No one knows how many people, particularly mature or older single women, were informally labeled "witches" by their fellow villagers, subjected to ridicule and humiliation, shunned and cast out of the community; no one knows the extent of the human cost in physical, psychological, and social abuse and suffering. Americans occasionally were prosecuted legally and even executed for witchcraft, the largest single number of them when the false accusations of a few hysterical girls resulted in the hanging of eighteen women and the crushing to death of one man at Salem, Massachusetts, in 1692.

7. Minority religions in America, especially new religions, commonly are labeled "cults," and there is organized opposition to them. Members of the anticult movement are highly vocal, politically active, and socially influential. The news media, some professionals, politicians, and other public officials take them seriously. Some police departments treat charges of satanic crime and ritual abuse as factual, and entire careers have been built on investigating them. Mental health professionals have responded in a similar fashion, and many of America's larger cities have psychiatrists, psychologists, and other counselors whose practices specialize in helping the victims of diabolical

witchcraft and abusive cults. Neopagan organizations, however, do not resemble the stereotypical public images of cults in any meaningful way. Wiccan groups are not headed by powerful, authoritarian personalities who brainwash mindless, sheeplike followers and force them to blindly obey orders to commit unmentionable crimes.

## STUDY QUESTIONS

1. What is the most prevalent form of paganism among contemporary EuroAmericans? Name several older traditions from which Wicca draws much of its practice.
2. What is the difference between religious belief and other forms of belief? Give examples of religious belief as opposed to other forms of belief.
3. Define animism, pantheism, and polytheism. Describe several ways in which these terms are related to Neopaganism.
4. What are three characteristics of the Great Goddess? Do these characteristics relate to your understanding of other deities from other traditions? from your own tradition? Be specific.
5. What are three aspects of the Great Mother? Do you see a natural connection between these aspects? In what ways does gender play a particular role in understanding the Great Mother and her relationship to the world?
6. What is the major principle from which Neopaganism derives its values and ethics? Name several implications that such a view has for issues concerning the environment, male/female relationships, ethnic diversity, and global warfare.
7. What is the function of Neopagan magical practices? Name several practices employed by Neopagans. How do these practices differ from your own religious traditions? How are they similar?
8. What are the characteristics of the typical American Neopagan? Are you surprised by these characteristics? Do they differ from other religious persons you know?

## FOR FURTHER READING

Adler, Margot. *Drawing Down the Moon: Witches, Druids, Goddess-Worshippers, and Other Pagans in America Today.* Boston: Beacon Press, 1986.

Butler, Jon. "Magic Astrology and the Early American Religious Heritage, 1600–1760." *American Historical Review* 84 (April 1979):317–46.

Jorgensen, Danny L. *The Esoteric Scene, Cultic Milieu and Occult Tarot.* New York: Garland, 1992.

Kerr, Howard, and Charles L. Crow, eds. *The Occult in America: New Historical Perspectives.* Urbana: University of Illinois Press, 1983.

Lozano, Wendy G., and Tanice G. Foltz. "Into the Darkness: An Ethnographic Study of Witchcraft and Death." *Qualitative Sociology* 13, 3 (1990):211–34.

Luhrmann, T. M. *Persuasions of the Witch's Craft: Ritual Magic in Contemporary England.* Cambridge, Mass.: Harvard University Press, 1989.

Russell, Jeffrey B. *A History of Witchcraft: Sorcerers, Heretics, and Pagans.* London: Thames & Hudson, 1980.

Starhawk. *The Spiral Dance: A Rebirth of the Ancient Religion of the Great Goddess.* San Francisco: Harper & Row, 1989.

# 6

## MOZELLA G. MITCHELL

---

# Religion and the Discovery of Self: Howard Thurman and the Tributaries of the Deep River

My discovery of my own ethical relation within my own [racial-ethnic] context was illumined by what I came to understand about the ethical impact of the religious experience of Jesus on his life as a Jew in Palestine. This became to me the one differentiating thing that was unique about my experience of the Christian ethic. And standing within that, whenever I met it in any religion in the world, the language was the same. And this gave me a sense of feeling at home. It also had to deal with a kind of despair that closes in upon you when you're trying to relate your life to the larger life without contamination.

God bottoms existences; therefore, the deeper down I go, the more into Him I find myself. None of the categories of classifications—of faith, belief, etc.—have any standing in the presence of this transcendent experience, because I think that whether I'm Black, White, Presbyterian, Baptist, Buddhist, Hindu, Muslim, that in the presence of God, all these categories by which we relate to each other fade away and have no significance whatsoever. For in his presence I am a part of Him being revealed to Him. And anything that I do that blocks that is sin because it is against God, and it is against life. And whenever in my experience with my fellows this can be awakened, then a door between us is opened that no one can shut. So I feel that the only and ultimate refuge that anyone has in this world is in another person's heart. Therefore, my feeling is that my heart must be a swinging door.

—*Conversations with Howard Thurman*

Throughout history, the religious experiences of oppressed peoples—those living, so to speak, with their backs against the wall—have demonstrated that the life of the oppressed is fertile ground for rich and power-ful religious development. This seems true especially where people in such conditions remain open to the workings of the spirit of life. Hope, faith, yearning for freedom for human and divine relatedness, and bonding together with one another in the face of overwhelming odds are among the characteristics of such groups as Jews, African Americans, Native Americans, Latin Americans, and women throughout the world and have been the source of great and powerful religious experiences and movements. One has only to look at the narratives of such figures as Moses, Daniel, Shadrach, Meshach, and Abednego, Ruth and Naomi, Esther and Mordecai, among the Jews; Black Elk among Native Americans; Frederick Douglass, Harriet Tubman, Sojourner Truth, and numerous others in American slave narratives, to see the powerful role religion plays in the life of the disinherited of the earth. African-American spirituals such as "Deep River," "Were You There When They Crucified My Lord?" and "Get Away Jordan," for instance, are a rich source for understanding the powerful religious imagination and insights possible among a people in restrained circumstances.

The history of African Americans, most of whom were brought to America in chains, stripped of all visible signs of their African religious and cultural background—language, family and other human organizational structures, religion—is one of struggle for survival in a hostile environment. Reduced to the level of chattel, near that of domestic animals, these people had great difficulty retaining their humanness. It was religion stemming from the African cultural context, kept within their minds, hearts, and souls, that they used to anchor them in their encounter with the Jewish-Christian religion in this new environment, and that enabled them to hang onto their humanness and peoplehood. Religion was everything to African Americans both during and after slavery. It helped them to withstand the violence and other extremes of servitude and to reorganize and structure their lives and society after Emancipation.

Howard Thurman is among the numerous African Americans—along with W.E.B. DuBois, Frederick Douglass, Harriet Tubman, Sojourner Truth, Booker T. Washington, John Henry Graham, Martin Luther King Jr., and Malcolm X—who opened themselves up to the religious experience and were thus able to rise above the greatest of obstacles surrounding them. By their actions they won a place in the social structure not simply for themselves but for their people, and they proved the human worth and values of all ethnic and racial groups. But Howard Thurman is unique in many other ways. Surely, religion played a major role in the formation of his character and worldview. He, however, through his quest for religious understanding, also played a major role in religious formation. From his own religious struggles, he was able to envision not a universal religion but a universal religious and human perspective that lends crucial meaning to the whole of human life.

The words quoted in the epigraph to this chapter summarize Thurman's discovery. But to grasp their significance, we should take a look at his life, which led him to this understanding and insight.

## THURMAN'S EARLY YEARS

To chart his journey, we must go back to his birth in Daytona Beach, Florida, in 1900. Thurman's boyhood was spent in a world surrounded by the Atlantic Ocean, Halifax River, and a large wooded area in which there were huckleberries, wild grapes, rattlesnakes, and live oaks dripping with moss. Thurman spent time fishing in the river, gathering orange blossoms, picking huckleberries, and exploring the woods with other boys his age. In his backyard was a large oak tree, a steadying force in his life when trials persisted. Watching the oak tree withstand the violence of summer storms gave him a sense of strength that helped him bear the storms of his own life, which were many for an African-American male growing up in a hostile Southern environment. He found in the tree and in other aspects of nature a deep companionship and comfort during his growing-up years.

Thurman often would sit with his back against the oak tree and talk about his problems. There he felt he could be heard and embraced. The dark nights, the quiet roar of the Atlantic, and the brilliant stars were a spiritual experience for him. From his earliest memory, he had a sense of being a part of the rhythmic flow of the life of nature around him. This experience of talking aloud with God while surrounded by nature was the earliest religious experience Thurman recalled. It had more religious meaning for him than what went on in church.

Thurman grew up in Waycross, one of three segregated black neighborhoods in Daytona Beach. The other two were Midway and Newtown. These sections were sealed off from the white world downtown, where young Thurman rarely ventured except to rake leaves for a white resident or do some other job; and even then, he was not allowed in any of these white sections after dark. But he had complete freedom to move among the neighborhoods of the black residents. These communities had their own civic, social, religious, educational, and recreational centers. Separated from the white world by a wall of hostility and overt suspicion, the African-American communities existed as extended families. They shared freely with one another in disciplining their children and helped one another at times of sickness and death and other needy occurrences.

The alienation and enmity between the black and white worlds of Thurman's youth are shown in his experience with a white family who had employed him to rake leaves. The family's five-year-old daughter would wait for him to come to his job and then follow him around all over the yard. Once, when he had made several piles of leaves for burning, the little girl decided to scatter the leaves to pick out a beautifully colored one to show him. Just as fast as he would rake them up, she would scatter them again. When he tired of her behavior and warned her not to do it again or he would tell her father, she drew out a straight pin from her pinafore and jabbed his hand with it. As he drew back in pain and chastised her, she replied, "Oh, Howard, that didn't hurt you! You can't feel!"

Thurman's own family consisted of his mother, Alice, and father, Saul Solomon Thurman; his two sisters, Henrietta and Madaline; and his maternal grandmother, Nancy Ambrose. He was the youngest sibling. He had a very carefully disciplined, supporting, self-affirming religious upbringing. His father, although not a churchgoing person, was a decent, religious, hardworking, dignified man; he died while Howard was yet a child.

Except for his father, Thurman's family were members of Mount Bethel Baptist Church in Waycross. Thurman was twelve years old when he confessed religion, was baptized, and became a member of Mount Bethel, but the strong religious training he received came through his mother's and grandmother's tutelage. His mother did not speak much about her religious life, but her church prayer made indelible impressions on young Thurman's mind.

An example of her influence occurred during the family's traumatic experience of Halley's comet in 1910, through which Thurman's mother shepherded him and conveyed to him a sense of sacred trust. Standing in the backyard with her, watching the comet as its tail spread out in a shimmering, fanlike shape over the sky, the ten-year-old boy was transfixed. In trepidation he said to her, "Mama, what will happen to us when that thing falls out of the sky?" Feeling her hand tighten on his shoulder, he looked up and saw her eyes full of tears but caught a rare expression of radiance and peace in her countenance. She replied at last, "Nothing will happen to us, Howard. God will take care of us." This experience had a lasting effect on Thurman throughout his religious journey.

Because Thurman's mother worked outside the home, the children were left largely to the care of their grandmother. It was she who had the most profound influence on the earliest shaping of Thurman's religious experience.

Nancy Ambrose was born a slave in north Florida, in a place called Moseley Hall, outside Tallahassee. With her deep sense of the value of life, education, and religion, she was an anchor in the Thurman family, who at times brooded over their lives. Knowing of the value of education because of the carefully orchestrated denial of it to slaves, she instilled in her daughter's children a great respect and desire for knowledge and training. She had rigorous requirements for their school attendance and class performance. In 1915, when Thurman left for high school in Jacksonville, the last thing she said to him was "Look up always, not down; look forward always, not back; and remember, everything you get you will have to work for."

There were many trying experiences and crises in Howard Thurman's life through which his grandmother brought him or for which she had prepared him spiritually. She was there to comfort and console him, for example, during his father's funeral. Because Thurman's father did not belong to the family's church, the pastor would not preach the eulogy. The funeral was held at the church because Thurman's grandmother insisted—but a traveling evangelist preached. This was Thurman's most disturbing and negative religious encounter as a boy. The minister's sermon literally put Thurman's father in hell because he "died out of Christ," meaning he was not a member of the church. Knowing his father to be a deeply religious man who had an "original mind" about religion, Thurman kept whispering to his grandmother, "He didn't know Papa, did he?" Though he never got a satisfactory answer from any of his family as to why the preacher acted this way, he appreciated his grandmother's tender touch and consolation. Still, the child Howard's reaction was a promise that if he grew up to be a man, he would have nothing to do with the church. It was one promise Thurman did not keep.

Nancy Ambrose awakened and nourished in Thurman a sense of his own inherent worth, meaning, and significance that did not depend on anything in his environment. Though the racial stigmas of Southern society were demeaning to young black males, Thurman was able to maintain a robust sense of personal dignity. This was stimulated by the religious orientation his grandmother gave to him and his sisters and further nourished by his own sensitive and perceptive experiences of nature.

Thurman's grandmother had a story, stemming from her religious experience as a slave, that she would tell the children of the family whenever she sensed life was becoming too burdensome. On the plantation where she lived, the slave master would allow a slave preacher from a neighboring plantation to come over and preach to his slaves once or twice a year. At all other times the slaves were required to attend services in segregated areas of the white churches and listen to sermons of white preachers, who urged the slaves to submit willingly to their status or risk eternal punishment in the afterlife. But hearing the slave preacher was a real treat for slaves, for he would speak to them as fellow human sufferers caught in a system of servitude from which God would surely deliver them, as God had done for the children of Israel in the exodus story. As was normally the case in the slave-preacher tradition, this preacher's style was dramatic and demonstrative. When he finished his dramatic portrayal of the gospel message, he would pause, scrutinize the faces of the congregation, and tell them, "You are not niggers! You are not slaves! You are God's children!"

Each time Thurman's grandmother told this story, she would repeat the slave preacher's message with such pride and conviction that the young people's spirits would be restored. For Thurman, experiences like this helped him feel rooted in the significance of all of life, which nothing in his environment could destroy.

The other great influence on Thurman was that of nature. He felt the nights and the rhythm of the sea were a part of what he was, all created by God. And once he internalized this feeling of oneness with all the creation of God, no negative attitude of people in his environment was able to destroy his sense of worth.

But the white world on the other side of Daytona Beach was a different arena of life. Almost nothing in Thurman's religious upbringing seemed to apply to that "other" world. As a boy, Thurman sensed that it was a world in which he needed to reduce his exposure to a minimum so that he might not unwittingly do something to bring all the potential violence of that world on himself. No sense of trust or confidence ever existed for him regarding the white world as he was growing up. The Christian ethic in his religious experience bound him to other black people but had no meaning for him as far as the white world was concerned. Later in life, when Thurman was one of two black men allowed to attend an otherwise all-white seminary in Rochester, New York, he began to address the ethical problems and issues in religious experience and practice regarding racial and ethnic relationships.

## THE DEVELOPMENT OF THURMAN'S RELIGIOUS VISION

Thurman finished high school the valedictorian of his class at Florida Baptist Academy in Jacksonville. He then enrolled at Morehouse College in Atlanta, majoring in economics. Morehouse is a prominent institution where many famous and outstanding African-American men, such as Martin Luther King, Jr., and Benjamin Mays, received their earliest academic training. It is also a college with rich and long-standing religious traditions. During his freshman year there, Thurman accepted the call to the ministry and was licensed to preach by Dr. Samuel A. Owens. Thurman was an eager, vigorous, and enthusiastic student at Morehouse, where he read every book in the library.

After graduating from Morehouse, Thurman entered Rochester Theological Seminary in New York in 1926 to prepare for a career in ministry. He became known in the broader community of Rochester, preaching sermons and lecturing on racial issues. While there, he was ordained into the ministry at First Baptist Church of Roanoke, Virginia, where he had worked as an assistant to the pastor, the Reverend A. L. James, for two summers. Dr. Owens preached Thurman's ordination sermon, coming all the way from Memphis, Tennessee, to do so. Beginning with his ordination, the laying on of hands became one of the high points of Thurman's religious experience.

Another significant event for Thurman was his memorable encounter with Dr. George Cross, one of his professors. Cross recognized Thurman's superior gifts and encouraged him in the development of the original gifts he was able to contribute to the spiritual life of the times. Cross urged Thurman not to give all of his time to the pursuit of racial questions but rather to devote himself to the timeless issues of the human spirit.

On graduating from Rochester Seminary, Thurman became pastor of Mount Zion Baptist Church in Oberlin, Ohio, where he continued to explore the nature of the religious experience. In 1929 he resigned from the church, after several years as its pastor, to study at Haverford College with the Quaker mystic Rufus Jones. Shortly after that experience, he accepted a joint appointment at Spelman College and Morehouse in Atlanta. He taught philosophy and religion at Morehouse and the Bible as living literature at Spelman, and he served as religious adviser to students and faculty. A year later, Thurman was given the responsibility of the chapel services at Morehouse.

It was at Morehouse and Spelman—and later, at Howard University, where Thurman became dean of Rankin Chapel—that he launched his endless quest for truth and authentic religious meaning, creatively and freely exploring the nature of the religious experience. In hopes of finding the idiomatic element of human experience that was primarily and uniquely religious, he would use literature—dramas (such as the plays of Shakespeare) and novels, for example—in the chapel programs. He was trying to discover the precious instrument that was time-transcendent and, to him, religious: the God-word as expressed in the minds of the novelist, the playwright, the philosopher, and the mathematician.

Thurman's quest led him on a lifelong mystical journey. In his travels to such places as London, Scotland, various African countries, and India, as well as in his other professional positions—his later role as pastor of the Church for the Fellowship of All Peoples in San Francisco, for example, and his deanship of Marsh Chapel at Boston University—he was in constant pursuit of that religious truth for which he yearned.

A pivotal point in his journey came during his teaching career at Howard University when, on behalf of the World Student Christian Federation, he chaired a delegation of African Americans in 1935, on a pilgrimage of friendship as guests of the Student Christian Movement of India, Burma, and Ceylon. Thurman took a leave from his position at Howard and spent the period from October 1935 to April 1936 on speaking tours, interpreting the Christian religious experience from the African-American perspective. He was accompanied by his wife, Sue Bailey Thurman, and by the Reverend Edward G. Carroll and his wife, Phenola Carroll. One of the high points of this tour was an audience with Mohandas (Mahatma) Gandhi in his ashram. In addition to the gratification of being in the company of such a renowned religious leader and political hero, during this visit Thurman received a challenge from Gandhi. The Mahatma posed questions to him and his delegation that cut to the foundations of the religious assumptions of African Americans.

The challenge from Gandhi came at the end of Thurman's travels in these Far Eastern countries, where he had frequently been asked similar questions. Many had wanted to know why Thurman's people, who were forcibly taken from Africa and enslaved in American by Christians, should embrace the religion of their slave masters. At least one questioner felt that Thurman, an intelligent man, was a traitor to all the darker peoples of the earth by his promotion of such a religion. Many thought that his being on a mission for Christianity among peoples who were, at the time, under colonial domination of the British Empire made him a tool of European whites. A key concern was that Christianity in America and the world was powerless before the color barrier of racism. Thurman's delegation was continually pressed about why this seemed to be the case.

In addition to these issues, Gandhi wanted to know why the slaves in America had not become Muslims. This was Gandhi's reason for the query: "The Moslem religion is the only religion in the world in which no lines are drawn from within the religious fellowship. Once you are in, you are all the way in. This is not true in Christianity, it isn't true in Buddhism or Hinduism. If you had become Moslem, then even though you were a slave, in the faith you would be equal to your master."[1]

Thurman was not able to answer satisfactorily the persistent queries of Indian students regarding Christianity and the color barrier in America. But en route back to America, Thurman experienced what he referred to as his "Khyber Pass vision." Standing in Khyber Pass, looking down into Afghanistan as a slow camel train went by on its way to India, he felt a strong sense of urgency that a way must be found to test whether or not it was possible in American society to have a religious institution that was not under external constraints and wherein people might experience a unity that would transcend race and class.

## THURMAN'S INFLUENCE
## ON THE RELIGIOUS LANDSCAPE

The opportunity to put his vision in action came not many years after Thurman's return to his position at Howard University. In 1944 he went to San Francisco, where he cofounded the Church for the Fellowship of All Peoples with Dr. Alfred G. Fisk, a Presbyterian minister and professor of philosophy at San Francisco State College. This became the first interracial, interreligious church in America. Most of the major Christian denominations were represented among the membership, and members of other religions, such as Jews, Buddhists, Muslims, and Hindus, shared in the worship and the intercultural and international activities. The church had local and national associate membership, among whom was Mrs. Eleanor Roosevelt.

The church was dedicated to worship that included many and varied experimentations with religious ideas that had bearing on opening up people's lives to the spirit of the living God. It was in this setting that Thurman discovered "the experiences of unity among peoples are more important and crucial than all the concepts, prejudices, ideologies, faiths, that may divide. And if you can multiply these experiences of unity over a period of sufficient duration, you can undermine any barrier that separates one person from another."[2]

In 1953, Thurman accepted an appointment as dean of Marsh Chapel and professor of Spiritual Resources and Disciplines at Boston University. He was the first African American to hold such a position at a major university. A large institution with a culturally, ethnically, and religiously diverse student body and faculty, Boston University became a testing ground for his religious ideas and vision. He was challenged to meet the religious and intellectual needs of such a diverse group of young minds. In the eleven years that he served in this position, Thurman grew immensely in popularity and power as a lecturer and preacher.

During his professional career, Thurman spoke at more than five hundred institutions, in America and abroad. He gave hundreds of lectures and meditations on radio and television stations in San Francisco and Boston and other places, reaching hundreds of thousands of people. He influenced numerous persons also through the more than twenty books and hundreds of articles he wrote. Retiring from Boston University in 1965, he returned to San Francisco and the Church for the Fellowship of All Peoples and established the Howard Thurman Educational Trust to provide financial aid to college students, support programs of intercultural understanding, organize and promote his own writings and other creations, and conduct religious seminars for persons of various backgrounds and interests.

Through all his efforts, Thurman realized the mission so well articulated by George Cross, his professor at Rochester Theological Seminary, to address himself to the timeless hunger of the human spirit. Thousands were drawn to Thurman as one may be drawn to a guru, holy man, or prophet. He has been described by various people as having had a mystifying presence, possessing profound eloquence and unusual charisma, being a creative interpreter of religion. He was able to lift persons, spellbound, to spiritual grandeur. Rabbi Joseph Glaser, for example, credits Thurman with being the major influence in Glaser's appreciation for his own Jewish faith and his commitment to becoming a rabbi.

One may wonder how Thurman could have had such a profound spiritual influence on millions of peoples of all religious and ethnic backgrounds. One important reason is that he put forth no particular system of beliefs or practices, so he could not be classified in one mold or another. All of his rich religious ideas grew out of his lived experiences. He rejected all labels, all categories. The title of one of his books, *The Search for Common Ground,* reflects his life's journey. In the book he sums up the nature of his journey, the many paths it took, and the wisdom he gained throughout. The central theme, as in his whole religious perspective, is the unity of all humankind.

Thurman tried to recall how he came to this belief in unity by means of his lived experiences. He did not remember exactly when he started experiencing the deep paradox at the very center of his conscious life. On the one hand, he had a fierce sense of privacy, of being isolated in the world and driven to experience his own "me-ness" as if he alone existed in the universe. He had to lay claim to the very root of his being—to hold it, experience it, taste it, feel it—so that none of the vicissitudes of life could tear it away from him and cause him to lose his deep sense of identity. He was speaking not of identity according to race or culture but rather of his identity as a living being, uniquely himself.

On the other hand, Thurman's quest was driven by a sense of the absolute necessity to relate to all the crucial elements in the external world— people, animals, plants, and so on—because we are all part of everything and, in a sense, part of everybody. Yet, he maintained, the only way a person can be at home everywhere is to be sure that she or he is at home *somewhere*. Drawing from his personal experience, Thurman stated:

> Deep within my own experience of myself, in the profoundest sense, is the key to experiencing any other living thing and every other person. The religion from which has come the great concept of universalism—I refer to Judaism, seventh-, eighth-century prophets, et cetera—is also the religion that is, in its genius, a very private, exclusive, unique religion. Within the tight circle of uniqueness, when you move down into it, you come up inside of every other living person. You don't go horizontally, which is the way of the sociologist, the political philosopher; the way of the person of religion is that he goes down within the self, and what one discovers there he universalizes. When he looks into the face of another person he sees his own face.
>
> I'm always on the lookout for the ——— I'm on my own scent all over the world, so that if I can't pick it up in you, then my sniffer is off.
>
> I deal with you not as I would have you deal with me but as I deal with myself.
>
> It is what I experience of my own essence that gives me my cue to what life is and what life is about.
>
> It goes back to my childhood, because I had constantly to affirm my own self in an environment that reduced me to zero, an environment in which I had no standing, as it were. I was driven to find in the grounds of my being that which transcended everything in my environment (external to me). Once I hit it, then I knew I was home free, that the environment could never destroy me because at my center I would never say "yes" to the external judgment of me [as a Black man].[3]

Thurman said that he began to look at the world and at the meaning of his experience, at his colleagues, at the meaning of the white people, and at the whole society. By affirming himself, he was able to affirm the whole world. But such an affirmation has to be achieved again and again, because certain events in life often throw one back into the dilemma of uncertainty. Thurman had to find ways to keep his self-affirmation nourished. That is why he enjoyed the silences and the dark nights in Florida, the Atlantic Ocean and the movement of the storms. All of this had a vitality that somehow swept into him, washing his shore of debris and giving him a fresh sense of his own "me-ness." In later years, such experiences became identified in his mind as the finger of God moving in his spirit.

## CONCLUSION

Throughout his work and experiences, Howard Thurman was able to break through the many barriers of race, religion, and culture and to experience and interpret religion for people of any religious persuasion. He has been called a prophet for our times because he was able to get at the core of religious and social meaning in our world and convey it to others. He did not try to impose any specific beliefs on others; instead, he spoke and acted in such a way as to lead or direct others on their own religious pathways. He has been called a modern-day, sophisticated shaman because, like the traditional shamans of African and Native American religions, he served as mediator between the individual or group and the sacred in their experiences of it. He helped all who heard his oral presentations or read his books to become open to the spiritual life. Perhaps Landrum Bolling (interviewer on *Conversations with Howard Thurman*) summed it up best when he said, "[Thurman] has attempted to speak through and above the noisy conflicts of nationality, culture, and ideology to what he has called the hunger of the human heart."[4]

## NOTES

1. *Conversations with Howard Thurman*. Part 1. Videocassette hosted by Landrum Bolling (San Francisco: The Howard Thurman Education Trust, 1978).

2. Ibid.

3. *Conversations with Howard Thurman*. Part 2. Videocassette hosted by Landrum Bolling (San Francisco: The Howard Thurman Education Trust, 1978).

4. *Conversations with Howard Thurman*. Part 1. Videocassette hosted by Landrum Bolling (San Francisco: The Howard Thurman Education Trust, 1978).

## STUDY QUESTIONS

1. What are three words that characterize oppressed people's religious experience? Why are these words particularly important to these persons' experiences?
2. Name at least three "disinherited" or "marginalized" communities. How do you define a marginalized community? Does this definition reflect your own tradition? Why? Why not?
3. What function did religion play in the lives of African Americans both during and after slavery?
4. What three words/phrases would you use to describe the religious life of Howard Thurman?
5. What lesson do you take away from Thurman's story about being jabbed with a pin only to be told, "You can't feel"? How does such a comment reflect the plight of oppressed persons?
6. Who had the most profound influence on Thurman's religious development? Why?
7. What important question did Mohandas (Mahatma) Gandhi pose to Thurman that became pivotal to Thurman's understanding of the African American's relationship to "white" Christianity? What was Thurman's answer to Ghandi's question? Do you agree with Thurman?

## FOR FURTHER READING

*Conversations with Howard Thurman.* Parts 1 and 2. Videocassette hosted by Landrum Bolling, San Francisco: The Howard Educational Trust, 1978.

Mitchell, Mozella. *Spiritual Dynamics of Howard Thurman's Theology.* Bristol, Ind.: Wyndham Hall Press, 1985.

Smith, Luther E. *Howard Thurman: The Mystic as Prophet.* Richmond, Ind.: Friends United Press, 1991.

Thurman, Howard. *The Search for Common Ground: An Inquiry into the Basis of Man's Experience of Community.* New York: Harper & Row, 1971.

———. *With Head and Heart: The Autobiography of Howard Thurman.* New York: Harcourt Brace Jovanovich, 1979.

# PART 2

## RELIGION IN THE POLITICAL REALM

# 7

**MICHAEL NOVAK**

# Religion and Political Economy

The most important thing a young person needs to know about religion is that religion is not outside of life, or above it, but within it, at the heart of everyday activities. Religion is in the middle of life as yeast is in dough and makes it rise as bread, as fire is in a white-hot ingot, as light is in the air between dawn and dusk, or as darkness fills the atmosphere at night. If a person is genuinely religious, you can see it in the way that person walks or listens or speaks. You can see it in the way a person buys things and uses things, and in the way he or she works. You can even seen it in the way in which people play. You can certainly see it in their sexual lives and in their families. But perhaps the most surprising thing of all is that you can see it in their politics and economics.

It is the last point that I explore in this chapter. Brazil and Japan are two nations with approximately the same population, about 140 million each as of 1985. In size, however, Brazil is immense, larger than the whole United States (without Alaska), whereas Japan is tiny, all its islands together amounting to not much more than California. In natural resources, Brazil may be the most blessed land on earth—certainly one of the top two or three. It has the largest rain forest, the greatest river, extremely fertile plains, a magnificent coastline, and vast mineral deposits of many kinds. By contrast, Japan is quite poor in natural resources. It is nearly 100 percent energy-dependent. Nonetheless, poor as it is in natural resources and small as it is in size (and largely uninhabitable), Japan is quite rich. It produces nearly 10 percent of everything produced in the world, whereas Brazil, despite its immense natural resources, produces under 1 percent, and the vast majority of Brazil's population counts among the world's poor.

So if wealth does not come from natural resources, and if a densely populated country like Japan can be rich whereas a sparsely populated nation like Brazil can be poor, where does the wealth of a nation come from? It is quite clear that the answer, at least in Japan, lies in the education, habits, spiritual attitudes, and self-organization of its people; in short, in *human* capital. In the creation of new wealth, what happens in the minds and souls of people seems even more important than the natural resources with which their countries are endowed. What happens in the human spirit seems to be at least as important as what is available in nature.

This should not surprise us. In many departments of life—in sports, for example—the human spirit counts more than brute strength. Freedom matters. Ideas matter. Being spirited, having a strategy, being attentive and intelligent rather than listless and passive—all these things matter, usually a great deal. A student who cares, like a teacher who cares, is utterly different from one who is merely going through the motions because they are required.

## THE ROLE OF RELIGION
## IN SHAPING HUMAN CONSCIOUSNESS

Religion is about how we organize our souls, how we order our spirits as well as our bodies, and about the point that we give to our lives (or perhaps, better, about how we recognize what has been *given* to our lives). Purity of heart, the great Danish religious thinker Søren Kierkegaard once wrote, is to will one thing. He might have written that religion is also to will one thing. In both Judaism and Christianity, for example, one of the greatest commandments is to love the Lord God, our Creator, with our whole heart, mind, and soul. It is to will one thing, thanksgiving and fidelity to God and to walk always in God's light and in God's ways. These are not easy religions, but they do give life a point.

These two religions furthermore have had a tremendous impact on economic and political life on this planet. They did not have this impact suddenly or all at once. Their impact, rather, has been felt gradually over time, like a seed dying slowly in moist and fertile ground, pushing out little roots, and then shooting up into a strong and spreading plant, a sturdy tree, perhaps, sheltering much of the earth.

Among all the world's peoples, the Jews are a quite tiny and in some ways humble group. Yet many historians have been obliged to notice that wherever they are to be found on earth, in however small a minority, dispersed over many countries, Jews seem to excel in many distinctive ways. We do not completely understand how to account for this, but it is impossible to deny that culture plays a very important role. There are ways, handed down from father to son and mother to daughter, in which children are brought up, certain habits encouraged, and a particular address to life imparted. Jews are a people shaped by the word of God, by Holy scripture and by Torah. Even if they are not religious, Jews seem to receive and pass along a remarkably strong set of attitudes toward life: a strong sense of family, hard work, and a desire to make a contribution and to excel. These attitudes patently lead to success in many worldly areas, both intellectual and practical.

Christianity, similarly, introduced new attitudes into the world, particularly concerning the important role to be played in history by each individual, as well as concerning important social ideals such as compassion, equality, and universality. Whereas Judaism seems to impart a stronger social sense—to be born of a Jewish mother is the first and most important way to become a member of the community—Christianity places central importance upon the experience of personal conversion. Being Jewish and being Christian are not in this sense, then, symmetrical. This lack of symmetry also is evident in the fact that Judaism, in its own self-understanding, does not need Christianity, whereas Christianity explicitly needs Judaism for its first set of premises and expectations. Without Judaism, Christianity does not quite make sense. By contrast, Judaism thinks of itself as self-contained. God's covenant with Israel is eternal and irrevocable; God's promises are always and forever valid.

The self-image of Christianity is that it is an offshoot of Judaism. Practically all that Judaism holds to be true, Christianity also holds to be true. The degree of overlap between these two religions is enormous. In contrast, however, Christianity historically distinguished itself from Judaism fairly sharply. One can read about its first struggles to do this in the Acts of the Apostles in the New Testament. Christianity saw itself as intended not only for those born of a Jewish mother but for all the human beings on earth. While the Christian church also regarded itself as a community and had its own powerful social sense, nonetheless it laid special emphasis on the call to the individual to be converted and to make the choice of accepting or rejecting that call.

Because of its emphasis on the individual, Christianity is usually credited with playing a vital role in introducing into history a focus on individuality and autobiography. St. Augustine's *Confessions* (ca. A.D. 400) is usually regarded, for example, as the first "modern" introspective biography; its emphasis is on the drama of the individual soul before God. Since one must choose to be a Christian, moreover, Christianity is largely responsible for focusing the world's attention on personal liberty. This emphasis is foreshadowed in the work of some of the ancient Greek and Roman writers, for example, in Socrates' famous aphorism. "The unexamined life is not worth living" and in Aristotle's emphasis on the personal appropriation of key civilizing virtues or habits. Such central words as *person, conscience,* and *will* received their classical exposition in Christian writings, especially in those of St. Augustine (A.D. 354–430) and St. Thomas Aquinas (A.D. 1224–1274). For such reasons, the great British historian of liberty Lord Acton (1834–1902) was obliged to observe that the history of the idea of liberty is virtually coincident with the peoples affected by Christianity and comes to other peoples from interaction with Christianity.

In treating the interpretation of religion and economics, however, the points I emphasize in this essay are equally valid for Christianity and for Judaism. Although I single out certain texts of Pope John Paul II (born in 1920, elected pope in 1978), the two chief religious ideals in question—creativity and community—derive from both Judaism and Christianity, even though they turn out to have universal relevance. (Isn't this exactly what we would expect from ideals derived from the Creator of all?) Ethics is not just about duties or rules; it is also about living up to ideals.

## ARISTOCRATIC IDEAL
## TO BUSINESS IDEAL:
## A MAJOR SHIFT IN THE
## HISTORY OF POLITICAL ECONOMY

Unless one understands the ideals inherent in or underlying a practice, ethical reflection about that practice is bound to seem uninspiring.[1] It is likely to have the effect of making ethics seem like an intellectual exercise rather than a way of life. It may make ethics seem like a list of obligations or taboos, without a vision. It may even prevent the crucial ethical questions from arising: Which way of life do I wish to choose for myself, among various alternatives, as I commit the larger part of my waking hours to this specific practical vocation? What are the ideals inherent in this vocation, that make it special among the many human vocations? What are its moral delights? What attracts me to it? What are its moral satisfactions? What are its specific betrayals?

The economy of the ancient (and even the medieval) world was quite different from that of the period after 1776. In earlier times, the chief form of wealth lay in the land and its fruits. While commerce, even international commerce, played a considerable role in ancient economies, the chief cause of wealth right up to the modern period lay in the productiveness of the land—in wheat, wool, grains, wine, olive oil, dates, forests, cotton, and the like. Invention and manufacture (in the modern sense) played a far lesser role. One of the chief, most common ways of acquiring new wealth was to acquire new lands, often by conquest. For this reason, wealth was typically associated with "taking"—with war, plunder, and booty. Cities needed to be walled against foreign invasion; aristocrats had to live in towered fortresses.

Nonetheless, the aristocratic life of the precapitalist era had its own specific aspirations, ideals, obligations, and duties. Not a few moral handbooks were written to guide the way of life of princes and other noble families, most of whom—in the beginning, at least—made their living from various branches of agriculture, husbandry, forestry, and the management of landed estates. Indeed, it was common for those engaged in such pursuits to be instructed in the proper ethical arts of "the noble way of life." Alexis de Tocqueville in *Democracy in America* has several elegant passages[2] on the differences between the ethos of aristocracy as he knew it in France and the ethos of the commercial republic he found in the United States—sometimes to the advantage of the one, sometimes to the advantage of the other.

Yet even now, some 160 years after de Tocqueville's magisterial volume, we still lack a well-formed philosophy (or theology) of business life. One reason for this, perhaps, is that philosophers and theologians still think of their vocations in the light of the aristocratic ideal (no doubt, quite properly so). Even common speech reveals aristocratic prejudices. For example, if someone says of you that you are a prince of a man, you are likely to feel flattered—no matter that the moral conduct of actual princes in history (murdering their nieces and nephews, plotting and scheming against their cousins) has been, to put it kindly, ambiguous. According to Shakespeare, and even more so according to Machiavelli, princes have seldom been moral giants; they put to death a great many of their own relatives, precipitated many wars of "honor," and employed their armed knights in countless acts of naked plunder. As a consequence, quite mistrustful of one another, most aristocrats were obliged to live in heavily fortified castles. David Hume remarks in his historical essays that princes are hardly in a position to present the aristocratic era as a shining model of benefits to be reaped by commoners.[3]

By contrast—so powerful is the hold of the aristocratic cast of mind on our common speech, even today—if someone in a university setting were to tell you that you had bourgeois tastes, you would suspect that you were being disparaged. You would suspect this (and it would be true) despite the fact that almost all the beautiful things that we associate with the aristocratic age—the best wines, the best cheeses, elegant cutlery, glittering armor, fine furniture, draperies, splendid gowns and capes and breeches, paintings, tapestries, and chandeliers—were actually developed, designed, and made by bourgeois craftspeople; that is, by persons who were neither serfs nor nobles but independent enough to have studios, shops, and trades of their own, and whose modest homes were usually clustered together in the towns and small cities that gave them the name *bourgeois*. These bourgeoisie were not lacking in taste; in fact, they created most of the tasteful objects in which the aristocracy took serene pleasure.

Despite these facts, through class prejudice the aristocracy looked down on craftspeople, artisans, and people of commerce. Aristocrats were, or pretended to be, focused on "things in themselves," *noble* things. People of the laboring and commercial classes were concerned merely with *utility*, with means rather than ends, and for the sake of vulgar profit. Besides, they often sweated and exhibited rude and lowly manners.

Alas, this aristocratic bias also infected the Christian moral tradition (but not, I think, the Jewish).[4] The historian Jacob Viner made this point succinctly in one of his notable essays on the history of economic thought:

> It was a commonplace of Greek and Roman thought, destined to be absorbed in the Christian tradition, that trade was either by its inherent nature, or through the temptations it offered to those engaged in it, pervasively associated with fraud and cheating, especially, according to Cicero, if it were "small," or retail trade. Horace decried trade as "unnatural" and "impious."
> . . . For the early Christian Fathers, as for the pagan philosophers, it was the element in trade of the pursuit of a middleman's profit which they found specially objectionable, as demonstrating "avarice," and therefore "sin." . . . Underlying this condemnation of trade was an implicit economic analysis which failed to see any possible counterpart in service to the buyer or the community for the gain of a merchant selling at a higher price than that at which he had bought. This came nearest to being made explicit in a passage of St. Jerome, destined to have a lasting influence: "All riches proceed from sin. No one can gain without another man losing."[5]

Needless to say, Marxist and socialist economic thinking owes not a little to this anticommercial strain in both Christian and aristocratic thought. Even thinkers who in their best moments favor democracy and capitalism, given the sorry alternatives, have not entirely broken free from these prejudices. Such terms as *money, wealth, profit,* and *entrepreneurship* still embarrass them somewhat.

In short, there are cultural reasons, reasons of history, for why we have been slow to reflect more profoundly on the transformation of values wrought in Western history by the replacement of the aristocratic ideal with the—dare I say it?—"business ideal." We have not been in a position to speak confidently of a business ideal. We tend to think that business lacks ideals; is merely utilitarian, concerned mainly with vulgar profit; and ranks considerably below a humanistic or Christian vocation. We tend to think of business, in short, as if we were aristocrats. This is false consciousness. It is also an anachronism. As Machiavelli coldly observed in *The Prince,* aristocrats were not at all lacking in self-interest. Nor is anyone else. "Self-love," the great reforming monk St. Bernard of Clairvaux taught his fellow monks, "dies fifteen minutes after the self." If it is so in monasteries committed to the pure love of God and fellow humans, it is no less so outside the monastery walls.

Following David Hume and Adam Smith in analyzing the rise of commercial society, I have sketched elsewhere[6] the great moral transformation in Western ethical reality—a transformation, Hume and Smith thought, for the better, especially from the viewpoint of ordinary people and the poor. It is quite important to grasp this moral transformation if one wishes to understand how business came to be regarded as the cutting edge of human progress. In seeking to establish the rule of law, liberty, and self-government, as well as to liberate the human race from immemorial poverty, writers since Baron Montesquieu (1689–1755) have looked to the business world to show the way. I cannot enlarge upon that historical background here; all I can do is summarize its relevant lessons.

## TWO MORAL IDEAS
## INHERENT IN BUSINESS

I am entirely in favor of the democratic project, by which I mean limited government, the rule of law, and the protection of individual and minority rights. Without an active business community, this democratic project is not empirically sustainable.[7] Without an active business community, national wealth can hardly be created or broadly distributed; opportunities for employment—jobs—must necessarily be few and low-paying; and vital moral habits necessary to republican self-government—the virtues of civic republicanism—are highly unlikely to flourish.[8]

Those on the American Left, Democratic presidential candidate Paul Tsongas said during his campaign in 1992, "would like to believe that they can create employment without employers. They're wrong." Let that commonsense warning serve as our transition. Business provides crucial services to the free society. That is its utility. But what are its internal moral ideals? We would be in a better position to develop a business ethnic nourished, guided, and corrected by those ideals if we actually knew what those ideals were.

Pope John Paul II, in *Centesimus Annus*, his 1991 encyclical, wrote quite eloquently about two ideals internal to the business vocation. No doubt, other ideals might be discerned, since it is not unusual for different personalities to be attracted to a specific vocation by different facets. Needing and drawing on a broad range of talents and temperaments, the business vocation is rich with possibilities and opportunities. For our purposes, however, it will suffice to make a beginning in the large task before us by limiting our attention to the two ideals singled out by John Paul II. The first of these is creativity; the second, community. In addition, the pope also highlights the specific virtues called upon by business.

### The First Ideal: Creativity

Many of us may first have learned to think about the ethic of capitalism by way of the analysis given by Max Weber in *The Protestant Ethic and the Spirit of Capitalism*.[9] Weber's great achievement was to bring to consciousness the fact that cultural—specifically, *religious*—forces are essential to the definition of capitalism. Capitalism is a system not solely about things but about the human spirit. Nonetheless, there is some question whether Max Weber actually caught the spirit of capitalism. I think it more exact to say that he scored a near miss.[10] The target he hit was "calculative rationality," the kind of thinking focused on efficiency and cost/benefits, which would confine human spontaneity within an "iron cage." He seemed to have in mind the huge industrial enterprises of the turn of the century, and he dreaded what he saw as the coming spirit of bureaucracy. In all this, he missed something much closer to the heart of the matter: discovery, invention, serendipity, surprise—what my colleague Rocco Buttiglione of the International Academy of Philosophy in Liechtenstein calls "the Don Quixote factor," the romance of risk and enterprise.

At the very heart of capitalism—its dynamic core, as the economists Friedrich Hayek, Joseph Schumpeter, and (in far greater detail) Israel Kirzner have shown—is the creative habit of enterprise.[11] Enterprise is the inclination to notice, the habit of discerning, the tendency to discover what other people don't yet see, as well as the capacity to *act* on insight, so as to bring into reality things not before seen.[12] As John Paul II observed:

> It is precisely the ability to foresee both the needs of others and the combinations of productive factors most adapted to satisfying those needs that constitutes another important source of wealth in modern society. . . . Organizing such a productive effort, planning its duration in time, making sure that it corresponds in a positive way to the demands which it must satisfy, and taking the necessary risks—all this too is a source of wealth in today's society. In this way, the *role* of disciplined and creative *human work* and, as an essential part of that work, *initiative and entrepreneurial ability* becomes increasingly evident and decisive.[13]

Many academic writers seem never to have imagined the sheer fun and creative pleasure involved in bringing a new business to birth. Such creativity has the stamp of a distinctive personality all over it. In the pleasure it affords its creator, it rivals, in its way, artistic creativity. To verify this, one only has to visit a business in the presence of its builder. It is quite possible that no diva was ever so pleased with what she had sung as an entrepreneur is with what she has built. (And it should be noted that a rapidly increasing proportion of entrepreneurs in the United States, in Latin America, and worldwide is female. Enterprise is a vocation made to order for newcomers into the market.)

As he approaches the question of creativity in section 32 of *Centesimus Annus*, the pope has just finished explaining how in history two factors—work and the land—are to be found in every society:

> At one time *the natural fruitfulness of the earth* appeared to be, and was in fact, the primary factor of wealth, while work was, as it were, the help and support for this fruitfulness. In our time, *the role of human work* is becoming increasingly important as the productive factor both of nonmaterial and of material wealth.[14]

Note that the pope has linked work today increasingly with knowledge. *And this is the crucial switch.* Unlike Karl Marx, who developed "the labor theory of value" (the theory that all economic worth springs from labor), the pope links value to knowledge: "Work becomes ever more fruitful and productive to the extent that people become *more knowledgeable* of the productive potentialities of the earth and more profoundly *cognizant* of the needs of those for whom their work is done."[15] The cause of wealth is knowledge. This cause lies in the human mind.

"What is the cause of the wealth of nations?" Adam Smith was the first to raise this question in 1776. Pope Leo XIII alluded to it in his 1891 encyclical *Rerum Novarum*.[16] Pope John Paul II has his own crisp reply:

> In our time, in particular, there exists another form of ownership which is becoming no less important than land: *the possession of know-how, technology and skill*. The wealth of the industrialized nations is based much more on this kind of ownership than on natural resources.[17]

The cause of wealth is intellectual capital. If the wealth of nations is based much more on intellectual property and know-how than on natural resources, then we can understand how some nations that are very wealthy in natural resources (such as Brazil) can remain poor, while other nations that have virtually no natural resources (like Japan) can become among the richest in the world.

In this respect, the pope differentiates the late twentieth century from two earlier periods:

> There are specific differences between the trends of modern society and those of the past, even the recent past. Whereas at one time the decisive factor of production was *the land* and later capital—understood as a total complex of the instruments of production—today the decisive factor is increasingly *man himself*, that is, his knowledge, especially his scientific knowledge, his capacity for interrelated and compact organization, as well as his ability to perceive the needs of others and to satisfy them.

These are exactly the factors in which Japan is preeminent: knowledge, scientific knowledge, a capacity for compact organization, and ability to perceive the needs of others and to satisfy them. Through these factors, the Japanese, who are extremely poor in natural resources, have made themselves preeminent.

Of course, natural resources are still important. But if human beings do not see their value and figure out ways to bring them into universal use, natural resources may lie fallow, forever undiscovered and unused, just as oil lay beneath the sands of Arabia, for thousands of years unused and treated as a nuisance, until human beings developed the piston engine and discovered the process of converting crude oil into gasoline. It was human beings who made useless crude into a "natural resource." In this sense, inanimate things are not the deepest, best, or most inexhaustible resource. The human mind is, as economist Julian Simon puts it, "the ultimate resource."[18]

It is not the things of earth that set limits to the wealth of the world. On this matter the Club of Rome, in its 1972 report predicting the exhaustion of natural resources in the near future, made an elementary mistake. Many of the things of this earth are useful at some times and not useful at other times (e.g., whale oil), depending on the value the human mind sees in them. In this sense, the human mind is the primary source of wealth.

And no wonder: it participates from afar in the source of all knowledge, the Creator. Thus, the pope says, "Indeed, besides the earth, man's principal resource is *man himself*. His intelligence enables him to discover the earth's productive potential *and* the many different ways in which human needs can be satisfied."

The pope sees three ways in which human knowledge is a source of wealth. First, "it is precisely *the ability to foresee* both the needs of others and the combinations of productive factors most adapted to satisfying those needs that constitutes another important source of wealth in modern society." Second, "many goods cannot be adequately produced through the work of an isolated individual; they require *the cooperation* of many people in working toward a common goal." This second kind of knowledge entails knowing how to organize the large-scale community necessary to produce even so simple a thing as a pencil.[19]

It does not ordinarily occur to theologians, but it is a matter of everyday experience to businesspeople, that even so simple an object as a pencil is made up of elements of graphite, wood, metal, rubber, and lacquer (to mention only the most visible and to leave aside others that only specialists know about) that come from vastly separated parts of this earth. The knowledge and skills needed to prepare these separate elements for the precise role they will play in the pencil represent a huge body of scientific and practical knowledge, which is almost certainly not present in the mind of any one individual but widely dispersed among researchers, managers, and workers in factories and workplaces in different parts of the world. All these factors of production—materials, knowledge, and skilled workers—must be brought together before anyone has a pencil in his hands.

For such reasons, the pope recognizes admiringly this second kind of wealth-producing knowledge: "Organizing such a productive effort, planning its duration in time, making sure that it corresponds in a positive way to the demand which it must satisfy, and taking the necessary risks—all this too is a source of wealth in today's society."

Thus far, the pope has discerned two ways in which knowledge is at work in human economic creativity: accurate insight into the needs of others and practical knowledge concerning how to organize a worldwide productive effort. But there is also a third way: the painstaking effort "to discover the earth's productive potential." Consider briefly three such discoveries, whose diffusion has done so much to change the world since Pope John Paul II first became pope in 1978: the invention of fiber optics, which in so many places are replacing copper (and thus contributing to the difficulties of Chile's copper industry); the invention of the word processor and of electronic processes in general, which are doing so much to shift the basis of industry from mechanical to electronic technologies; and the use of satellites and electronic impulses to link the entire world in a single, instantaneous communications network. All three of these breathtaking discoveries are the fruit of "man's principal resource," humanity's own creative intelligence. The human discoverer is made in the image of God (*imago Dei*). To be creative, to cooperate in bringing creation itself to its perfection, is the human vocation.

In this light, we see that it is no accident that a capitalist economy grew up first in the part of the world deeply influenced by Judaism and Christianity. Millions of people over many centuries learned from Judaism and Christianity to regard this earth not merely as a region of taboos, never to be investigated or experimented with, but rather as a place in which to exercise human powers of inquiry, creativity, and invention. The philosopher Alfred North Whitehead once remarked that the rise of modern science was inconceivable apart from the habits human beings learned during their long centuries of tutelage under Judaism and Christianity. Judaism and Christianity taught humans that the whole world and everything in it are intelligible, because all things—even contingent and seemingly accidental events—spring from the mind of an all-knowing Creator. This teaching had great consequences in the practical order. The belief that each human being is *imago Dei* was bound to lead, in an evolutionary and experimental way, to the development of an economic system whose first premise is that the principle cause of wealth is *caput* [Latin, "head"]: human wit, human creativity.

### The Second Ideal: Community

Already in section 31 of *Centesimus Annus*, Pope John Paul II noted that, nowadays, "it is becoming clearer how a person's work is naturally interrelated with the work of others. More than ever, work is *work with others* and *work for others*: it is a matter of doing something for someone else." From the very beginning, the modern business economy was designed to become an international system, concerned with raising "the wealth of nations," *all* nations, in a systematic, social way; it was by no means merely focused on the wealth of particular individuals. In section 32, Pope John Paul II picks up this line of thought: "Mention has just been made of the fact that *people work with each other*, sharing in a 'community of work' which embraces ever-widening circles." The pope then notes that "many goods cannot be adequately produced through the work of an isolated individual; they require the cooperation of many people in working toward a common goal." So again he comments, "It is man's disciplined work in close collaboration with others that makes possible the creation of ever more extensive *working communities* which can be relied upon to transform man's natural and human environments."

In a word, the person in business is constantly, on all sides, involved in building community. Immediately at hand, in his or her own firm, a person of business must build a community of work. Next, for its practical operations this firm depends on a larger community of suppliers and customers, bankers and government officials, transport systems, and the rule of law. And furthermore—as we saw in the example of the pencil—modern products derive from every part of the planet. The modern business system expresses the interdependence of the whole human race. In all these ways, then, business is a community activity. Capitalism is not about individualism. It is about a creative form of community.

Indeed, even in making a point about the role of profit (in section 35 of *Centesimus Annus*), the pope shows that the business firm, in its internal composition, is primarily a community of persons. He writes, "In fact, the purpose of a business firm is not simply to make a profit, but is to be found in its very existence as *a community of persons* who in various ways are endeavoring to satisfy their basic needs, and to form a particular group at the service of the whole society."

Precisely because even the business firm should be understood primarily as a community, the pope is able to write in the same section that

> the Church acknowledges the legitimate role of profit as an indication that a business is functioning well. . . . But profitability is not the only indicator of a firm's condition. It is possible for the financial accounts to be in order, and yet for the people—who make up the firm's most valuable asset—to be humiliated and their dignity offended. Besides being morally inadmissible, this will eventually have negative repercussions on the firm's economic efficiency.

In brief, the institution that is capitalism's main contribution to the human race is the private business corporation, independent of the state— and the main thing to notice about it is that it is a new and important form of human community, one of whose main social purposes is to make a profit, that is, to create new wealth beyond the wealth that existed before it came into being. The pope notes this aspect with approval: "When a firm makes a profit, this means that productive factors have been properly employed and corresponding human needs have been duly satisfied."[20] In other words, through the exercise of knowledge, the business firm uses the productive factors of the earth properly; it well discerns and satisfies human needs. By this path, it is "at the service of the whole of society." The economic and the ethical point of a business corporation is to serve others. So even in itself, the business firm represents a novel but important form of human community.

In fact, in section 32 of *Centesimus Annus* the pope goes to quite daring lengths in describing the modern business process. He sees that the modern business process "throws practical light on a truth about the person which Christianity has constantly affirmed," and for this reason "it should be viewed carefully and favorably." The truth he sees reflected is this: *the person working in community with other persons and for the sake of other persons*. This creative community is the greatest transformative power of the earthly order: "It is man's disciplined work in close collaboration with others that makes possible the creation of ever more extensive *working communities* which can be relied upon to transform man's natural and human environment."

## THE VIRTUES OF BUSINESS LIFE

Immediately after the last quoted passage, the pope goes on:

> Important virtues are involved in this process, such as diligence, industriousness, prudence in undertaking reasonable risks, reliability and fidelity in interpersonal relationships, as well as courage in carrying out decisions which are difficult and painful but necessary, both for the overall working of a business and in meeting possible setbacks.

At first glance, these virtues sound like a list taken from Max Weber's famous book *The Protestant Ethic and the Spirit of Capitalism*. But one sees on reflection that the context and meaning are utterly different. Max Weber saw the roots of capitalism in the negative attitude held by Protestants toward creation: in their sense of self-denial, their asceticism, and their sense of the depravity of natural man. By contrast, Pope John Paul II sets these ordinary, kitchen-variety virtues in the context of the basic goodness of creation as it springs from the hands of the Creator and in the light of the *imago Dei* impressed on man's nature. These virtues are not negative, repressive, or ascetic—or at least not primarily so—for they entail invention, serendipity, surprise, and the sort of romance that leads many to risk their shirts.

This is a considerable contrast to Weber's understanding, and thus one might speak, quite accurately, of "the Catholic ethic and the spirit of capitalism." This is the new ethic that the pope recommends for the Catholic nations of the world, from the Philippines through Latin America and on into central and eastern Europe—all those nations that are just now beginning to make the transition from a socialist or precapitalist, third-world economy to a capitalist economy.

## CONCLUSION

These, then, are the basic ideals around which the pope orients his approach to business ethics: creativity and community, and the virtues involved in them. The first two are extremely demanding principles. They will require great changes in the workings of the economy. They especially require change in all those economies that do not yet promote the right to personal economic initiative among all citizens, universally.

Every single person, no matter how poor or unlearned, is made in the image of God. Each has a right to exercise his or her own personal economic creativity. Therefore, existing economic systems that repress the right to personal economic creativity must be reformed, because they abuse the image of God endowed in all. They abuse that image by making the incorporation of small businesses prohibitively difficult; by failing to provide sources of cheap credit to poor people (while credit is the mother's milk of new enterprises); by failing to provide universal education, particularly in the creative and practical skills of economic activity; and by not cherishing human capital and intellectual property as the primary sources of wealth. Indeed, to fulfill the pope's vision of a genuine ethic of capitalism, a peaceful but profound revolution will be necessary throughout much of the third world. In the developed world, too, great changes will be necessary, particularly in the moral and cultural area; but that is another and larger subject than the foundations of business ethics.

The implication of the pope's argument is that true development must begin from the bottom up. It must be universal. It must allow every person, no matter how poor or unlearned, to participate in economic activism. Thus, every free society must examine all its institutions to see whether they are promoting or repressing human creativity. The test of a business system is what is happening among the able-bodied poor. Here in the United States, we must ask ourselves, Are we doing enough to draw the poor into business activities, to include them? Are current government programs, intended to help the poor, actually an aid to the poor, or are they an obstruction?

*Centesimus Annus* is a marvelous and revolutionary piece of work. It is original, clear, and compelling. It sets before us a huge agenda and offers no grounds for complacency. It does what no other religious document has done before: it grasps the interiority of the life of business, the excitement of it, the idealism of it, the challenge of it.

Men and women of business *enjoy* creating something that did not exist before. In Pope John II, business leaders have at last found an ecclesiastical leader who sees clearly what moves them, who speaks of that spirit affirmatively, and who sets great challenges in front of them. There is nothing business leaders like better than challenges. So it will be surprising if men and women of business are not stimulated by the pope's words to become more creative than ever and to lead the way to the revolution in the world's economy that the pope envisages.

For Pope John Paul II, business ethics means a great deal more than obeying the civil law and not violating the moral law. It means imagining and creating a new economic order, one based on the principles of individual creativity, community, and the special virtues of enterprise. It means respecting the right of the poor to their own personal economic initiative and their own creativity. It means fashioning a culture worthy of free women and free men—to the benefit of the poor, and to the greater glory of God.

## NOTES

1. What follows is adapted from the Hayek Memorial Lecture presented by Michael Novak in London, England, June 22, 1993. Part of section 4 of this chapter appears in modified form in Michael Novak, *Business as a Calling: Work and the Examined Life* (New York: Free Press, 1996).

2. See especially book 3, chapter 2, "How Democracy Renders the Habitual Intercourse of the Americans Simple and Easy"; and book 2, chapter 19, "What Causes Almost All Americans to Follow Industrial Callings."

3. See "Idea of a Perfect Commonwealth" in David Hume, *Essays: Moral, Political, and Literary* (Indianapolis: Liberty Classics, 1987), 528.

4. See Irving Kristol, "The Spiritual Roots of Capitalism and Socialism," in *Capitalism and Socialism: A Theological Inquiry,* ed. Michael Novak (Washington, D.C.: American Enterprise Institute, 1979), 1–14.

5. Jacob Viner, "Early Attitudes towards Trade and the Merchant," in *Essays on the Intellectual History of Economics,* ed. Douglas A. Irwin (Princeton, N.J.: Princeton University Press, 1991), 39–40.

6. This development is traced in Michael Novak, *This Hemisphere of Liberty* (Washington, D.C.: American Enterprise Institute, 1992), chap. 7, "Wealth and Virtue—The Development of Christian Economic Teaching" (63–88).

7. In the sociologist Peter Berger's formulation, "Capitalism is a necessary but not sufficient condition of democracy. . . . As to falsification of the above hypothesis, the most convincing one would be the emergence, in empirical reality rather than in the realm of ideas, of even one clear case of democratic socialism" (*The Capitalist Revolution* [New York: Basic Books, 1986], 81).

8. For a full consideration of the civic dimension of Adam Smith's thought, see Jerry Z. Muller's *Adam Smith in His Time and Ours* (New York: Free Press, 1993).

9. Max Weber, *The Protestant Ethic and the Spirit of Capitalism*, trans. Talcott Parsons (New York: Charles Scribner's Sons, 1958).

10. My appreciation and critique of Weber is developed at greater length in Michael Novak, *The Catholic Ethic and the Spirit of Capitalism* (New York: Free Press, 1993), esp. 1–14.

11. The most developed treatment of this point is to be found in Israel Kirzner, *Discovery and the Capitalist Process* (Chicago: University of Chicago Press, 1985).

12. For a fuller treatment of enterprise, see Novak, *This Hemisphere of Liberty*, chap. 4, "The Virtue of Enterprise" (25–35).

13. John Paul II, *Centesimus Annus* (Boston: Daughters of St. Paul, 1991) sec. 32.

14. Ibid., sec. 31.

15. Ibid. Emphasis added.

16. For a discussion of this point, see Oswald von Nell-Bruening, S.J., *Reorganization of Social Economy* (New York: Bruce Publishing, 1939), 131–32.

17. John Paul II, *Centesimus Annus*, sec. 32. Hereafter, unidentified quotations in the text are found in sec. 32.

18. Julian L. Simon, *The Ultimate Resource* (Princeton, N.J.: Princeton University Press, 1981).

19. See Leonard Read's classic essay of 1958, "I Pencil," reprinted in *Imprimis* (Hillsdale, Mich.), June 1992.

20. John Paul II, *Centesimus Annus* sec. 35.

## STUDY QUESTIONS

1. What is the most important thing a young person needs to know about religion, according to Novak? Do you agree? Why? Why not?
2. What defines the wealth of a country? Defend your answer by comparing Japan and Brazil.
3. Give three characteristics of the relationship between Judaism and Christianity. What is the significance of this relationship?
4. What text is considered the first "modern introspective biography"? Why is it described this way?
5. What was the chief form of world wealth prior to 1776? In what ways has such an evaluation of wealth changed? Be specific.
6. What three moral ideas are inherent in business? Describe each one. Are you comfortable with these relationships between wealth and values? Why? Why not?

# 8

## ROBERT WUTHNOW

# "We Prayed They Would Win": How Christians Become Political Activists

Conservative, Bible-believing Christians used to stay at home, read their Bibles, and attend church on Sundays. Politics was remote, a worldly activity that did not interest them much. Now things are different. Christians who call themselves "fundamentalists" and "evangelicals" have become quite active in American politics. They threw their votes heavily in favor of Ronald Reagan, George Bush, and other Republican candidates. They have lobbied hard to prevent homosexuals from gaining greater influence in society, have worked to curb pornography, and have come out strongly against abortion.

The New Christian Right, as it has been called, shows that religion can have a strong impact on the public life of our nation. Many people may believe that faith is strictly a matter of the heart and that each person should believe whatever he or she wants to believe. But religious organizations remain quite strong. More people attend religious services each week in America than in virtually any other country in the world. They hear sermons that may not tell them exactly how to vote but that may encourage them to favor one position more than another. They may also be involved in religious groups that talk about politics and, on occasion, mobilize their members to become actively involved in political efforts.

There is nothing illegal about this. Indeed, most observers believe that our society is stronger when groups of all kinds, including religious

I wish to thank Natalie Searl, for her assistance on the various research projects that produced some of the material included in this chapter, and the Lilly Endowment, for its funding of this research. The characters featured herein are real people; I have changed their names and disguised some of the details in order to preserve their anonymity.

groups, take an interest in public policy. Such involvement is vital to the democratic process. It is nevertheless important to know that millions of Americans who had never voted before, and who had never been very interested in politics, became increasingly concerned about political issues in recent years as a result of their churches. How does this happen? What is the process? Let us consider a revealing case.

## ONE WOMAN'S STORY

"My childhood was terrible—tough, just really tough." This is Annalee. She is twenty-eight, married, the mother of two small children. She grew up in Virginia and now lives in Pennsylvania. Her childhood was tough because her father was an alcoholic. He stayed sober all week, but when he came home from work on Fridays, he was drunk; and he stayed that way until Monday morning. He was never physically abusive, but he yelled at Annalee and her two sisters all the time, telling them how stupid they were and that they were no good. Annalee says her self-image was just rotten.

It was a long road from that environment to the fundamentalist church Annalee now attends. She is a deaconness and a faithful member of the women's Bible study group. She feels better about herself now. She works hard at being a good mother to her children and a good wife for her husband. She has also become more interested in politics. What worries her most is the moral decay that seems to be corrupting America. She is glad there are conservative Christians who are beginning to speak out about these problems. Randall Terry of Operation Rescue is one of her heroes; James Dobson of Focus on the Family is another. She is one of a growing number of young women and men at her church—and across our nation— whose religious commitment has started to have political overtones.

To understand why Annalee, like millions of other Americans, has become sympathetic to conservative Christian politics, we must look more closely at the journey she has undertaken since those traumatic days as a child in Virginia. Annalee's mother, as if to compensate for her husband's inattention, always paid special attention to the needs of her daughters. Although she worked full time at a poultry-processing plant near their home, she poured her life into her girls, doing things for them, helping them with their homework, and making sure they were involved in school activities. An active Catholic, she also sent her daughters to mass every Sunday and made sure they knew the catechism. All three girls made straight As in high school and went on to attend local community college, which was what the family could afford. And they took practical courses. Annalee graduated with a certificate in dental hygiene.

The best thing that ever happened to Annalee, she says, was meeting John. When she was a little girl, she used to pray every night that someday she would find a husband, a good man who would be different from her father. Then one day during her senior year in high school, she was working at the local doughnut shop, and John came in with a couple of his buddies. They started talking to her, and John asked her out. A year later they were engaged, and the next year Annalee had a baby. Two weeks later, John married her. She says he is indeed everything her father was not: "He's a family man. He's loving. He's religious."

With a husband to support her and a baby to care for, Annalee decided she needed to get away from her father. She told him they were leaving and never wanted to see him again unless he stopped drinking. He did stop, too—at least for a while. But the scars in their relationship remained, and he had relapses and still smoked two or three packs of cigarettes a day.

When Annalee and her husband settled in Pennsylvania, John worked as a carpenter, making kitchen cabinets. He did this for two years before he was laid off. Then he got a job installing security systems, but it lasted only a year. For the past five years, John has been driving a delivery truck to local restaurants and bars. He likes the work because it is steady and he's on his own most of the time. There is a lot of lifting, but John is muscular and still takes pride in the fact that he was a high school football player.

Five years ago, when John got his new job, he and Annalee moved to their present community. She had been working part time as a dental hygienist, but shortly after they moved, their son was born, and Annalee had to quit. She intends to get a job again in a few years, but with two young children and her husband putting in twelve-hour days, she has not been able to yet.

The first thing John and Annalee did when they settled in their apartment complex was to look for a nearby church. Annalee's childhood training in the Catholic church had not been without effect. As a child, she had trouble thinking of God as a father figure because her own father was so mean. She did, however, believe in God, and she gradually came to regard God as the loving father she wished she had. She went through confirmation class, took her first communion, and was still attending church regularly when she met John. Looking back on it, Annalee notes it probably seems strange that she started sleeping with John, especially as he was a

Christian too. She figures she just wanted to be loved so badly that she didn't really stop to think about it.

John's parents were conservative Baptists and were not, to say the least, happy with his decision to marry a Catholic. John himself did not see what all the fuss was about. As long as people were Christians, he figured, what difference did it make? But to please his parents, Annalee became a Baptist. She remembers that at the first church they attended in Pennsylvania, every Sunday evening the minister preached a long sermon and then asked if anyone would like to come forward. One evening Annalee did. She felt that she was already a Christian, but she had never really made a personal commitment to Christ, as most of the Baptists had done. She admits she understood little of what she was doing, but she wanted the church people to accept her.

She and John chose their present church, an independent Bible church, because it was adjacent to their apartment complex, they liked the preaching the first time they visited, and it had a children's Sunday school program that looked good. They tried some Baptist churches in the area as well, but these were either too large or too small. They also talked it over with John's parents, who said, Annalee recalls, that "it doesn't matter the denomination as long as it's a Bible-believing church and they're preaching from the Bible." Annalee feels the church is, indeed, quite oriented toward the Bible. When she first came, she says, she could hardly find the various books of the Bible, but now she knows exactly where they are. And, more important, she feels she has a better understanding of what the Bible means.

The main reason Annalee feels this way is the women's Bible study group she joined about a month after she and John started attending the church. The group meets every Tuesday morning for two hours. About fifteen women attend regularly, and another five to ten come occasionally. Annalee is one of the regulars. She was attracted by the fact that several other young mothers were nursing their infants the first time she came. There is babysitting now, to give her a couple hours free from "Mommy, this and Mommy, that." She has learned a lot from several of the women, who have children just a few years older than hers. And she especially likes the leader and a couple of the older women who attend. They know the Bible a lot better than she does and have interesting stories to tell about their lives.

The group spends about half its time each week studying some passage from the Bible or some other inspirational book or study guide. In recent months they have, for example, worked through booklets on Christian homemaking, motherhood, and the book of Esther, as well as others on the book of James and on maturity as a Christian. The discussions are loosely structured, usually emphasizing personal applications more than abstract knowledge. The leader, for instance, will throw out a few points and then ask if anyone has had an experience that would illustrate a point; from there, the discussion wanders to a conversation at the supermarket, a recent argument with one's husband, or a cute anecdote from one's three-year-old. The remainder of the time is spent in prayer and fellowship. Each woman mentions several prayer requests, taking the opportunity to update the group on what has been happening in her life during the previous week. The group members then pray for one another, and after visiting for a while over coffee, they return to their homes. Many, of course, see one another again at the services on Sundays and may call one another during the week.

Annalee's life now revolves around her children, her husband, and her Bible study group—in that order. She is concerned, above all, about being a good Christian and a good mother. Politics is not a major part of her life. Nor is politics the glue that holds her Bible study group together; they meet mostly to study the Bible and to talk about their personal problems. Yet the group does encourage its members to become more politically involved than they otherwise would be and, indeed, more involved than many of their unchurched neighbors are. Group discussions reaffirm members' beliefs on certain publicly contested issues. For example, it is abundantly clear from week to week that the group is adamantly opposed to abortion. Anyone whose views were waffling would soon find herself confronted with strong pro-life arguments. Indeed, Annalee admits this was her own experience. "I used to think that abortion was okay and that it was no big deal," she explains. But she says that being in the group has "really made me see that that is a live baby in there and it's wrong and you're killing a human being."

Unlike some churches, Annalee's does not load its members onto buses to participate in anti-abortion rallies. But the women in her Bible study group are encouraged in quieter ways to be vigilant and to stay involved. They talk about bills being presented to the state legislature and discuss issues confronting the local school district. There are often petitions in the church lobby for members to sign. And at election time, members quietly find out how the others are voting; they identify candidates with conservative, pro-moral, and pro-family reputations and support them in the voting booth and in their prayers. Annalee recalls, "Yes, on election day we got together and we prayed about who God wanted to be in office. We prayed they would win."

## RELIGION AND POLITICS

Religious faith has generated political action periodically throughout history. In the Middle Ages it prompted the Crusades, carried out by knights from England and France who sought to liberate Jerusalem from Muslim Turks in the name of Christianity. Joan of Arc led her troops into battle during the Hundred Years War because she heard voices—the voices of three saints, whose statues decorated her church—telling her to do so. In the sixteenth and seventeenth centuries, Protestants fought Catholics across the face of Europe in the name of different beliefs about worship.

The political landscape of our own country has also been deeply influenced by religion. The Revolutionary War came shortly after a period of intense religious revival and may have been encouraged by the zeal for independence that was being preached in New England pulpits. Early in the nineteenth century, many of the political reforms during the Jacksonian era were led by preachers and religious activists who wanted to build a society that was more compassionate toward the poor and who hoped that middle-class morality could be extended to new immigrant workers. The movement against slavery owed much to the religious revivalists, who held tent meetings in the 1830s and 1840s.

In recent decades, religion has again inspired a wide variety of political activities. The United States Constitution keeps church and state separate, thus preventing religious groups from taking control of the government or gaining special benefits for themselves through legislation. However, separation of church and state does not mean that religiously motivated people are denied their right to speak up for what they believe is right. Thus, during the Civil Rights movement, many religious leaders, including Dr. Martin Luther King, Jr., became actively involved in pressing for greater racial equality in America. During the Vietnam War, campus ministries often played a role in organizing protest demonstrations among students. Throughout the cold war era, many pastors, priests, rabbis, and other religious leaders worked actively to halt the nuclear arms race. And during the 1980s, groups such as Moral Majority, Christian Voice, and Religious Roundtable became active in lobbying for such causes as the right to pray in public schools, prohibitions against abortion, and restrictions on the activities of homosexuals. The political concerns that Annalee and millions like her have come to talk about in recent years are thus only the latest instances in a long history of political action that has been encouraged by religious faith.

It is impossible to draw generalizations about the ways in which political action may be influenced by religion. Political views that in their day were considered quite conservative have been encouraged by religious groups, but so have views that were quite liberal or radical. In some cases, believers took up arms and fought wars to protect their beliefs, but in our own society it has been much more common for religious groups to fight causes the same way as everyone else—by voting, lobbying, sending in petitions, staging peaceful demonstrations, and, perhaps most often, simply by preaching, teaching, and praying.

We can, however, understand some of what it takes for religious people to become politically involved by considering some of the factors we have already seen at work in Annalee's case. Five factors in particular deserve our attention: social support, a sense of threat, leadership, religious belief itself, and communication.

### Support

The Bible study group is Annalee's most immediate and important source of support. Living in a different state from her parents and trying to raise her children differently than she was raised, she looks to the group as her main source of practical, moral advice. It is where she goes to talk about how to potty-train her children and to vent her fears about the consequences of letting them play with toy guns or Barbie dolls.

The group is doubly important because her husband, John, is away much of the time, and because he is not nearly as conservative in his religious views as she. Part of the difference is that he grew up in a conservative family, whereas she is a convert to conservatism. Therefore it means more to her. Moreover, he is trying to loosen up, giving his children more freedom than he had growing up, whereas she is deeply concerned about teaching them absolutes.

John's religious views are also shaped by the fact that he is in a work setting all day, instead of staying at home with the children. He says he tries to witness to people he sees just by being nice to them, sometimes by striking up a conversation about religion, and by playing the Christian radio station in his truck. But his deliveries take him into bars, a couple of go-go joints, and even one place he suspects is a house of ill repute. He says he thinks sometimes that he should go in and yell at these people, telling them how sinful they are. Then he remembers, however, that keeping his job is important, so he stays quiet. He and Annalee are able to discuss these issues. But it is usually she who becomes more vexed by them, and when she does, she finds kindred spirits in her group.

## Threat

It takes support to get things done, but the motivation to do them is often heightened when one's way of life seems threatened. Annalee is a vivid example because she illustrates how vulnerable even conservative, church-going Christians are to prevailing social trends. She is one of the many Americans (estimates range from one-fourth to one-half the population) who have been exposed to alcoholism in their immediate families. As a teenager, she suffered from low self-esteem and then became pregnant out of wedlock. She went to college, acquiring more education than either of her parents, yet she and her husband are well down in the pecking order in the largely professional and managerial community in which they live. They are struggling to pay their bills and worry that bankruptcy, which has already hit some of their friends in the church, may happen to them.

When Annalee and the other women in her Bible study group think about what is happening in the wider society, they clearly feel threatened. They do not see and then lust after glitzy homes, Rolex watches, Lexus ES300 sedans, high salaries, and advanced degrees. Instead, they see moral corruption. At one of the meetings, for example, a young woman in the group ventured the following observation: "What's happening now is your big colleges and schools are handing out all those big degrees, but they're not teaching the morals that need to be taught."

They also worry that the corruption they perceive in the wider world is causing decay within their own ranks. "My husband was watching this program on CNN the other day," one woman told the group. "It was about these virgins in California. They were born-again Christians. And they were practicing all these alternative forms of sex that allowed them to still be virgins. But that's not right in God's eyes." She said she didn't want to go into detail, but she wondered what the Christian community was coming to.

This story prompted Annalee to lament that even the church was often not taking the stand on moral issues that it should. "It is to blame," she remarked, "because we allow too many gray areas." Noting how the church no longer came out strongly against drinking and dancing, she added, "I like black and white. Tell me yes or tell me no. I think we need to take stands. We have to stop with this gray stuff. It really upsets me."

## Leadership

Although they may feel threatened, people nevertheless need leaders to prompt them to take action. In Annalee's Bible study group, leadership functions in three important ways. First, there is a leader of the group itself. She is an older woman who is highly respected by all the members. She plays a prominent role in selecting topics for the group to study and in guiding week-to-week discussions. When conversations roam away from the topic, she draws them back. She is not as conservative as some of the other members, so she does not prompt them to think in absolute terms or to become more concerned about political issues. She does, however, drive home many of their own observations, cautioning them to be vigilant against evil and to speak out against it.

Second, the group has connections with leaders external to it. Unlike many such groups, this one is not supervised by the pastor. It has few connections with him, and he is too preoccupied with other matters to take an active role in public affairs. If he did, the group would probably become much more active as well. One woman in the church, however, ran for a seat on the local school board; the Bible study group prayed repeatedly for her success, and some of its members helped with her campaign. External leaders also include national figures in the New Christian Right. James Dobson is a favorite because many of the group's members receive his program on their cable channels, and others subscribe to his newsletter. Charles Colson, Pat Robertson, Oliver North, and others are mentioned from time to time as well. The group leader often announces to the members that they should watch certain programs that feature these leaders.

Third, the group is quite mindful of leadership patterns within the home. As conservative Christians, they think it is divinely ordained that husbands be leaders of their wives and children. Therefore, the women seldom take it on themselves to become directly involved in political activities (except the one who ran for school board), but they encourage one another to speak to their husbands, to bring issues to the attention of their husbands, and to make sure their husbands vote, sign petitions, and keep abreast of important public policies. As one member remarked in her prayer one day, "Men are the leaders over us, and without their leadership, we will fail."

### Religious Beliefs

Political action is also motivated directly by religious beliefs. What distinguishes fundamentalists most from other Christians is their emphasis on the Bible. They believe that God's truth is contained totally, most clearly, and without error in the written words of the Bible. This becomes their basis for certainty in life. If they have any questions, all they need to do is turn to the Bible. Having been raised in the Roman Catholic Church, Annalee is quick to draw a contrast between that church and her present one. She is not a rabid anti-Catholic. Indeed, she now feels that the church she was raised in taught many good things, and she was simply not at a place in her own life to understand them. She admits she would like to attend mass again, from time to time, and is curious about what is happening at the Catholic church near her apartment complex. Yet she also has harsh words to say about Catholicism in comparison with her present beliefs. "There were deceptions and there were lies," she says. "We were just told what the Catholic Church believes, and nothing was based on anything. The pope said it, and he told the monsignors, and they told the priests, and they told us. And you never questioned, you never asked, and you never disagreed. You just accepted it."

That, of course, sounds like the way many people would describe fundamentalists. But Annalee sees a difference. To her, the Bible is a valid and trustworthy source of authority. If you have a question, she says, people respond by saying, "Well, let's look in the Bible. What does it say about that?" For her, this is comforting. "It's backed up with scripture, whereas in the Catholic Church it never was. Never learned a verse. Never was asked to memorize. Never was given a Bible."

Fundamentalists believe that the Bible is literally true and that each word therefore should be regarded as divinely inspired. But how do they get from that position to specific points about public policy or, for that matter, about personal morality? One view is that they have philosophical arguments for why the Bible is true and then find in the Bible specific rules to apply to their daily lives.

This view probably does not capture what the rank-and-file fundamentalist actually does. In Annalee's case, at least, she discovers God's truth in the Bible by listening to the stories the women in her group tell. She knows God can heal people, for example, because she has heard people in her group say so. She has also heard them point out that God does not always provide healing but that believers can find comfort in God anyway. She believes the book of Proverbs is literally true when it says, "A soft answer turns away wrath" (15:1), because her group discussed this verse last week and everyone could cite examples proving that this advice worked. She believes that abortion is always wrong because the same people have pointed to a verse in Psalms that talks about the person existing in the womb.

In short, fundamentalists do not have a tightly woven view of the universe that includes a rule book for all situations. Instead, they have groups of respected peers who validate one another's beliefs by providing examples of how things have worked in their own lives. Their faith is pragmatic in two senses: it is true because it works; and if it is truly true, then it should work.

In keeping with the latter sense, fundamentalists are concerned that many people, as the Bible says, call on God but do not follow God's commands. An issue they believe to be morally right, such as a stance against abortion, therefore can also become a test of whether or not one is a genuine Christian. One day the discussion at Annalee's Bible study group focused on the ways in which things were different now from the time of King David's reign in Israel. One member commented that it was harder now, because so many people called themselves Christians, went to church, and tried to live a good life but probably were not true followers of Jesus. That remark prompted another member to encourage the group to watch a James Dobson film she had seen recently. She said the film showed a lot of people who, when interviewed, said they believed in God and went to church; but when the same people were asked if abortion was murder and if it should be outlawed, they said no. "So," she concluded, "there was no application of what they supposedly claimed. What they believed had nothing to do with their everyday life." Before concluding the meeting, the leader reinforced the point. She mentioned a book on the subject in the church library that everyone should read and reminded them that being a Christian means having the courage to speak out on controversial issues.

### Communication

Finally, political action depends on having ways to communicate. When communication is mentioned, it is easy to think of news reports or factual information being passed along, for example, about when the next pro-life rally is going to be held. And that sort of communication is important in mobilizing people for political action. During a recent presidential campaign, church lobbies and parking lots became prime targets for political operatives who wanted to pass out leaflets showing why their candidate was better. But there is another form of communication that is probably far more powerful. It involves telling stories—personal anecdotes that carry a punch because they are personal but that also make a moral or political point.

In Annalee's Bible study group, this kind of communication is vital. Members tell stories about themselves, asking the group to pray for them, and in the process they provide anecdotes about how to raise children, how to respond to abusive husbands, or how to deal with worldly neighbors. Sometimes these stories also reinforce the group's political orientations.

Two weeks after the group's conversation about abortion, the discussion again turned to the problem of people believing one thing and doing another. One member offered the following example. A very close friend of hers, she said, was doing a lot of good work protesting against abortion. He was a Christian, she observed, and her tone of voice made it clear that she admired his political activism. His own daughter, however, had become pregnant out of wedlock, and this man had faltered in his convictions. He had encouraged his daughter to have an abortion. The group member shook her head, and several others did the same. "That's the problem with situation ethics," the leader remarked. "Our beliefs are absolute; we have to base our decisions on them, even if it is inconvenient."

Annalee couldn't agree more. She wants to see the moral corruption in our society cleared away. When she votes, signs petitions, and talks about politics in her group, that goal is uppermost in her mind.

## STUDY QUESTIONS

1. Name two ways that you see religion having a strong impact on political life. Can you think of specific examples?
2. In what three ways does conservative Christianity give stability to Annalee's life? What basic needs does the church supply Annalee?
3. Try to think of three events in U.S. history that were both political and religious. In each case, is it possible to separate religion from politics? Are church and state really separate in contemporary society, in particular, in the United States? Why? Why not?
4. What are five factors that motivate religious persons to become politically involved? Discuss each one. Be specific.

# 9

## JOHN L. ESPOSITO

---

# Jihad:
# The Struggle for Islam

Events in the Muslim world in recent years have underscored the extent to which Islam is a way of life, a worldview that shapes and directs the lives of one billion Muslims. The resurgence of Islam has revealed the struggle within the global Islamic community to define—or redefine—Islam as a comprehensive way of life, a religion that both nurtures the inner life of the believer and shapes the institutions and public policy of Muslim society.[1] However, the impact of Islam on Muslim politics and society also raises profound questions about the relationship of religion to state and society and about the capacity of religion to be a source of social justice and conflict resolution rather than political and social conflict and instability. Governments and opposition movements in the Muslim world have appealed to Islam for legitimacy and to mobilize popular support. Rulers, reformers, and revolutionaries have appealed to God (Allah) and the Qur'an as well as the sword (armies and militias) to retain or gain power, advocate sociopolitical reforms, act in self-defense, as well as wage war and commit acts of terrorism.

The Islamic resurgence across the Muslim world, from North Africa to Southeast Asia, has challenged the once-pervasive belief that modernization required a clear Western, secular path and orientation in nation building.[2] Governments and Islamic movements (moderate and violent extremists) have appealed to Islam to enhance their legitimacy and authority, buttress nationalism, legitimate policies and programs, and mobilize popular support. The struggle—jihad—to follow or spread Islam has been interpreted in multiple ways by diverse interest groups, and thus to determine who is in the right is often a challenge. The line between the use of religion and its manipulation, between charismatic leader and demagogue, between secular and religious authoritarianism, between self-defense and aggression, and between holy warriors/freedom fighters and terrorists is often blurred.

The response of Western governments and their citizens to political Islam has often been confused and ambivalent. While Americans and the West abhorred the nightly television images of Americans held hostage in Tehran and Ayatollah Khomeini's desire to spread his holy war to the Persian Gulf and beyond, they cheered another holy war, providing money and arms to support the Afghan mujahideen (holy warriors) in their struggle (jihad) against Soviet occupation. Ironically, after years of Western support to Iraq as a buffer to Iranian expansionism in the Persian Gulf, Iraq turned upon its supporters, annexed Kuwait, and declared a jihad against the United States and the West. Having mounted an offensive to liberate Kuwait and protect Saudi Arabia from Iraqi incursions, Americans and Europeans have been tentative and contradictory in their responses to the plight of Muslims in Bosnia and Kashmir and to the Algerian military's cancellation of election results in which the Islamic Salvation Front swept parliamentary elections.

From the Iranian Revolution in 1978–79 to the World Trade Center bombing in 1993, America and the West have experienced the wrath of "militant Islamic fundamentalism." Media headlines such as "Islam's War against the West," "Beware of Religious Stalinists," "Roots of Muslim Rage,"and "Jihad against the Jews"; terrorist attacks by Jihad organizations in Egypt, Lebanon, Gaza, and the West Bank; and television programs with ominous titles such as "The Sword of Islam" and "Jihad in America" portray Islam as and often reduce it to an international crusade by religious extremists who engage in a holy war that threatens global stability and security.[3] As a result, Islam and the vast diversity of Muslim believers are often equated simply with fundamentalism, radicalism, and terrorism. Since *fundamentalism* has become a catchword for religious extremism and terrorism, it is better to speak of Islamists or Islamic activists when referring to those who wish to implement Islam socially and politically. Then, basing evaluations on individual cases, we can make specific judgments about individual leaders, governments, and organizations, as to whether they are moderate, extremist, violent, revolutionary, democratic, or otherwise.

The reality of Islam and its relationship to peace and conflict, like that of Muslim politics, is complex.[4] The second largest of the world's religions, *Islam* means "peace" or submission to God's will. It is a religion that speaks of God as merciful and compassionate; its greeting is "Peace be upon you" (*Salaam alaykum*). At the same time, Islam relates happiness in the next world not only to piety and submission to God but also to action, following God's will or law, and the mission of the Muslim community to spread God's word and rule. Muslims, as individuals and as members of a global community of believers (*ummah*), are to serve as an example to other communities, to strive and struggle to implement a global order based on God's will and social justice in this world.

A central belief in Islam is that all Muslims must strive or struggle (*jihad*) to follow, to spread, and to defend God's will and rule. Historically, jihad has had three meanings. First, it refers to the struggle of all believers to be faithful and to lead virtuous lives. Second, it means the struggle or process of understanding and interpreting (*ijtihad*) Islam. And third, jihad means the sacred struggle both to defend and to spread Islam. It is the last meaning that has been equated with holy war. While some Muslims have used jihad to legitimate aggression, others have argued that it should be used only in self-defense, in defense of Islam and Muslim territory.

The best vantage point for understanding the nature and dynamics of contemporary Islam is one that combines theory and practice, doctrine and action. Contemporary Islam is the product of religion and politics, faith and the political and economic realities of Muslim societies. The challenge for many Muslims today, as for all religious believers, is to discover and articulate the relevance of their faith to the realities and demands of modern (or postmodern) life. If the tendency in some Muslim societies has been to separate religion from public life, to attempt to restrict religion to personal belief and practice, other Muslims have reasserted the belief that Islam is a comprehensive way of life, with guidance and norms that affect personal and public issues: from diet, dress, women's status, and family values to politics, economics, and international affairs.

In recent decades, various Islamic movements have sprung up throughout the Muslim world. They have been inspired and influenced by the Muslim Brotherhood of Egypt and the Jamaat-i-Islami (Islamic Society) of South Asia, which have often provided the ideological and organizational inspiration and models for other organizations to build on. Yet there has been no monolithic movement or ideology, no single answer or model, no unified international network or headquarters. Many contending and contentious voices exist; differences abound; conflict, violence, and extremism have existed alongside prayer and piety. Perhaps the best way to see and appreciate the many faces and voices of contemporary Islam is to witness the diversity of the Muslim experience and struggle in Egypt.

## EGYPT: FROM ARAB NATIONALISM
## TO POLITICAL ISLAM

Egypt has long been regarded as a leader in the Arab world, politically, militarily, religiously, and culturally. Among the most modern of Muslim countries, it has experienced the full array of Islamic revivalist activities. It once offered a barometer for a process of modernization that was predominantly Western and somewhat secular in orientation. In recent years, Egypt has provided a full-blown example of the more complex—and at times, volatile—experience of Muslim societies, as many Muslims attempt in a variety of ways to integrate their Islamic heritage and values in their sociopolitical development.

During the late 1950s and the 1960s, Arab politics was dominated by Arab nationalism and socialism, which proved popular and effective. Revolutions in Egypt, Syria, Iraq, Libya, the Sudan, and Algeria were legitimated in the name of revolutionary socialism. The 1952 Free Officers Revolution in Egypt elevated Gamal Abdel Nasser, whose charisma made him a hero at home and abroad. Nasser simultaneously championed Egyptian and Arab nationalism and socialism. His desire to unite the Arabs under his leadership proved a sufficient threat to conservative Arab monarchs that Saudi Arabia's Prince (later, King) Faisal countered with a Saudi-sponsored alternative, pan-Islam. Condemning narrow forms of secular nationalism and socialism as un-Islamic, the Saudis spoke of the transnational Islamic nation of which Arabism was a part. Saudi Arabia created and funded international Islamic organizations, for instance, the Organization of the Islamic Conference to foster cooperation among Muslim governments; the Islamic Development Bank, to sponsor economic development projects in the Muslim world; and the Muslim World League, to preach and promote Islam and Islamic causes worldwide. Oil wealth enabled the Saudis to assert their international Islamic leadership and exercise significant influence in the Muslim world.

The Arab defeat in the 1967 Arab–Israeli war, in which the combined forces of Egypt, Syria, and Jordan were routed by the Israelis, did much to discredit Arab socialism and triggered an identity crisis that led many in Egypt and throughout the Arab world to question the path and direction of political and social development and to turn inward for strength and guidance. The Western-oriented policies of Arab governments and elites appeared to have failed, as demonstrated by Arab impotence in the war, commonly referred to as "the disaster" or "the catastrophe." Military failure combined with the knowledge that Western allies supported Israel, and not the Arabs, to contribute to the identity crisis.

The soul-searching in Egypt and the Arab world embraced a broad spectrum of society and raised many questions about the direction and accomplishments of development. Politically, regimes seemed less successful in establishing their legitimacy and an ideology for national unity than in perpetuating autocratic rule. Despite parliamentary systems of government, governments were headed by authoritarian rulers, often propped up by Western governments and multinational corporations.

Economically, both Western capitalism and Marxist socialism seemed incapable of effectively reducing poverty and illiteracy. Capitalism in particular was regarded as the system of special interests and new elites that had produced a society driven more by materialism and conspicuous consumption than by concern by equity and social justice. Young people in particular found themselves in a world that offered a dim future. Idealism, study, and hard work were rewarded by unemployment, housing shortages, and a lack of political participation that increased the sense of frustration and hopelessness. Neither liberal nationalism nor Arab socialism had fulfilled their promises.

Socioculturally, modernization was seen as a legacy of European colonialism, perpetuated by Western-oriented elites who imposed and fostered the twin processes of Westernization and secularization. As dependence on Western models of development was blamed for political and military failures, so, too, cultural dependence resulted in what some authors called the Westernization of Muslim societies or the "disease" of "Westoxification." The resultant sociomoral decline was seen as a major contributor to the breakdown of the Muslim family, to more permissive, promiscuous societies, and to spiritual malaise.

Finally, American ignorance and hostility toward Islam and the Middle East, often critiqued as a "Christian crusader" mentality influenced by Orientalism and Zionism, were blamed for misguided U.S. political-military policies: support for the "un-Islamic" Shah of Iran, massive military and economic funding of Israel, and the backing of a Christian-controlled government in Lebanon.

If the late 1960s were the nadir of dejection and uncertainty in the Muslim world, identity and pride seemed to be restored by events in 1973 and 1979. The humiliation of the 1967 war and the discrediting of Arab socialism were reversed by the moral victory of the October 1973 Egyptian–Israeli war. Egypt's Anwar Sadat cast the war in an Islamic mold; it was represented as a sacred struggle—jihad, or holy war. It was the Ramadan

War, named after the sacred month of fasting during which it occurred; its battle cry was *Allahu akbar* (God is most great), the traditional Islamic battle cry; its code name was Badr, the first great Islamic victory led by the prophet Muhammad. The relative success of Egyptian forces in acquitting themselves on the battlefield and penetrating Israeli territory, coupled with the economic impact of the Arab oil embargo, constituted a source of enormous pride.

The Arab world, like the Middle East in general, was now the focus of greater world attention and concern, an area of increased geostrategic significance. The stereotype of the bedouin and camel was replaced by that of the wealthy oil sheikh. An area and people long rendered impotent by European colonialism, by successive defeats at the hands of Israel, and by their status as a pawn in the battle of the superpowers now commanded recognition, if only, at times, in the form of begrudging acknowledgment.

The restoration of wealth and power to some sectors of the Arab world seemed to symbolize that the centuries-long decline and subservience of the Arabs were now in eclipse and that God would restore Muslim fortunes. The "Islamic revolution" in Iran in 1978–79 provided the political victory and proof for many that a return to Islam was the antidote to the ills of society. Islamic renewal and reform, it was felt, could work miracles, restoring Islam and the Muslims to their precolonial, centuries-long position of political and cultural dominance. Iran seemed to serve as an example, an explicit critique of the inner weakness of Westernization, and clear proof of the unlimited power of Islam.

If Arab socialism was the dominant ideology in Egypt during the 1950s and 1960s, Islamic revivalism or fundamentalism emerged dramatically as an ideological and political force during the 1970s. Anwar Sadat's rule (1970–1981) was characterized by two policies: an appeal to Islam and a welcome to Western economic and political interests. Faced with succeeding the popular and charismatic Nasser, Sadat turned away from Arab socialism and the Left and sought both to establish his own, independent political identity and legitimacy and to garner popular support by enhancing his Islamic image. He capitalized on his reputation for personal piety and cultivated a public image of Islamic leadership. Sadat appropriated the title of "believer-president," was photographed at prayer, peppered his speeches with religious phrases, provided substantial support for the building of mosques, and relied heavily on Islamic symbols (as in the 1973 Egyptian–Israeli war) to legitimate his policies.

In addition, Islamic organizations such as the Muslim Brotherhood, which had been suppressed by Nasser, were rehabilitated. Leaders who had been imprisoned or driven underground or into exile were freed and permitted to function again in Egyptian society. Sadat also fostered the growth of Islamic student organizations (*gamaa islamiyya*) on campuses, to counter the influence of Nasserites and leftists. He marshaled the support of the Islamic religious establishment (1) to legitimate key government policies, such as the Camp David Accords; (2) to legitimate reforms in Muslim family laws (that area of Islamic law that governs marriage, divorce, and inheritance); and finally, (3) to support Sadat's condemnation of militant activists who challenged his rule from the mid-1970s onward.

By 1974, Sadat's controlled use of Islam began to deteriorate as the government found that Islam was indeed a two-edged sword, capable of legitimating and delegitimating, effective in the hands of both governments and opposition movements. The Muslim Brotherhood and the government-supported Islamic student organizations, having gained their own momentum, were increasingly critical of Sadat's policies, such as his support for the Shah of Iran and bitter denunciation of the Ayatollah Khomeini, his "sellout" at Camp David, and what they regarded as his "Westernizing tampering" with Muslim family law. Moreover, a new crop of secret, more radical Islamic organizations, some founded by disaffected Muslim Brothers, began to violently attack the government, charging that its use of Islam was hypocritical and self-serving. Like many moderate Muslims, radicals cited the government's failure to implement Islamic law as clear proof of Sadat's disingenuousness. In 1974, Muhammad's Youth (Shahbab Muhammad), also known as the Islamic Liberation Organization (ILO), attempted a coup d'état. In 1977 another extremist group, the Society of Muslims, also known as Takfir wal Hijra (Excommunication and Emigration), kidnapped and executed a former minister of religious affairs. When the ILO's leaders were executed, many members joined other underground groups that were now mushrooming, such as the Army of God (Jund Allah) and the Holy War Society (Jamaat al-Jihad).

Given the stereotypes that governments and the media have often used to describe militant organizations, it is perhaps surprising to consider the conclusion of an Egyptian sociologist and expert on such organizations:

> The typical profile of members of militant Islamic groups could be summarized as being young (early twenties), of rural or small town background, from middle or lower middle class, with high achievement motivation, upwardly mobile, with science or engineering education, and from a normally cohesive family. It is sometimes assumed in social science that recruits of "radical movements" must be somehow alienated, marginal, anomic, or oth-

erwise abnormal. Most of those we investigated would be considered model Egyptian youth.[5]

Despite their differences, all militant Islamists condemned Sadat and Egyptian society as un-Islamic, politically corrupt, controlled by infidels (that is, people who were not "true believers"), and dominated by alien and decadent Western laws and lifestyles, which fostered secularism, materialism, and a spiritually lax and permissive society. They believed that the task and duty of all true Muslims was the liberation of Egyptian society through armed struggle, or holy war, against a regime they regarded as oppressive, atheist (un-Islamic), an ally of Israel, and a puppet of the West.

In the late 1970s, Sadat's government became increasingly authoritarian and began to crack down on all forms of dissent. This merely broadened the base of his critics, secular and religious; increased broad-based discontent; and often earned militant Islamic groups at least a modicum of admiration from many Egyptians. The militant groups seemed to be the only effective voices against a ruler who was disparagingly referred to as "Pharaoh." The widespread suppression of dissent came to a head in 1981, when government security forces imprisoned more than fifteen hundred people from a cross-section of Egyptian society, including Islamic activists, lawyers, doctors, journalists, professors, and former government ministers.

On October 3, 1981, as Anwar Sadat sat in the reviewing stand at ceremonies commemorating the October 1973 war, he was assassinated by members of al-Jihad, whose leader cried out, "I am Khalid Islambuli, I have killed Pharaoh and do not fear death." Sadat's popularity in the West and his portrayal by Western media as a flexible, enlightened leader sharply contrasted with his growing unpopularity at home. For many in Egypt, "Khalid therefore appeared as a sort of 'right arm' of the popular will, and not merely as a militant exponent of an Islamicist group."[6]

The 1980s revealed new ways of operating, both for the government and Sadat's successor, Hosni Mubarak, and for Islamic activists. Mubarak pursued a path of greater political liberalization and was careful to distinguish between political and religious dissent on the one hand and direct threats to the state on the other. He crushed violent outbursts and riots fomented by militants but, at the same time, allowed religious critics public outlets for their opposition. On the one hand, between April and August 1989, more than two thousand fundamentalists were imprisoned, and in September twenty-six members of Salvation from Hell were sentenced on charges that they had established a paramilitary organization and attempted to assassinate two former cabinet ministers. On the other hand, the government sponsored television debates between Islamic militants and representatives of the religious establishment; and government-run television and newspapers regularly featured religious programs and columns that were often independent in their tone and commentary.

If Islamic revivalism in Egypt had seemed to be dominated by confrontation and violence, the 1980s actually witnessed a broader-based, quiet revolution that had often been eclipsed by the conflict between Sadat and his militant Islamic opposition. Islamic revivalism became part and parcel of mainstream society, rather than a merely marginal phenomenon. Greater Islamic consciousness and identity were expressed not only in formal and informal religious practices (prayer, fasting, Sufi gatherings, Qur'an study groups) but also in social services offered by psychiatric and drug rehabilitation centers, hospitals, dental clinics, legal aid societies, as well as organizations that provide subsidized housing and food distribution.

Islamic private volunteer organizations filled a void and thus were an implicit critique of the government's inability or failure to provide adequate services, in particular for the nonelite sectors of society. Their network of services provides for the middle class an alternative to expensive private institutions, and for the poor, to overcrowded public facilities, so that in 1988 an analyst could write:

> This strand of Islamic activism has therefore set about establishing concrete Islamic alternatives to the socio-economic institutions of the state and the capitalist sector. Islamic social welfare institutions are better run than their state-public counterparts, less bureaucratic and impersonal. . . . They are definitely more grass roots oriented, far less expensive and far less opulent than the institutions created under Sadat's *infitah* (open-door policy), institutions which mushroomed in the 1970's and which have been providing an exclusive service to the top 5% of the country's population. Apolitical Islamic activism has thus developed a substantial socio-economic muscle through which it has managed to baffle the state and other secular forces in Egypt.[7]

In the 1990s, Islamic revivalism ceased to be restricted to small, marginal organizations on the periphery of society. Revivalism instead became a visible and prominent part of *mainstream* Muslim society, producing a new class of modern-educated but Islamically oriented elites who work alongside—and at times, in coalitions with—their secular counterparts. Revivalism continues to grow as a broad-based religio-social movement in Egypt and in virtually every Muslim country, and transnationally. It is a vibrant, multifaceted movement, whose goal is the transformation of society through the Islamic formation of individuals at the grassroots level and sociopolitical action. *Dawah* (call) societies work in social services (hospitals, clinics, legal aid societies), in economic projects (Islamic banks, investment houses, insurance companies), in education (schools, child care centers, youth camps), and in religious publishing and broadcasting. Their common programs are aimed at young and old alike. At the same time, Islamists became major actors in electoral politics.

## DEMOCRATIZATION

The clearest evidence of the mainstreaming and institutionalization of Islamic revivalism, or activism, was the emergence of the Muslim Brotherhood as a political force in electoral politics. In the mid- to late 1980s, moderate Islamic activists in Egypt and other parts of North Africa and the Middle East demonstrated a gradualist, bottom-up approach to political change, a willingness to participate within the political system.[8] While banned as a political party in Egypt, the Muslim Brotherhood formed coalitions with political parties and emerged as the strongest political opposition group.

Egypt's Islamic organizations in recent decades have spanned the spectrum in their politics as they have in their tactics and use of force. Radical organizations such as Muhammad's Youth, Takfir wal Hijra, al-Jihad, and the Islamic Group have sought to overthrow the government and reject democracy outright. The attitude of the Muslim Brotherhood toward democracy has varied over the years. In the early decades of its existence, the Brotherhood's ambivalent attitude toward democracy was part and parcel of its belief that the Islamic world struggled to survive in the midst of the global civilizational threat of the cold war. They believed that Muslims were caught between a capitalist West, with its emphasis on secularism, individualism, and materialism, and a communist/socialist, atheistic East, marked by dictatorship and tyranny.[9] Both alternatives, which possessed systems of political participation, were judged as doomed to failure and, at the same time, regarded as a threat.

Increasingly, as the Brotherhood, after its reemergence in the 1970s, clearly chose participation rather than violent revolution, it invoked democracy both to critique the government and as a means to achieve its goal or best to wage the struggle for Islam. Under the Sadat and Mubarak governments, the Brotherhood sought recognition as a political party and participation within Egypt's multiparty system. The Brotherhood joined with the Wafd Party in the 1984 elections, and the coalition won 65 of 450 seats to become the largest opposition group in the parliament. Subsequently, the Brotherhood formed a new coalition, the Islamic Alliance, with the Labor Party and the Liberal Party in the 1987 elections. Campaigning with the slogan "Islam is the solution" and calling for the implementation of Islamic law, they won 17 percent of the vote, emerging as the chief political opposition to Mubarak's government. Brotherhood candidates held thirty-eight of the Alliance's sixty seats.

The moderate, gradualist approach of the Brotherhood was reflected in a platform that, while critical of the status quo, did not reject society as un-Islamic. It did not call for revolution but rather for a process of Islamic reform, in which Islamic values would inform the political, economic, social, and educational spheres, as well as the media. The Islamic Alliance was inclusive rather than exclusive. It included Christian Copts on its list of candidates and in its 1989 program affirmed that "brother Copts in particular and the people of the book in general have the same rights and obligations as Muslims."[10]

Muslim Brothers and other Islamic activists also became a major force in professional associations—democratic and voluntary associations of teachers, lawyers, doctors, and journalists. These professional organizations are a pillar of Egyptian civil society, "the most advanced sectors of public life in Egypt, enjoying high status and speaking with an autonomous and respected voice."[11] The successes of Islamic activist sociopolitical mainstreaming included a significant increase in an Islamically oriented professional class, reflecting the numbers of young professional graduates. In September 1992, the Muslim Brotherhood won a majority of the board seats in bar association elections, long regarded as a bastion of liberalism. This victory reflected the growing number of younger, Islamist-oriented professionals, the appeal of the Brotherhood to professional classes as the only credible opposition, the indifference and reluctance of many professionals to vote in association elections, and the ability of a well-organized, highly motivated minority to "get out the vote" and work with purpose and persistence. Operating within the political system, moderate activists such as the Muslim Brotherhood have couched their criticisms and demands within the context of a call for greater democratization, political representation, social justice, and respect for human rights.

## MUBARAK'S WAR AGAINST THE REASSERTION OF RELIGIOUS EXTREMISM

Radical, violent alternatives, relatively silent in the early Mubarak period, boldly and directly challenged and attacked the regime in the late 1980s and in the 1990s. Islamic student organizations once again dominated university student unions in the cities of Assyut, Al Minyā, Cairo, and Alexandria. They pressed for an Islamic revolution, the implementation of Islamic law, curriculum reform, separation of the sexes in classes, restriction of mixed socials, and the banning of Western music and concerts. Their growth was fed by the government's inability to address chronic socioeconomic realities that had a disastrous effect on the more than half of Egypt's 50 million citizens who were under the age of twenty. Hundreds of thousands of university graduates found jobs and housing impossible to obtain. Young couples often lived with their families or delayed marriage for years until they could find adequate housing.

The government attempted to control a breeding ground for Islamic militancy by nationalizing Egypt's mosques. The vast majority of Egypt's mosques were private—and thus independent in terms of their preachers and the content of sermons and activities—rather than state-controlled. In October 1992, Mubarak's ministry of religious affairs announced that all sermons at state-controlled mosques would be subject to approval by government-appointed officials, and that the building of private mosques would be curbed.

The chief militant Islamic challenge to the Mubarak government has come from the Gamaa Islamiyya (Jamaat Islamiyya, or Islamic Group) and from al-Jihad, who became locked in a deadly battle with security forces and police during the early 1990s. The Gamaa Islamiyya evolved (or perhaps more accurately, "devolved") from student groups active on university campuses and in politics in the early Sadat days to an umbrella organization that includes a host of underground extremist groups active in Cairo, Alexandria, Assyut, Al Minyā, and Fayyum. Its membership today is younger (with a heavy component of adolescents as well as university students and graduates), less educated, living in more desperate conditions of poverty and unemployment, more radical ideologically, and more random in its use of violence than in the past. Whereas the Gamaa in the Sadat days was urban and university-based, today it is a clandestine movement, many of whose members are of high school age and active in small villages and towns, as well as urban areas, in Egypt. The Gamaa regards as its spiritual leader Sheikh Omar Abdel Rahman, the blind cleric who was arrested, tried, but released in the trial of the assassins of Anwar Sadat and who is currently implicated in World Trade Center bombings in the United States. Bent on destabilizing the Egyptian economy and overthrowing the government, the Gamaa have attacked and murdered foreign tourists, Coptic Christians, and government officials and have bombed banks and government buildings. They attack the cinema, theater, magazines, books, and associations that popularize modern concepts such as individualism and Western culture.[12] Militants believe the liberation of Egyptian society requires that all true Muslims undertake an armed struggle, or holy war, against a regime they regard as oppressive, anti-Islamic, and a puppet of the West.

The Mubarak government has aggressively responded to what it clearly perceives as the major threat by Islamic radicalism to the stability of the government and to regional security. More ominously, in June 1994 the Mubarak government extended its actions to include not just the terrorism of the Gamaa Islamiyya but also Egypt's strongest opposition group, the Muslim Brotherhood. In what seemed like an all-out war, it moved "to curtail not only those movements that have carried out violent attacks, but also one that has come to dominate many municipalities, professional and labor associations and university faculties."[13] In the process, the lines between radical and moderate Islamists, state security and the limits of state authority, and the prosecution of criminals and human rights have often been blurred. In its war against "terrorism," the Egyptian government's crackdown on and massive arrests of suspected extremists and sympathizers have included not only extreme but also moderate Islamists and family members of suspects, in an attempt, many believe, to silence and intimidate all Islamic opposition.

Too often in the 1990s, extremists and the government have been locked in a "holy war" in which the government's police and security forces as well as the militants have had a hit list for murder and assassination, rather than for arrest and prosecution. An Amnesty International report noted that security forces "appear to have been given a license to kill with impunity."[14] Special military courts, which do not permit defendants a right of appeal, have been created to try civilians accused of terrorism. These courts quickly, and often quietly, mete out swift, harsh sentences. The number of those executed under the Mubarak regime has vastly exceeded the number executed in the past for politically motivated crimes, such as the attempt to kill Nasser or the assassination of Sadat. Defense lawyers often charge that they have been permitted only limited access to their clients and that their clients have been tortured. Lawyers for suspected militants have themselves been arrested. Systematic torture, long-term detention without charge, taking family members of suspected Islamists or terrorists "hostage" to force their relatives to surrender, and press censorship have led officials of international nongovernmental human rights organizations to declare, "This poor human rights record has yielded resentment, the narrowing of civil society, religious intolerance and erosion of the rule of law in Egypt—and fertile ground for the growth of extremist alternatives."[15]

## CONCLUSION

Islamic activism in Egypt, as in much of the Muslim world, has not receded. Rather, it has rooted itself more deeply and pervasively in Egyptian society. Its variety and diversity, its many faces and postures, have long been overshadowed by its equation with a monolithic, radical, fundamentalist threat. The broader significance and impact of Islamists can be seen by the extent to which they have gained cultural legitimacy, have become part of mainstream Muslim life and society, and are not solely members of marginalized and alienated groups. Secular institutions are now complemented or challenged by Islamically oriented counterparts that provide much-needed educational and social services and underscore the limitations and continued failures of government. The Muslim Brotherhood and other activists became dominant voices in professional organizations and syndicates of lawyers, doctors, engineers, and journalists.

Islamic awareness and activism have grown among the lower and middle classes, educated and uneducated, professionals, students, and laborers, young and old, women and men. The emergence of modern-educated but more Islamically oriented professionals in society offers a political and social alternative elite that challenges the Western, secular presuppositions and lifestyles of many in the establishment. These professionals present their criticisms and demands within the context of a call for greater democratization, political representation, and respect for human rights.

Contemporary Islamic activism provides an alternative system or infrastructure, an implicit critique of the failure and inability of the state to respond adequately to the needs of its citizens. This, combined with the remarkable growth of Sufism and other nonpolitical religious organizations and societies, creates a potential pool of politically and nonpolitically oriented Muslims. Given the right conditions (failure of the governmental system, lack of viable political or Islamic alternatives), these Muslims can be politically mobilized to vote for those who proclaim, "Islam is the solution."

The secular presupposition of the separation of church and state has increasingly been challenged throughout much of the world as major world religions (Hinduism, Buddhism, Judaism, Christianity, and Islam) have experienced a revivalist impulse. Islam provides a full-blown example of the variety and diversity of revivalist themes, organizations, strategies, and tactics.

The reassertion of Islam has caused many issues to surface:

the extent to which religion is a way of life, a worldview that informs both personal and public life;

the degree to which religion not only is a system that informs and guides the belief and practice of a community but also is the product of social contexts and realities;

the extent to which the reassertion of religion in public life is a source of unity or division, of greater community vitality and cohesion, social justice and peace, or conflict and violence;

the compatibility of religion with democracy, political participation and pluralism, and human rights.

These issues, in turn, raise fundamental questions: Whose Islam? Who is to interpret the tradition—religious scholars and clergy, laity, political leaders, elected parliaments? What Islam? What interpretations (doctrines or laws) are to be implemented in society? And finally, does the struggle to inform society with religious values mean a reimposition of classical or medieval laws and doctrines, or does it require a reformation, a bold reconstruction and reapplication of religious doctrine?

## NOTES

1. For studies of these developments, see John L. Esposito, *Islam and Politics*, 3d ed. (Syracuse, N.Y.: Syracuse University Press, 1991); John O. Voll, *Islam: Continuity and Change in the Modern World*, 2d ed. (Syracuse, N.Y.: Syracuse University Press, 1994); and James P. Piscatori, ed., *Islam in the Political Process* (Cambridge: Cambridge University Press, 1983).

2. See, for example, Daniel Lerner, *The Passing of Traditional Society: Modernizing the Middle East* (New York: Free Press, 1958); Manfred Halpern, *The Politics of Social Change in the Middle East and North Africa* (Princeton, N.J.: Princeton University Press, 1963); Donald Eugene Smith, *Religion and Political*

*Development* (Boston: Little, Brown & Co., 1970). For an analysis of the factors that influenced the development of modernization theory, see Fred R. von der Mehden, *Religion and Modernization in Southeast Asia* (Syracuse, N.Y.: Syracuse University Press, 1988), 2.

3. John L. Esposito, *The Islamic Threat: Myth or Reality?* (New York: Oxford University Press, 1992).

4. John L. Esposito, *Islam: The Straight Path* (New York: Oxford University Press, 1991); Malise Ruthven, *Islam in the World* (London: Penguin Books, 1984); Frederick M. Denny, *An Introduction to Islam* (New York: Macmillan Publishing Co., 1985).

5. Saad Eddin Ibrahim, "Egypt's Islamic Militants," *Middle East Report* (MERIP) 103 (February 1982): 11.

6. Gilles Kepel, *Muslim Extremism in Egypt: The Prophet and the Pharaoh* (Berkeley: University of California Press, 1986), 192.

7. Saad Eddin Ibrahim, "Egypt's Islamic Activism in the 1980's," *Third World Quarterly* (April 1988): 643.

8. For an analysis of this issue, see John O. Voll and John L. Esposito, *Islam and Democracy* (New York: Oxford University Press, 1996), and "Islam's Democratic Essence," *Middle East Quarterly* 1 (September 1994):3–11; John L. Esposito and James P. Piscatori, "Democratization and Islam," *Middle East Journal* 45 (summer 1991):427–40; John L. Esposito, "Islam, Democracy, and U.S. Foreign Policy," in *Riding the Tiger: The Middle East Challenge after the Gulf War,* ed. Phebe Marr and William Lewis (Boulder, Colo.: Westview Press, 1993).

9. Richard Mitchell, *The Society of Muslim Brothers* (1969; reprint, New York: Oxford University Press, 1993), 226.

10. Voll, *Islam,* 116.

11. Sami Zubaida, "Islam, the State and Democracy: Contrasting Conceptions of Society in Egypt," *Middle East Report* (November–December 1992): 8.

12. Amira El-Azhary Sonbol, "Egypt," in *The Politics of Islamic Revivalism,* ed. Shireen T. Hunter (Bloomington, Ind.: Indiana University Press, 1988), 25.

13. Christopher Hedges, "Egypt Begins Crackdown on Strongest Opposition Group," *New York Times,* June 12, 1994, 3.

14. Christopher Hedges, "Seven Executed in Egypt in Move to Suppress Islamic Rebel Group," *New York Times,* July 9, 1993.

15. Virginia N. Sherry, "Egypt's Trampling of Rights Fosters Extremism," *New York Times,* April 15, 1993.

## STUDY QUESTIONS

1. Why have Muslim believers often been equated with Islamic fundamentalists? Is such a description valid? Why? Why not?

2. What are the multiple meanings of jihad? Were you surprised that jihad had so many meanings? Does such a discovery remind you to be cautious when describing other persons' religious traditions? Explain your answer.

3. What is the best vantage point for understanding the nature and dynamics of contemporary Islam? Explain your answer.

4. For what reasons did countries like Egypt resist modernization? Do you agree with these reasons? Why? Why not?

5. What events occurred in 1973 and 1979 to restore identity and pride to the Muslim people of Egypt? Discuss why?

6. What two policies characterized Anwar Sadat's rule of Egypt from 1970 to 1981? Why would such policies earn Sadat the title "Believer-President"?

7. What were the causes of Anwar Sadat's declining influence in Egypt by the mid-1970s? Why is he now characterized as un-Islamic? What role did religion play in his downfall?

8. Describe the contemporary Islamic revolution. What are the goals of Islamic revivalism?

9. Who is the Muslim Brotherhood? What role is this Islamic organization playing in contemporary society? What role does democracy play in the Brotherhood's political decision-making?

# PART 3

---

# ON LIVING JUSTLY WITH OTHERS: GENDER, FAMILY, AND THE ETHIC OF CARE

# 10

## SUSAN BROOKS THISTLETHWAITE

# Religion and Gender

There is a certain relation between any religious unit and its power to direct the movement of its most precious human resource, women.

*—Dominique Zahan*[1]

## WHAT IS GENDER?

Human beings are born with a biological sex, but they are trained to become one gender or the other. Biological sex is simply the number and arrangement of your chromosomes, an arrangement that determines your external sex characteristics. Gender, however, is the way in which the social relations of a society—economic, political, or familial—are divided by that society for the different sexes.

For most of human history, it was thought that the sex of a human being determined his or her social role. Whether through the control of a god or gods or by nature, the different social roles played by men and women in a particular society were deemed to be given and unchangeable.

In the nineteenth century, however, new fields such as sociology, anthropology, history, and psychology began to reveal that human behavior according to sex has been anything but fixed and eternal. Different cultures in different periods of human history around the world, it was discovered, have arranged behaviors according to gender in very different ways.[2]

How do people of different sexes learn the gender roles expected of them in a given society? Young children are socialized from the moment of birth into their society's appointed gender roles. In Western culture, boys are often dressed in blue and encouraged to like "snakes and snails and puppy-dog tails." In short, they are socialized to aggression and domination. They are given GI Joe dolls to play with and are told that "big boys don't cry." Baby girls are often dressed in pink and encouraged to like "sugar and spice and everything nice." To be compliant, to be passive, to be "nice," is the gender role expected of girls. There was recently an outcry against the Barbie doll who talked and exclaimed, "I don't like math!" Is it "natural" for girls to fall behind boys in math in school, or is this the result of gender socialization?[3]

Gender socialization also presumes a universal heterosexuality, and gay men and lesbians, as they develop, report feeling tremendous conflict in a forced socialization into heterosexual gender.[4] Feminist theory, too, has articulated the struggles of women to resist gender stereotyping.[5] Girls who have a good throwing arm in sports are told approvingly, "You throw like a boy." How is a girl to understand herself as being both good at sports and a girl? And boys who do not like sports are often ridiculed and called "wimps" for liking reading or painting. They grow up with the fear of being "unmanly." The modern men's movement has addressed itself to the contradictions in male socialization.[6]

Religion is the most powerful way people are introduced to and maintained in the social roles of their society. Religion is the repository of the values held to be of supreme importance in a given society. Religious texts, rituals, rules, and even, in theocratic societies, laws dictate conduct deemed appropriate. The gender divisions of society occupy a prominent place in all the major world religions. In fact, "ethnographers have provided richly detailed descriptions of myths, rituals, and everyday life in societies that are preoccupied with separating men and women."[7]

## GENDER AND RELIGIOUS SYMBOLISM

The division of human beings into two biological sexes has had a strong impact on the development of human consciousness. The fact that human beings have two separate sets of external sex characteristics and perform different, and opposite (or complementary, depending on your interpretation), reproductive functions has become a metaphor for difference.

What is a metaphor? "Most simply, a metaphor is seeing one thing *as* something else, pretending 'this' is 'that' because we do not know how to think or talk about 'this,' so we use 'that' as a way of talking about it."[8] The power of metaphor comes from the creative tension between the fact that there *is* a likeness between the metaphor and the idea it seeks to communicate but that there also *is not* a likeness between them.

People's sexual differences have become a metaphor for difference itself. Take language again. In many languages around the world, grammar has a gender. In French, for example, the word for "table" is *la table* and takes the feminine gender. Yet the French do not claim that tables have female sex characteristics. They use masculine and feminine grammatical gender as a way to divide words into different classes. In this way, the grammatical case structure of French both is *like* gender difference and is *not like* gender difference (i.e., words have no sex characteristics).

In the same way, religious language, rituals, roles, and symbols draw on the powerful human experience of sex differentiation and use it as a metaphor for division or separation. The metaphorical function of gender in religion has generated powerful religious symbols organized by sex difference. This powerful metaphor of human difference has produced several unfortunate by-products: the value ascribed to each sex has not been equal; the emphasis on difference has obscured the way in which sexual difference is not the only human characteristic, and that human beings, male and female, are more alike than different; and it has often made heterosexuality equivalent to the order of the cosmos.

## A HIERARCHY OF RELIGIOUS VALUE

In the past, women from all traditions have been regarded not only as inferior beings who were not likely to have the capacity to experience ultimate reality, but also as actual obstacles to men's spiritual progress.[9]

The history of the major world religions begins with a period in which the so-called higher religions and civilizations emerged, an age that shaped the identity of the world's "great" religions—the male-dominant ones. The *axial age*, a term coined by Karl Jaspers in the 1940s, has been elaborated on in the sociological work of Shmuel Eisenstadt. The axial age was the time of great civilizations, such as ancient Israel, Greece, Persia, early imperial China, and India. This period is seen as peculiarly focused on the development of the higher religions, those that made transcendental claims to universality, beyond tribes or clans, and that emerged in the midst of imperial civilizations. Within a few centuries of each other appeared such figures as the Hebrew prophets, Gautama Buddha, Confucius, Plato, and Jesus. The axial age, it is claimed, through its religious innovations brought new ethical insights to higher civilizations, an insistence on the need for values such as nonviolence, justice, and compassion.

In effect, the religions of the axial age emerged as a protest against the problems caused by what preceded them: extensive military activity, highly stratified societies, the exploitation of the disadvantaged, slavery, the political ideologies of imperialism, and the social chaos that follows warfare. These religions protest by presenting a critical, reflective challenge to the actual world and a new vision of what lies beyond it.[10]

Religions have changed since that time, of course. They have changed enormously. But if we are to ask how the peculiar relation of gender and religion came about, we need to look at religions during a formative stage in their development and evolution.[11] The approach is analogous to the examination of the early, formative years of an adult, an examination that often provides important clues to the structure of a personality and its achievements. In addition, the axial-age religions are not without significant contradictions. In fact, the ambiguity of male-dominant religions in relation to women is evidenced by the ways in which they teach negative attitudes about women's sexuality and bodies and expect the subordination of women to male authority at the same time that members of the same religions organize to help women and children escape violent exploitation.

Many anthropologists would argue that the chaos and suffering inflicted by military violence and feudal hierarchies were late developments in human evolution, preceded for 99 percent of human life on earth by egalitarian, cooperative hunter-gatherer societies, of which very few now survive.[12] Religion in such societies is characterized by its closeness to the immediate forces that govern human life—the weather, vegetation, animals, birth, illness, sex, psychic forces, and kinship. Spiritual forces are observable and grounded in human experiences of what gives and takes life, of what heals and makes sick. These religious systems tend to have a high tolerance for ambiguity, humor, individual idiosyncrasy, and tragedy; and they focus ritual on the production of shamanic, ecstatic, healing, trance-induced, and visionary experience. Magic, philosophy, and religion are not differentiated. One might call these religious systems "immanental" or "cosmologically horizontal." They understand the existence of a spiritual world outside ordinary experience, but their understanding of that world is in terms of concrete human experiences. These early systems did not give birth to axial-age religions.

As societies grew to more advanced organizations, their religious systems also evolved. The development in agrarian societies of class stratifications, centers for the distribution of goods, specialized roles and tasks, and one-crop agriculture produced religious systems and temples for re-producing fertility, the elevation of gods for certain functions and groups, and the connection of political power to religious functions. Queens be-came goddesses and kings became gods. Temples managed rites of sacred sex and ritual sacrifice, and people participated differently in religion, based on their social status and functions. Religious authority became more hierarchical as natural symbols and spiritual forces were increas-ingly located in the hands of a religious leadership and removed from the daily life of ordinary people. As locations of sacred rites were more cen-tralized, the categories of "sacred" and "profane" grew in importance. In addition, as a more diverse population was included within the expansive reach of centralized power, ideologies of universalism or ideas to organize unrelated collectives became important for social harmony.

Sociological work on the axial age provides some important clues to the context that produced the "higher" religions, especially in Asia and Mesopotamia. As the political systems of such societies gained controlling power, another group of elites began to compete with those powers. These new elites developed moral and legal systems outside the usual structures of kinship and custom, including religio-philosophical systems necessary to the ambitions of large, centralized empires. The elites criticized existing political powers but based their critique on ideologies that devalued the natural world as incomplete, inferior, and in need of transformation. They asserted "vertical cosmologies," transcendent rational and supernatural spiritual principles that gave them hierarchical leverage in criticizing their political rivals. They stressed "the existence of a higher, transcendental moral or metaphysical order that is beyond any given this worldly or other-worldly reality."[13]

Because spiritual power is removed from ordinary planetary and hu-man life cycles, a fundamental and unstable tension is created within the structure of personality. That instability creates the need for salvation that bridges the chasm between the natural and preternatural worlds by re-constructing the personality according to the "precepts of the higher moral or metaphysical order. While the concept of immortality in these civilizations may or may not still be tied to bodily images and to ideas of physical resurrection, the very possibility of some continuity beyond this world . . . was always torn by many internal tensions."[14]

The elites controlled access to this salvation, even as they defined it. It became their means of leverage both into the power of and against the abuses of political systems. Rigid social stratification was relativized by salvation, so that those who were closest to the resolution of the tension—that is, closest to salvation—become "endowed with a special autonomous aura."[15] Their status superseded status according to birth.

This abstract split between transcendental religion and the actual world takes on crucial importance when the actual world is dominated by political systems that are dehumanizing and totalitarian. The religion of the Hebrew prophets and that of Jesus of Nazareth and his community are scathing critiques of divine kingship and totalitarian rulers. In India, Gautama Buddha and his monks walked away from political power to seek spiritual answers to suffering, and in China, Confucian scholars created a political philosophy of benevolent order in the midst of a century of warring chaos. Justice, liberation, benevolence, and compassion became important principles by which to measure politics and to compete with it for loyal followers. It is no accident that in circles of interfaith dialogue, common ethical concerns have been noticed in the world's higher religions.

Yet these religious innovations have had important negative consequences. Because, in male-dominated societies, the religious elites are men, they are more easily coopted into broader social systems of power and privilege. Rather than identifying male dominance, politics, and militarism as problems, the religious systems metaphorically appropriate these to represent their own power. Women are used to symbolize the problematic world, the natural world of menstruation, birth, sex, desire, and sickness. Women *as women* have little place in these preternatural systems, which ground salvation in transcendence of the body and of the earth itself. The worlds and work of women remain outside these new religious systems, except as they are taken in abstractly to serve masculine functions. Otherwise they are simply polluting or evil. The earth and its cycles are no longer the human home but a way station to be endured or conquered for something higher, better, and more real. Bodies must be left behind to achieve a "pure" knowledge of reality, abstractly defined.[16]

In the so-called higher religions, therefore, female gender is a symbol of nature, of the cycles of birth and death, and, ultimately, of that which is antithetical to the "spiritual," or indeed the antithesis of what is most profoundly religious.

This is not to say that women have had no role in the world religions but rather that, symbolically, gender as a metaphor for difference has been used to define religion and social roles and to establish boundaries, in both religion and society, based on sexual difference.

## GENDER AND RELIGION:
## THREE EXAMPLES

Let us look particularly at three religions—Islam, Christianity, and Confucianism—and at how gender and religion are constructed in each. There are three especially important markers of the relation between religion and gender in the religious construction of human experience: economics, power, and hierarchy. The discussion of power and hierarchy requires a discussion of the legitimation of force, since it is through force, or the threat of force, that power and hierarchy are maintained in a society. The legitimation of violence against women by religion is a major barrier to the transformation of religion and society to greater gender equality.

### Islam

To the Western feminist eye, the image of the Muslim woman with her head, and sometimes her whole body and even her face, covered with the traditional chador or *burka* can appear as an archetype of women's oppression. Many Muslim women, however, feel that the Western feminist view that equates the wearing of the chador and the seclusion of women with oppression is prejudiced, the product of Western individualism. In their view Western individualism has not worked out particularly well for women. In the West there is a lack of respect for women in public places (witness the high incidence of sexual harassment), a neglect of the family and children, and the famous double shift that mothers who work outside the home have to put in. At a conference at Chicago Theological Seminary (CTS) titled "Muslim Women on Islam," these points were made with some frequency.[17]

The Holy Qur'an still forms the basis of prevailing family law in most areas of the Muslim world. These are the divine revelations from God that were given to humanity in the seventh century A.D. through the vehicle of God's final prophet, Muhammad. The Muslim women at the CTS conference pointed out that the Qur'an brought important improvements to the lives of women who, with the exception of queens or other elites, were little more than chattel.

There are important financial injunctions for women in the Qur'an. For example, women are permitted to inherit and own property, which is considered a big advancement, though women inherit only half of what their male relatives inherit. This is considered only correct, since women are not financially responsible for the maintenance of the family and can keep their inheritance intact. In Islam, marriage is not a sacrament but a legal contract, and according to the Qur'an, a woman has clearly defined legal rights in negotiating this contract. She can dictate the terms and can receive the dowry herself. This dowry she is permitted to keep and maintain as a source of personal pride and comfort. Economically, then, Islamic women historically were far ahead of Christian women in their ability to achieve some degree of financial independence.

Yet it must be said that, practically speaking, Muslim women have only infrequently exercised the rights given in the Qur'an for their financial independence. The tradition of marriage at a very young age and the lack of education for women, including learning about their own rights given by the Qur'an, mean that their fathers have practically negotiated the marriage contract, and their husbands have managed their funds, often without their knowledge or consent.

The basic message of the Qur'an is the oneness of God and the inevitability of God's judgment. All persons, men and women, are to respect these realities. Islam has a tradition that Umm Salama, one of the wives of the prophet Muhammad, reminded him that he was saying "men" only, after which the Prophet clearly identified both believing men and believing women as fully responsible for their religious duties and fully accountable at the time of the final resurrection and judgment. In terms of the duty to God, men and women are equal.

Yet the financial obligation men have to support women also means that men are given authority over the females of their families. At 2:228 the Qur'an says that, for this reason, men are a step above women. Regarding divorce, in the Islamic world only Turkey has a secular family law. For the rest of the Islamic world, the Qur'an is the guide to family law. The Prophet was clearly against divorce, and the dreaded "triple statement," whereby the husband can say three times to his wife, "I divorce you," was tantamount to sin on the part of the husband. Yet it is fair to say that this kind of repudiation, either immediate or over several months, has been far too frequent. Women technically have the right to divorce, but (1) often have not been informed of the possibility, (2) have been prevented from carrying it out, and (3) have found that the possibility of divorce needed to have been stated in the marriage contract. Moreover, a divorce initiated by a woman must have specific grounds, such as desertion, physical abuse, lack of maintenance, insanity, or impotence, to name some of the acceptable reasons.

Polygamy is permitted by the Qur'an, though today for a man to have more than two wives is extremely rare. In Turkey and Tunisia, multiple marriages are illegal. As economic conditions change, however, some of the countries in which women work outside the home show a rise in multiple marriages, apparently undertaken to increase the family income.

Power relations, then, are structurally hierarchical. Women have some financial rights but often are prevented from actually exercising them.

Islam has no actual peace tradition, though there are multiple writings on the need for Muslims to maintain harmony with other Muslims. The "just war" and crusade traditions are strong in Islam and provide most of the basis of thinking on the permissibility of force. But there is little evidence that either the just war traditions or pacifism has ever been applied to family life as they have been to public life.[18] While there are no extensive studies of violence against women in Muslim societies, anecdotal evidence suggests that it is widespread. Public force against female violation of religious dress codes is permitted in Islamic fundamentalist societies such as Iran, where a woman can be hit on the legs with a cane by a specially designated religious patrolman for dress-code violation. And jail terms are not unknown for women violating such codes.

### Christianity

Christianity, like Islam, has elements of female subordination and male hierarchy, as well as elements of possible egalitarianism and female independence. This statement is a broad generalization that applies to Roman Catholic forms of Christianity as well as to Protestantism.

Certainly, the subordination of women in the order of creation has been a major fault line in Christian theology, from the biblical period on. Male headship in the order of creation, based on only one of the creation stories in Genesis—at 2:18–25, the story of Eve's subordination to Adam in the creation—along with the doctrine of the Fall, for centuries has justified female subordination. In fact, because this order of male headship is considered to be God-given, any change is considered sin. I worked with a battered woman whose husband used to say to her, while he was beating her, "Your bones are my bones, just like it says in the Bible."

The identification of women as the origin of sin has been interpreted to indicate women's moral inferiority to men: women lack control over their passions and appetites; they willfully tempt males, and therefore they need to be kept under close control, so that they do not disturb even further male capacities for rationality and virtue.

Because women are required by the order of creation to obey their husbands, there developed in Christianity what theologian Mary Potter Engel has called a "Just Battering tradition," where Christian theology permitted and sometimes even required the physical abuse of women. For example, despite an undertone of pastoral care, the Protestant reformer John Calvin wrote to a female parishioner who implored him to help her because her husband beat her:

> We have a special sympathy for poor women who are evilly and roughly treated by their husbands, because of the roughness and cruelty of the tyranny and captivity which is their lot. We do not find ourselves permitted by the Word of God, however, to advise a woman to leave her husband, except by force of necessity, and we do not understand this force to be operative when a husband behaves roughly and uses threats to his wife, nor even when he beat her, but only when there is imminent peril to her life, whether from persecution by the husband or by his conspiring. . . . We exhort her to bear with patience the cross which God has seen fit to place upon her; and meanwhile not to deviate from the duty which she has before God to please her husband, but to be faithful whatever happens.[19]

The divine ordering of creation, so evident in this Calvinist double predestination, makes God the ultimate author of the battering of a woman, because it is a "cross which God has seen fit to place upon her." Clearly, it is sinful to resist the actions of God; even Jesus was supposed to submit to the cross, according to the penal theory of the atonement. The hierarchy of creation theology presented here by Calvin, though common throughout Christian theology, makes God into the abuser of women.

Yet, as in the Muslim traditions, there are other trajectories in Christianity. A return to the original scriptural texts is often a way to make an interpretive shift, and Christian feminists have often pointed out that Jesus' attitude toward women challenges patriarchal assumptions about their subordination. For example, the rabbi Jesus defends Mary's right to study with him and contrasts her studying unfavorably with Martha's kitchen duties in Luke 10:38–42. It is important, however, that the price of Jesus' egalitarian attitude toward women not be the painting of other rabbis as unredeemably patriarchal. As biblical scholar Judith Plaskow points out, this makes feminist interpretation of the Bible anti-Semitic.

It is pointed out often as well that the historical Paul, as opposed to the authors of letters attributed to Paul, was more inclusive than formerly thought. The later Pauline epistles, or letters, are influenced by the household duty codes of the surrounding Greco-Roman world. The letter to the Ephesians, for example, with its hierarchical arrangements of men over women, parents over children, slave owners over slaves, took Roman social hierarchies directly into Christian theologies of the relationship of Christ and the church. It is important to remember that it is not the egalitarian Jesus or the early Paul who prevails in Christian theologies of the family but the Roman hierarchies.

The right of women to control their dowries or inherit property is not affirmed in the Christian scriptures or the Hebrew Bible (Old Testament), unlike in the Qur'an. The marriage ceremony is a sacrament in Catholicism. Yet contracts of property exchange did exist through the High Middle Ages, and there is evidence that some ruling-class women, at least, managed their own property and often their husband's property when he was off waging war. Abbesses often gained considerable economic independence, and the female monastery became a self-governing female world. The Beguines were a crafts guild of single women in the Middle Ages who were not cloistered but who bound together to produce goods and to follow a monastic rule. Their independence was eroded by male ecclesiastical authority—there was tremendous hostility to the "irregularities" of the Beguines—and was banished outright in Protestantism.

The view that Protestantism improved the lot of women is not supported by data. In fact, women lost political and economic rights, and there is evidence during the rise of Protestantism of Protestant as well as Catholic persecution and murder of women as witches. It was often the somewhat economically independent widow who was accused of witchcraft. While Protestants such as Martin Luther concurred that there had been an original equivalence of women and men, they argued that women lost this equality, due to their fault in the Fall. Note Luther's comments:

> The rule remains with the husband, and the wife is compelled to obey it by God's command. He rules the home and the state, wages war, defends his possessions, tills the soil, builds, plants, etc. The woman, on the other hand, is like a nail driven into the wall. She sits at home. . . . The wife should stay at home and look after the affairs of the household as one who has been deprived of the ability of administering those affairs which are outside and concern the state. . . . In this way Eve is punished.[20]

Luther also admitted to giving his wife Katie a slap when the occasion demanded.

The rise of capitalism and the increased independence of women in the workforce coincide with the gains of Protestantism in Euro-Atlantic cultures. Protestantism accommodated secularism and the separation of economies from religion, as has been well documented. This is a mixed blessing for women, for while economic independence does correlate with reduced violence against women in the home, it is also true that sexual harassment in the workplace often takes the place of, or even supplements, battering in the home. This helps to maintain a "culture of battering."

Christianity, while it does have a tradition of legitimating the use of force against women to maintain power and hierarchy, also has various peace traditions from the first three centuries of its existence, from the left wing of the Reformation, and from radical Catholic groups. The methods of conflict resolution that have emerged from these traditions, however, are ordinarily applied to the public sphere, and even pacifist communities report incidents of violence against women in the home.

## Confucianism

The patriarchal Confucian culture restricts and subjugates women in Korea and in Northeast Asia. Many folk stories about ghosts feature women. Unjustly treated and murdered victims come back as ghosts, demanding justice. . . . A typical story goes as follows. In ancient days, the traditional marriage was arranged by the family and the young couple never met each other until the wedding day. They did not know what their spouse would look like, nor did they know what kind of person the partner would be.

On the wedding night in the bridal chamber, so the story goes, a bride was sitting dressed in her bridal garment, waiting for the groom to tell her what to do. The groom felt the need to go to toilet which was in the courtyard. He stood up and opened the door. It was wintertime. A strong wind blew. His clothes became caught on the doorknob and were torn. He thought the woman was vulgar and not endowed with the feminine virtues of passivity and subservience. He became angry at her and decided not to return to her.

The bride's family became anxious and sent members from her family to find out what had happened. One by one as they tried to open the door of the chamber, the family members died. The room was abandoned for 40 years.

The groom decided after 40 years to revisit the fatal place. As he opened the door he found a piece of his torn clothing hanging from the doorknob. He realized that it had not been the woman's doing. He found her body sitting as she was on her wedding night, still in her bridal garment. He felt great sympathy for the unfortunate creature. He approached her and tenderly caressed her shoulder. At that moment she collapsed and turned to dust.[21]

Early Confucianism was primarily a practical moral philosophy, not unlike Greek Stoicism—a way for running the household and the state. Later, in its conflicts with Buddhism, neo-Confucianism struggled to articulate the deeper spiritual problems of the human being, and these problems were distilled into the problem of controlling human desires and passions.

While early Confucianism was primarily about harmonious (through hierarchy) human relations, later Confucianism became deeply suspicious of relationships, stressing control over one's desires as central. The neo-Confucian therefore saw women as the activators of male desires, and so later Confucianists became obsessed with female chastity, especially that of widows. In the *Elementary Learning*, the Chinese primer for young men compiled by Chu Hsi (1130–1200), the most famous Sun dynasty neo-Confucian, the emphasis on female chastity is extreme:

> In one case, we have a woman who progressively mutilates her body with each new exertion of pressure by her parents to remarry. First she cuts off her hair, then her ears, and finally her nose, all the while defiantly asserting her determination to remain faithful to her dead husband. Another example is of two unmarried sisters who are abducted by bandits. They both resist rape, the first by hurling herself off a high cliff and the second by dashing herself on the rocks (there is plenty of blood and gore in these tales) (*Hsiao-hsueh*, 6:11a–12a).[22]

The impact of the neo-Confucian philosophy was to make the female body, particularly in sexuality, the property of the male members of her household. "Once women's sexuality and chastity belonged to her family, women had to live under severe sexual censorship because, under the Confucian social order, losing her virginity hurt the social advancement of male members of her family,"[23] writes feminist theologian Chung Hyun Kyung. "The young girl's sexual desire was the object of her family's fear."[24]

This extreme fear of uncontrolled female passion resulted in a severe restriction of female bodily movement, to the point where women were physically imprisoned in their homes or even forced to commit suicide if they were widowed. What happened culturally, of course, is that the general resentment at the restrictions of Confucian regulations about all aspects of human life became referred specifically to the female body, and the female body, once controlled, channeled this anger.[25]

The hierarchy of women beneath men in Confucianism is cosmic. The cosmic order is comprised of heaven, earth, and the human. The heavens and earth do not get out of order and into chaos when each maintains its proper sphere. Human beings who stay in the right relationship will have harmony with themselves, with the earth, and with the larger cosmos.

The title of Chung Hyun Kyung's book, *The Struggle to Be the Sun Again*, shows the cosmic dimension of women's subordination in Confucianism. Men are the sun and women are the moon, only passively reflecting male light. In the yin-yang, which depicts the energy of the cosmos, the feminine as yin constitutes the earth—lowly, inferior, yielding, receptive, and devoted. It is inferior to the male principle, the heavenly, active initiator.

And women in the home were subject to three obediences: as a daughter, subject to her father; as a wife, to her husband; and as a widow, to her son. The wife had no grounds in Confucianism to initiate divorce, and even after death she was supposed to remain faithful to him and never remarry.

The legacy of Confucianism in the modern period is complicated. In China, poverty, overpopulation, and corruption caused a revolution that turned on Confucianism as one of the prime sources of the problems. Perhaps never has such a widespread attack on a religion been conducted. And the results of the 1949 Chinese revolution were a marked elevation of women's position in the society, the elimination of foot-binding (the breaking and wrapping of female children's feet, to keep them small into adulthood) and near elimination of female infanticide, and an end to the buying and selling of women. (Actually, with regard to female infanticide, population limits have kept the practice alive in the rural areas, and the use of amniocentesis and abortion in the city has caused the birth rate of males to triple, even quadruple, compared to that of females in some areas of Asia. The rise in the male birth rate has been so great that newspapers now concern themselves with whether many men will ever find anyone to marry.) Mao Tse-tung saw women as an untapped revolutionary source, and China under Mao made sweeping reforms to improve the status of women. Often, however, the independence of married women carries with it the double work shift. And outside China, the buying and selling of women continues, especially in the flourishing sex trade in Asia.

Is Confucianism irredeemably inimical to women's safety and life? There are elements of Confucianism—and Asian feminists point them out—that could be mined to improve women's lives. Its profound humanistic spirit and its sense of religious practice as building the human community and of the relational qualities of all things, in heaven and on earth, could be springboards for such improvement.

## CONCLUSION

Gender is a symbol for human difference. As employed by the major world religions, this difference has been given a particular value, with the male assigned to represent the transcendent or spiritual plane, the female to represent the material plane. The origins of modern religions in the social and political turmoil of the axial age are translated today in the arrangement of human society according to hierarchical power relations of men over women, both in the public sphere of economics and politics and the private sphere of home and marriage.

Yet all religions also contain the germ of protest against inequality and its maintenance by force. To challenge the unequal power relations of gender in religion requires us to explore religions for their subversive elements.

## NOTES

1. Dominique Zahan, cited in Ursula King, ed., *Women in the World's Religions, Past and Present* (New York: Paragon, 1987), 7.

2. See Margaret Mead's landmark study *Male and Female* (1949; reprint, New York: William Morrow & Co., 1975). See also Charlotte O'Kelly and Larry S. Carney, *Women and Men in Society: Cross-Cultural Perspectives on Gender Stratification* (Belmont, Calif.: Wadsworth Publishing Co., 1986).

3. Dory Adams, "Women + Science = Math?" published and distributed by National Association for Independent Schools, 1620 L Street NW, Washington, D.C. 20016-5605.

4. See Gary Comstock, *Gay Theology without Apology* (Cleveland: Pilgrim Press, 1993).

5. See the articles in *Gender and Society*, the Journal of Sociologists for Women and Society, published by Sage Publications, 2455 Teller Road, Newbury Park, California 91320.

6. See Robert Moore, *King, Warrior, Magician, Lover: Rediscovering the Archetypes of the Mature Masculine* (San Francisco: HarperCollins, 1990).

7. Scott Coltrane, "The Micropolitics of Gender in Nonindustrial Societies," *Gender and Society* 6, 1 (March 1992): 87.

8. Sallie McFague, *Metaphorical Theology: Models of God in Religious Language* (Philadelphia: Fortress Press, 1982), 15.

9. King, ed., *Women in World's Religions*, x.

10. For a thorough discussion of Karl Jaspers and the religions of the axial age, see Shmuel Eisenstadt, "The Axial Age: The Emergence of Transcendental Visions and the Rise of Clerics," *European Journal of Sociology* 23, 2 (1982): 294–314; and the entire spring 1975 issue of *Daedalus*. The significance of the axial age for the construction of the relation of women and religion was first pointed out to me by Dr. Rita Nakashima Brock, and this argument is taken from our book *Casting Stones: Prostitution and Liberation in Asia and the United States* (Minneapolis: Fortress Press, 1996).

11. Shmuel Eisenstadt, *Revolution and the Transformation of Society: A Comparative Study of Civilizations* (New York: Free Press, 1978), 60–70.

12. See O'Kelly and Carney, *Women and Men in Society*; and Peggy Reeves Sanday, *Female Power and Male Dominance: On the Origins of Sexual Inequality* (Cambridge: Cambridge University Press, 1981).

13. Shmuel Eisenstadt, "Religious Diversity," in *The Encyclopedia of Religion,* ed. Mircea Eliade 12: 313.

14. Eisenstadt, "Axial Age," 297.

15. Ibid., 304.

16. See Plato, *Phaedo* 2.65c–67d.

17. "Muslim Women Scholars on Islam," *Chicago Theological Seminary Register* 83, 1–2, (winter–spring 1993).

18. See Roland Bainton, *Christian Attitudes toward War and Peace* (New York: Abingdon Press, 1960), or Richard B. Miller, *Interpretations of Conflict: Ethics, Pacifism, and the Just War Tradition* (Chicago: University of Chicago Press, 1991).

19. *Letters of John Calvin,* ed. Jules Bonnet (Philadelphia: Presbyterian Board of Publications, 1858), col. 539.

20. Martin Luther, "Lectures on Genesis, Gen. 3:16," in *Luther's Works,* ed. Jaroslav Pelikan (St. Louis: Concordia Publishing House, 1958), 1:202–3.

21. Sun Ai Lee Park, "Theology of Han from a Woman's Perspective," privately circulated paper, 1990.

22. Arvind Sharma, *Women in World Religions* (Albany, N.Y.: State University of New York Press, 1987), 156.

23. Chung Hyun Kyung, "'Han-pu-ri': Doing Theology from Korean Women's Perspective," in Virginia Fabella and Sun Ai Lee Park, *We Dare to Dream: Doing Theology as Asian Women,* published by Asian Women's Resource Center, 566 Nathan Rd., Kiv Kin Mansion, 6/F, Hong Kong.

24. Ibid.

25. The importance of recognizing this anger at women and the resulting resentment women feel at being so designated is interpreted as *han.* According to theologian Suh Nam-Dong, *han* is "the suppressed, amassed and condensed experience of oppression caused by mischief or misfortune so that it forms a kind of 'lump' in one's spirit" ("Towards a Theology of Han," in *Minjung Theology* [Singapore: Christian Council of Asia, 1981], 65).

## STUDY QUESTIONS

1. What is the distinction between sex and gender?
2. How do persons learn their gender roles? Give specific examples for both male and female roles.
3. Define gender stereotyping. Give three examples of stereotypes associated with gender. Can you think of others? Have you ever been the victim of gender stereotyping? If so, in what way?
4. What is a metaphor? What makes a metaphor powerful?
5. What is the axial age? What is the focus of the axial age? Who were several typical "male" leaders of the axial age? In relation to gender, how does religious metaphor develop from this period of our history? Be specific.
6. Define the role of women in each of these traditions: Islam, Christianity, and Confucianism. How do women's roles differ among these three traditions? How are women's roles similar in each tradition? What role does hierarchy play in each tradition? Be specific. Give examples.

# 11

## BONNIE J. MILLER-McLEMORE

# Protestantism and the European-American Family: Like Oil and Water

Distinct from the often relentless stream of pro-family rhetoric in evangelical and fundamentalist Protestantism, old-line liberal Protestant Christianity has molded family life silently, subtly, and most important—ambiguously. When I was asked to write about the religion I "know best" and "what it does" in terms of the family, I have to admit that no clear outline came to mind. Unlike those schooled in conservative evangelical James Dobson's Focus on the Family, I have little conscious memory of anything explicitly taught about the family per se in the Christian Church (Disciples of Christ) in which I grew up. Today, neither my denomination nor old-line Protestantism in general has made the family a central topic of discussion, despite recent political fervor surrounding related issues such as homosexuality and abortion.

I include this instance of writer's block not to warm to the topic but because it is important to the theses on religion and the European-American family that eventually emerged. The murky relationship between old-line Protestant Christianity and the family is not just a personal conundrum. Ambiguity, paradoxical commands, and conflict between faith claims and family claims lie at the heart of Christianity both today and in the past. Furthermore, to a greater extent than Catholic theologians, old-line Protestant theologians have been hesitant to delimit the place of the family in their understanding of the whole of the Christian life.

Ultimately, these and other abiding convictions allowed me to proceed. The Protestantism I know exerts a powerful influence over family life, sometimes endorsing and protecting and sometimes seriously undercutting it. Protestant women, moreover, traditionally relegated to a secondary status and often caught between conflicting commitments of family, work, and faith, have thus far experienced the ambiguities of the Christian family tradition to a far greater extent than most men have.

## PROTESTANT CHRISTIANITY
## AND FAMILY: A DOUBLE MESSAGE

Christianity has been the source of two, often diverging forces. On the one hand, it has functioned to build and sustain conventional, socially established relational structures and dynamics, whether in the form of the medieval sanction of celibacy and monastic life or the more recent influential image of the "traditional" family of breadwinner husband and homemaker wife. Indeed, it was precisely Christian endorsement of white, patriarchal, bourgeois family and economic structures that led many people in both feminist and black liberation movements in the 1960s and 1970s to attack Christian belief as an oppressive ideology.

On the other hand, Christianity has served to undermine and transform conventional understandings of family life through other ideals internal to the Christian gospel—justice, the kingdom of God, baptism in Christ, *imago dei* (image of God). We can find equally powerful countermovements of feminist theologians, such as Elisabeth Schüssler Fiorenza and Rosemary Radford Ruether, and civil rights activists, such as Martin Luther King, Jr., who have seen Christianity as a source of revolutionary, liberational commands for love, equality, and justice in family and society.

With regard to the family, then, as well as to other issues, Christianity has been a complacent, sometimes moderate, and sometimes militant force. This divergent agenda of both building and breaking orthodox ideals of the "good family" is partially covert, because Christianity exerts its influence not just through its theology and Holy Scriptures but through religious traditions and practices and, more exactly, through congregational and familial life. Beliefs are embodied not just in formal religious dogmas and institutions but in the interactions around the communion table and around the hearth. This chapter illustrates these generalizations, both through historical material and through some of my own life experiences.

## A BRIEF HISTORY OF
## PROTESTANTISM AND THE FAMILY:
## A CASE STUDY IN AMBIGUITY

From its beginnings, Christianity was not merely ambivalent about the social institutions of marriage and family; in some ways, it was hostile to them. In this it is distinct from other ancient religious practices. In the

Hellenistic era, both Jewish and Greco-Roman religions sanctioned the family and home as a site for daily and weekly prayers and for celebration of annual religious festivals. In Greco-Roman culture, this included worship of ancestors, gods, and goddesses, who protected the home. In Israelite religion, the extended family unit played an important role. Religious traditions were handed down from generation to generation; hence, religious education was located at the heart of home life. By contrast, Christian beliefs have often compelled family members to put their hearts in loyalties beyond the homestead.

In the Gospel narratives and in the early Christian community, biblical and theological claims about the kingdom, the "household of God," and the "new life in Christ" shift the locus of religious life from hearth to extrafamilial relationships. In vigorous, vivid hyperbole, Jesus declares in the Gospel of Luke, "Whoever comes to me and does not hate father and mother, wife and children, brothers and sisters, yes, and even life itself, cannot be my disciple" (Luke 14:26; cf. Matt. 10:37).[1] In another scene recounted in three Gospels, a crowd around Jesus tells him his mother and brothers are asking for him. Repudiating the claims of biological kinship, Jesus declares, "'Who are my mother and my brothers?' And looking at those who sat around him, he said, 'Here are my mother and my brothers! Whoever does the will of God is my brother and sister and mother'" (Mark 3:33–35; cf. Luke 8:19–21 and Matt. 12:46–50). Later, from the height of the cross, Jesus creates new postfamilial bonds, telling the "disciple whom he loved" and his mother, "Woman, here is your son"; "Here is your mother" (John 19:26–27).

The focus here and elsewhere in Jesus' teachings is not on familial ties per se but on a personal relationship of an analogous but transcending sort. In early Christianity, the Christian congregation itself was treated as a larger family-type community, organized into "house churches" and sometimes assemblies of radical equality, with women in important leadership roles (Rom. 16:3). As recorded in Acts 4:32, "No one claimed private ownership of any possessions, but everything they owned was held in common." When Ananias and Sapphira deviated and Peter declared their deceit before God, they "fell down and died" (Acts 5:5, 10).

The antifamily sentiment and egalitarian counterculture of early Christianity created and, I argue in this chapter, continues to create certain social tensions. Over the centuries, Christian faith has asked people to "'hate' father, mother, spouse, children, to 'forget' wives or husbands they had married, to leave all things in pursuit of something greater than ordinary family life."[2] New Testament passages and the early church itself functioned to subvert the patriarchal households of Jewish and Greco-Roman societies. Both Christian martyrdom and the later monastic movement are examples of the rejection of family responsibilities for the sake of a more radical testimony. In Roman Catholicism, marriage has almost always been a lesser calling. Although this judgment is largely a result of the connection between marriage and the long-standing negative evaluation of sexuality, the secondary station of the family in the Christian life has served to decrease further its role and value.

Then and now, the Christian community, not the family, is essential to Christian life. In theory at least, people do not think of faith as transferred from generation to generation. Believers are created anew through conversion to Christ by the grace of the Holy Spirit, regardless of family history and situation. Today, congregations continue to create a different kind of familial community, which often stands in partial tension with the biological family or kinship group.

Yet also from the beginning, countermovements sought to reconnect social customs and Christianity. Next to the rejection of his original kindred we find Jesus helping his mother and blessing wedding wine and children. Unique among religious figures, he rebukes his disciples when they try to prevent people from bringing their children to him, telling them, "It is to such as these that the kingdom of God belongs" (Mark 10:14). His comments on family-related matters such as divorce and adultery reflect an opposition not to the family per se but to conditions that violate divine laws of creation, such as the joining of husband and wife as one flesh. When asked about divorce, Jesus registered his opposition by remarking, "But from the beginning of creation, 'God made them male and female.' . . . Therefore what God has joined together, let no one separate" (Mark 10:6, 9). Rather than rejecting family, he is intent on putting family claims in proper order and perspective.

In addition, the pseudo-Pauline authors of the household codes (epistles attributed to Paul but written by others in his style), concerned about the acceptability of Christianity within the Roman Empire, hoped to mitigate the socially disruptive effects of the egalitarian, antifamily trends within the early Christian community. Ephesians 5:21–6:9, equating male headship with Christ's headship of the church and requiring female submission, is among the most representative and influential of these codes. It mixes fresh, vivid ideals of husbands loving wives "as they do their own bodies"—becoming "one flesh"—with the hierarchical family order familiar to antiquity. On the one hand, rather than ruling over his domestic household as the designated autocrat of Jewish, Greek, and Roman patriarchy, the husband is admonished to imitate the cherishing, protecting love of Christ. Yet, on the other hand, he is required to serve as the head. Here, side by side, we find at once a challenge to the patriarchies of the ancient world in the high ideal of husbandly benevolence and a concession to them with the return of the language of male headship and female submission. Theologian Rosemary Radford Ruether calls this "love patriarchalism" because, at one and the same time, it "modifies traditional patriarchy" yet "nevertheless fundamentally discards the original Christian vision of equality in Christ."[3]

The patriarchal model of male headship perhaps triumphed above all when it became the family model so enthusiastically affirmed by the Protestant Reformers. Reformation theologians took the household codes as a definitive Pauline statement on the relationship between church and family. Embracing this particular, limited model as *the* biblical family was part of a dramatic divergence from the Roman Catholic Church that, in a more positive vein, reclaimed the value of family. The family, previously relegated to a secondary, profane status, was given a new, sacred role within the Christian life. Martin Luther categorically rejected celibacy and embraced family life as a font of religious inspiration. In his theology, there is no higher social calling than marriage. He himself left monastic life and raised a large and boisterous family. In his view, raising children was the "noblest and most precious work of them all."[4]

The family became "an *ecclesiola in ecclesia*," a "little church," with the father as household minister gathering his flock—his wife, children, and servants—around the hearth for scripture reading and prayer. Notably, while the wife became the "religious companion to her husband," women also lost the significant alternative avenues of religious fulfillment, education, and relative independence provided by monastic life.[5] Women were to keep silent in church, to abstain from public teaching and preaching, and to seek godliness through the roles of mother and wife—avenues that proved limited, given the changes over the next several centuries.

For various, complicated reasons external and internal to church life, the Reformed Protestant effort to redeem family life has had trouble succeeding. External to the church, the public world of material production and the private world of domestic reproduction were severed from each other in the industrialization of the nineteenth century. The domicile was designated as the women's sphere, subordinate to the men's sphere and to the public worlds of church and society. In this century, technology, science, and political separation of church and state relegated religious piety and the church itself to the private realm. The marginalization of the family and the church as secondary, "feminine" institutions deeply undercuts a theology built on their essential value.

Both women and men were misled by increasingly impossible vocational ideals and roles. Women received a double message. Unlike men, they were called both to transcend family life and to sacrifice almost everything for its sake. And many did so, losing sense of their own worth and rightful needs. Under the auspices of the Protestant work ethic, a religious value system in which hard work and prosperity were seen as reflecting God's blessing, men were called to transcend family life through vocational labor, and they did, but not as originally understood. The work ethic degenerated from a communal dedication to the creation of God's elect kingdom to the individualistic pursuit of personal achievement and material wealth of capitalist societies. Family duties held importance only insofar as they supported the ultimate cause of economic prosperity and success in the workplace.

Internal to Reformation theology, the very emphasis on freedom in Christ and the priesthood of all believers stained family loyalty. This Protestant principle subjects all human commitments to prophetic rebellion in the name of a righteous God. In the Anabaptist tradition, for example, in the covenantal relationship of marriage, the primary commitment is to God rather than to one another or to any human community.[6] Practical theologian Janet Fishburn's *Confronting the Idolatry of Family* reminds contemporary Protestants of this heritage: "If love of family is stronger and deeper than love for Jesus Christ, this is family idolatry."[7] When Christians link happy, churchgoing families with the prosperity of a Christian nation, they commit the blatant error of "religious familism" grossly misusing religious language and rituals to serve family and national needs, rather than for the glory of God.

Ultimately, the Protestant restoration of the family also collapsed because it was built on a precarious model of male headship and human sexuality that has come under attack from both within and without the Christian tradition. In the very process of reclaiming the import of the family as a sacred realm alongside other realms of human and Christian life, Reformation theology gave a diminished religious role to women and instituted social subordination as a divinely mandated order of creation. Moreover, while the Reformers affirmed marriage and children, they did little to change the negative evaluation of sexuality as shameful and unruly. As a result, despite women's proximity to the family and children, upheld by Luther and others as noble callings, the fate of women, perceived as closer to nature, childbearing, and the temptations of the flesh and the devil, changed very little. In some cases, like that of the Puritan witch-hunts of New England or today's isolated housewife or abused spouse, female destiny deteriorated.

Nonetheless, a Christian trajectory present from the start, emphasizing not hierarchy but equality, collaboration, and the vitality of human embodiment in family, faith, and church, has had a steady, albeit silenced, influence and has acquired more prominence in the latter half of the twentieth century. Over against social convention, in recent years liberal Protestants have harkened to a revolutionary creed at the center of life in Christ: "As many of you as were baptized into Christ have clothed yourselves with Christ. There is no longer Jew or Greek, there is no longer slave or free, there is no longer male and female; for all of you are one in Christ Jesus" (Gal. 3:27–28). Some have struggled to embody this imperative for the coequal discipleship of women and men in families and churches.

While an ethic of male dominance stands behind Protestantism and is alive and well in much of recent evangelical fundamentalism, old-line denominations have struggled to alter such definitions of the family. The 1980 United Methodist Church *Book of Discipline* (p. 89), for example, states this:

> We understand the family as encompassing a wider range of options than that of the two-generational unit of parents and children (the nuclear family), single parents, couples without children. We affirm shared responsibility for parenting by men and women and encourage social, economic, and religious efforts to maintain and strengthen relationships within families in order that every member may be assisted toward complete personhood.

This emphasis on fostering the personhood of all humans, on social and religious justice, and on the equal claim of all persons to the love and acceptance of the church has pervaded denominational statements on the family from the liberal branch of Protestant Christianity in the last two decades. On related family issues, such as divorce, abortion, and homosexuality, statements of the Presbyterians, Lutherans, United Church of Christ, Methodists, and so forth reflect the need for greater openness and relative legitimation—however cautious, ambiguous, and anguish-ridden.[8]

Beyond that, however, overt controversy surrounds many related family matters, such as the use of abortion as an acceptable contraceptive method, the chastity and ordination of homosexuals, women as senior pastors of affluent and influential congregations, and female god imagery, to name a few issues. Across the board, such debates have led to the development of conservative caucuses within many denominations, often with separate, well-organized gatherings, mailings, and magazines.

Groups such as Disciple Renewal, Methodist Good News Movement, and Episcopalians United for Revelation, Renewal and Reformation often make family-related causes a central part of their protest of liberal church tenets, policies, and hirings. As of yet, however, none of these parties has led members in a mass exit to join denominations such as the Nazarenes or the Southern Baptists, who adamantly advocate male headship and female submission as the God-given family pattern and who oppose divorce, abortion, and homosexuality.

In one way or another, most North American Protestant families are caught in the age-old, still unresolved tensions between ideals of equality and ideals of male responsibility and between the claims of faith and the claims of family. Indeed, determining *the* Christian view of the family is currently at the center of a hot debate or "culture war," as sociologist James Davison Hunter contends. When he uses this term, he means a conflict that is not simply over public policies or the politics of, say, abortion, homosexuality, values in schools, and sexual harassment but is over "*how we as Americans will order our lives together.*" It is a debate over some very basic, nonnegotiable moral convictions and deeply embedded religious worldviews. And the family is, in Hunter's words, "the most conspicuous field of conflict."[9] In fact, the way people answer the most intimate questions of how authority, power, responsibility, obligation, and sexuality are ordered in family life may be pivotal to the outcome of these other more political battles mentioned above.

Although old-line Protestantism is reluctant to enter the fray, the battle will continue to determine North American images of the "good family" and the "good life," and religious belief will make a difference. In the culture war, the influence of religious traditions on the family is quite a bit like the air we breathe and the gravity beneath our feet; we sometimes fail to notice how much we rely on them and how much force they really exert.

In the battle over who defines *the* Christian view, the sides are not equally well organized and represented. Liberals are far more concerned with respecting diversity—racial, ethnic, gender, sexual, and so forth—than with arriving at a uniform family platform and theology. The press consistently gives greater coverage to conservative rhetoric on patriarchal family forms as representative of "Christian family values" than to the apparently out-of-fashion old-line Christian rhetoric of equality, justice, and acceptance as equally important Christian family values.

Fair or not, the culture war over the definition of the Christian family continues. As sociologist Judith Stacey observes, we are living in the very midst of a "transitional and contested period of family history, a period *after* the modern family order, but before what we cannot foretell."[10] We have come to a stage when the "logical progression of stages breaks down." No wonder my mind went blank. These are perplexing times for Protestantism and family. However, if this quick reading of the diversity of views of the family in Christian history shows anything, it is that old-line, liberal Protestantism continues to have an important role to play.

## AN AMBIVALENCE LIVED:
## A PERSONAL CASE STUDY

Protestant heritage has undoubtedly shaped my convictions about the elements of a faithful generative life.[11] I can readily identify four premises that have crept into my living and being: (1) family and parenthood are valued as vocations in their own right, as worthy as celibate religious life; (2) love and children are signs of God's gift and blessing; (3) work is valued as a way people sustain themselves, provide for others, and otherwise collaborate with the living community—never simply as a means for making money; and at the very same time, (4) the call to follow God relativizes all familial and vocational commitments as secondary to the reign of God, the coming of the kingdom, and the new ecclesia (new church), with its reconstituted family of another sort.

As powerful as these ideals are, I know them as much from my academic study of religion as from any graphic memory of lessons taught and learned in worship or Christian education. And there is little in current old-line Protestant practice that offers guidance to the way these ideals are best embodied in the midst of contemporary conflicts. Even worse, a great deal I have learned about exhaustive self-sacrifice, sinful self-assertion, the dangers of sexual, bodily pleasure, and the secondary place of women and mothers in biblical stories and religious traditions serves me very poorly indeed.

As a white feminist mother with Protestant convictions, I stand upon several thresholds, caught between cultures. I am neither inside nor wholly outside the traditions and cultures that have held me and those that have liberated me. On the one hand, despite my best intentions, I still wrestle with the resilient cultural ideals of the "father-knows-best" family that gripped the heart of American Protestantism in the 1950s with a fierce tenacity. On the other hand, I live, albeit uneasily, with the new, still sketchily drawn ideals of equality and working women. I feel caught in a vicious circle that the women's movement identified: women's stories have not been told and have not shaped cultural myths; without them, a woman is lost; women need stories that value their experiences.

For the most part, the task of arbitrating the contradictions between cultures has been up to individuals. My own efforts have been strained at several points. Daily, I get entangled in the so-called oppositions between public and private life. On the one hand, my "private" vocation as devoted mother collides head-on with my religious and feminist hopes for justice and equality in a "public" world not structured for, and even hostile to, children. On the other hand, my "public" vocation as professor clashes with my religious and maternal desires for creation, nurturing, and sustenance in the "private" world of child-play and domestic routine. My life refuses to fall into the traditional dichotomy between private and public arenas that Western society has fostered.

I face a double bind. My heritage as a Christian feminist mother involves a forceful dual disinheritance. First I question marriage and motherhood and fear the entrapping snares of domesticity, and then I find myself questioning tactics for success in a male-defined economy and materialistic society. Coming of age in the 1970s, I was acutely aware of the entrapments of home and children. But the birth of children and the admission of Christian faith reinforced my disinclination to become an "honorary man" in a world organized and run by men, the power of money, and the lure of status. Both the conventional "marriage plot," which assigns women the script of taking care of the private world, and the "quest plot," with its scripts of heroic adventure in public life, have valid appeal but serious flaws. Yet if neither of these narratives fits today's world, what's the new plot, for women and for men alike?

Resolution of the daily conflicts leads inevitably to contradictions, frustrations, ambiguous solutions, and hard choices. I recall one day, while trying to revise a manuscript during the nap time of one of my sons, feeling torn between my desire for total, uninterrupted silence and horror at my fantasy that a capricious god might grant me my impulsive wish and I would lose my children forever. This moment, indelibly stamped on my memory, illustrates vividly the dilemmas of creativity and procreativity that I seek to portray: one moment, I want to drop the whole project to turn to household matters of grave importance; the next, I want to see the project through, for its own value and for the love of my vocation. A hundred times—and not for the last time, by any means—I have wondered, Am I attempting a self-defeating task, trying to "conceive" in professional and familial ways at the same time? No matter how a mother designs her life—whether she stays home, works at home, works outside the home—most would admit that conflicts plague their resolutions to questions of family and vocation.

Family role distinctions, however distorted and unjust, remain a backbone of social order, undergirding not just society's reproductive arrangements but, more plainly, how people see and understand the world. People and institutions have a heavy investment in perpetuating these distinctions. Ambiguity in gender identity, from the dilemma of mothers who work to the ambiguity of transsexuality, is amazingly "difficult to tolerate," observes feminist sociologist Cynthia Fuchs Epstein in *Deceptive Distinctions*. As the movie *The Crying Game* proves so powerfully, people are terribly disturbed when known gender categories are disrupted. They are uncomfortable with the inconsistency, the lack of clarity, and the impossibility of closure. Although adults learn far more sophisticated ways than do children to camouflage their uneasiness when a young father arrives at a preschool tea and his wife comes and talks about her profession, or when an unmarried woman talks about her child-rearing plans, they are just as uncomfortable. In the end, Epstein remarks, society tends to "punish those who deviate" from general practices.[12]

Almost immediately between my husband Mark and me, the physiological disparities of bearing and nursing children necessitated a reappraisal of the mutuality internal to our relationship. However, these differences did not lessen our religious and cultural commitment to partnership. Nor did the differences lessen my desire or need for my own work. Rather, they intensified my vocational pursuit and began to teach us the complicated lessons of the arduous practice of a mutuality that embodies more fully the tension inherent in the biblical commandment to "love your neighbor as yourself" (Mark 12:31). In retrospect, the period of acute physical difference was relatively brief and gave way to the trickier problems of socialized gender differences. This phase proved a worthy testing ground for the breadth and depth of our commitment to a joint participation in parenting.

We discovered that the mutuality we wanted to maintain could not be spelled out as easily as kitchen duty (and that wasn't easy), but it required a measured and steady response to the constantly emerging, evolving needs of our children for love and our need to love ourselves, as parents and otherwise. Actualizing this mutuality amid the flux and disparities between us required compensation for the person who had given too much. It required flexibility, improvisation, and support. Daily, we tried to find ways to balance the inequities of the demands that my physical proximity to the children created for both of us and to build avenues for common participation, often with little outside encouragement and few supportive structures. This sometimes meant intentionally inverting and overriding what seemed our natural impulses. When it seemed right and necessary, it even meant overriding the real, physical inclinations of the "gut" with an affirmation of the deeper realities that our socialization had denied us—Mark's physical experience of the lure of our children and my experience of a desire for creative work.

In other words, something more than a "revision of household rules and the alternation of household roles" is required for equality in contemporary families. Biblical scholar William Countryman argues that complex moral and religious shifts are necessary:

> It involves new understandings of manliness and womanliness that can come about only with some pain and anxiety as well as some sense of liberation and joy. If the husband gives up the image of himself as sole ruler . . . he must also give up its spiritual equivalent—the image of himself as the family's unique sacrificial sustainer, isolated in his moral strength and grandeur. If the wife gives up being the servant of all . . . she must also give up the spiritual vision of herself as the one who gives all for others' good. . . . None of this will be easy.[13]

Learning new moral and religious values and virtues is never easy.

Our choices have assumed a basic responsiveness on the part of our respective employing institutions—the church in Mark's case and the seminary in mine—that does not prevail in most working institutions. While seldom articulated, this responsiveness has something to do with our employers' identities as religious institutions. While valuing family and work, Protestantism recognizes the limits of earthly devotions and the dangers of idolatry, whether it be excessive concern with material wealth, workaholism, or even excessive familism. Church teachings juxtapose the "treasures on earth," which moths and rust consume and thieves break in and steal, with the "treasures in heaven" (Matt. 6:19–20). One cannot "serve God and wealth" (Matt. 6:24b). One ought not be solely loyal or even heavily committed to the limited, albeit worthy, values of one's own work *or* one's family. In this vein, religiously committed people with whom we have worked have understood our mutual commitment to the less tangible, less material rewards of family life.

At the same time, there have been limits to this understanding. There have been times when the institutions did not want to budge, as with certain requests for paternity leave and reduced time, and we simply had to live with our frustrations. More profoundly, I have found the practices of old-line churches in general peculiarly less receptive to the struggles of people in their midst and more resistant to challenging the status quo than I anticipated. While national denominational meetings may use inclusive language and elect women officials, when women arrive at the communion table as elders in local congregations, they often still pray to a "Father God." When my first son reached age three, he insisted that God is male. Who could blame him for claiming what he had inevitably heard and seen? Sociologist David Heller's study of *The Children's God* reveals that my son is not unique.[14]

Old-line Protestant traditions have been especially quiet about generative responsibilities. In contrast to more conservative traditions, many people in old-line congregations now admit that fathers do not always know best. But they have not determined who does if fathers don't or, more precisely, they no longer know exactly what *is* best. Many people in the pews, especially those under age fifty, consider theological doctrines of male headship and female submission, narrowly extrapolated from Ephesians 5:22, to be wrong. When these household codes appear as part of the worship lectionary, if they are read at all, one can practically feel the dissent as telling looks between mothers, daughters, and, sometimes, husbands and fathers ripple through the congregation. Women and men, most seem to agree, are equal before God.

Exactly what this means, however, for the common life of work and love in churches, in families, and in jobs is less clear. In contrast to early feminist efforts, the ambiguous meanings of equality surface not so much around still unresolved questions about inclusive God language or even female leadership but most explicitly when concrete chores arise, whether within the home or within the church community itself. Women are elders, even ministers, and we may have fewer prayers directed to "Our Father," but who runs the Sunday school program now?

The caring demands of the institutional church, from nursery duty to funeral meals, assume a woman's active participation. Most women under fifty now work. In the next decade, 80 percent of these working women will be of childbearing age, and 90 percent of those will become pregnant. Most continue to take on major responsibilities with their families. Yet the traditional expectations of women in churches have not adapted to changes in women's lives. Women still usually fix the funeral meals, staff the nursery, cook the potlucks, clean up, teach Sunday school, run rummage sales, and now, in addition, take on new roles of leadership.

One male minister, who identifies the "changing role of women" as a "convenient" point of entry into his discussion of the major changes he has witnessed in a few decades of parish life, sees the problem from the other side. Sadly, he is not particularly concerned about the reconstruction of a healthy theology of the family and its practice or, for that matter, about the fact that feminism has not had much impact on liturgical language or women's groups in his congregation. What bothers him is the decline of "numerous, reliable, and ambitious" volunteers and the difficulty of church attendance on Sundays when parents work.[15] There are no bodies to run the programs. A female minister displays the same blindness to the need to reconceive Protestant views on the family in her recent article "Serving Potlucks and Pulpits."[16] Contrary to the impression left by the title, she voices no concern at all about the implications of this double load for women and focuses entirely on the ways in which the women ministers can now get along with the women in pews. She, too, overlooks the nature of the conflicts.

Many ministers and old-line congregations have lost touch with the women and men in their midst who have felt the impact of the revolutions in family life of the past two decades. Mary Guerrera Congo, feminist Roman Catholic and mother of two, connects her crisis of faith directly to her new powers and burdens as a laboring, caring mother:

> It would gradually become painful and then intolerable for me to sit in church and watch robed men, who had cooks and housekeepers running the rectory for them, playing out the supposedly sacred roles of giving "new life" to children in baptism, children they had never labored to birth, and feeding such children with sacred bread they had never labored to bake.[17]

This robbed her of any sense of her own essential place as a mother in the church and in religion.

Although on one level I knew that it is God who gives new life and new hope in baptism and communion, on another level I experienced a disenchantment similar to Guerrera Congo's when I looked upon a crèche scene of kings, shepherds, and father, absent of women except for Mary, who in Protestant sanctuaries fades away into the shadows. Carrying thirty extra pounds of baby, and later, bearing the sticky weight of nursing, told me I knew something about the giving of one's body and blood that did not seem reflected in the way the rituals of communion and baptism are enacted. It seemed as if in its most powerful rituals and stories, a male church had forsaken women and then wrongly appropriated the bounty of female bodily knowledge.

Conservative churches clearly advocate a return to the so-called traditional family. Old-line churches stand in the cross fire between the feminist revolution and conservative trends. When all is said and done, they pay little heed to the transformations of the former and to the hazardous retrenchments of the latter. The moral majority claims the image of Eden as home, while radical feminism claims the exodus story. In this scenario, a woman must either return home to save the family from decline, observes theologian Elisabeth Schüssler Fiorenza, or she must abandon the oppressive confines of home and church as hopelessly corrupt.[18] Most women in old-line congregations are caught somewhere in between.

A "conspiracy of silence," in Janet Fishburn's words, enshrouds what happens in the family lives[19] and, I must add, in the work lives of church members. Many old-line clergy and members have relegated family and work problems to the private realm. They seldom question deeply entrenched conventions about family privacy and unwritten rules about what can and cannot be discussed. During the "Joys and Concerns" segment in the small church worship service I attend, certain events such as anniversaries, deaths, acceptable illness, and hospitalizations are mentioned, but many authentic concerns such as divorce, infertility, abortion, domestic stress and violence, teen–parent conflicts, and vocational conflicts and choices are taboo.

Immense anxieties surround these issues, especially when changes in images of family mean giving women new voice and authority and diminishing the assumed priority and prerogatives of men and men's work. If nothing else, for many men, women's equal participation in life remains an intrusion and a hassle. The intrapsychic discomfort of changes in family role expectations runs far deeper than most people anticipate. Some of the apprehension is also intergenerational. Since most congregations are communities of many generations, members are most resistant to changes of any kind that expose generational differences. And changes in family relations today do just that.

Two different groups characterize my congregation: those born after and those born prior to World War II. By and large, the latter group assumes, even if its members do not practice, a homogeneous, unified moral code. Among other things, this moral code prohibits masturbation, premarital intercourse, extramarital intercourse, and homosexuality and discourages interracial marriages, divorce, and even discussion of suicide, adultery, children out of wedlock, and other misfortunes. The younger generation is less likely to be imbued with most of the same moral ideals, professing a relative acceptance for many, if not all, of the behaviors that those born before World War II forbid or dispute. For most people born after World War II, "no moral issue has the kind of black-and-white clarity . . . that it had for those who came of age before 1960."[20]

People across the generations may not fully understand or accept one another's worldview. Usually, people prefer to operate as if nothing has changed. But a great deal has changed. Younger members' work and family lives follow new moral codes, in which sexual relations have changed, the woman is no longer the "keeper of the springs," the man has more responsibilities than "bringing home the bacon," and unexpected, unheard-of complications arise. Pure rational discussion is inadequate to the task of intellectual and practical change. Change requires a new level of engagement, conflict, and empathy that many old-line congregations and families are bound to find most trying.

Going to church was what my mother called a "good habit." Although I remember few explicit church teachings on the family, beliefs were enacted. I recall vividly my ten-year-old cognitive dissonance when the church voted to allow women as deacons and then elders. To young eyes adapted to only men marching down the aisles in dark suits, these women looked starkly out of place. Now this memory simply serves to remind me of the extent to which resistance to gender inclusivity and the equal status of women and men is deeply embedded in the human psyche and social systems, including religious traditions.

In contrast, although Fishburn derides the "family pew" as a sign of the "domestic captivity" of the church, that we—my mother, father, brothers, myself—sat together honored the value of human vulnerability and connection within the family fold. Going to church was one of the primary activities we did together as a whole family, with few other parallels. My parents' care for my brothers and me, however limited by their own foibles, was an essential context in which they practiced what they believed and I learned about the love of God. The rites of passage of church education, youth Sunday, church camp, communion, and, most significantly, adult baptism were offered to me equally, as to my brothers, with no distinction based on my sex, thus verifying my place as a child of God within life and within the kingdom. Our congregation created a new and different kind of familial community oriented toward looking beyond individual, familial well-being and toward working together in the wider community for the common good. Different from school and neighborhood, in church I made friends and commitments I might not have otherwise.

## CHANGING OLD HABITS

This excursion into Protestant history and my own case illustrate the ambiguous relationship between family ideals and Christian faith. The tension between family claims and faith claims is influenced both by cultural pressures and by theological interpretations of original doctrines and beliefs.

On the one hand, Protestantism has honored children as models of righteousness and the family as a place where other-centered love can be learned and practiced. Over against the pressures of a fast-paced, product-oriented, technological society, Christian rituals, symbols, and stories point to divergent values about life's priorities and ultimate meaning. Captured in key scripture verses, these values strengthen families as they negotiate the demands of contemporary life—"Love one another" (John 13:34); "You cannot serve God and wealth" (Luke 16:13); "The last will be first, and the first will be last" (Matt. 20:16); "Let the little children come . . . for it is to such as these that the kingdom of heaven belongs." (Matt. 19:14). More general beliefs about justice, kindness, and walking humbly with God and about the kingdom and Christian baptism validate the worth of all of human creation and the equal engagement of both men and women in securing human fulfillment. Beliefs about divine creation, sustenance, and redemption sustain families through normal life-cycle transitions and through unexpected disruptions and tragedies. Christian tradition provides human connection, stability, and meaning, within families and between families.

Yet Christian ideals and structures of stability have also lent themselves to exploitation, oppression, and violence. Over the course of its history, Christianity has reinforced a culturally inherited patriarchal structure for the family. This model rears its ugly head in the New Testament household codes. It comes to fruition in Reformation Christianity and ripens in conservative circles today. Unfortunately, ideals of male headship and female submission have served as a reinforcement of, rather than a challenge to, violent behavior in families. Church affiliation has been correlated with statistics for wife abuse and father–daughter incest.[21] In the end, the church as family and the models of family that Christianity has endorsed over the past two thousand years remain flawed and limited institutions, as Christ himself knew and proclaimed.

In a real sense, although family life and family churchgoing can be important avenues for learning about and practicing Christian faith, rigid, religiously ordained family structures and "family pews," when unreflected on and approaching idolatry, are not good habits. Changing old habits to bring in the kingdom remains an arduous task. Within Christianity, however, there remains an important liberating precedent for breaking the ties of bondage, whether of kings or fathers, and creating new households of freedom.

## NOTES

1. All scripture quotations are from the New Revised Standard Version of the Bible, copyright © 1989, Division of Christian Education of the National Council of the Churches of Christ in the United States of America.

2. Margaret Farley, "The Church and the Family: An Ethical Task," *Horizons* 10, 1 (1983): 50–71, esp. 53.

3. Rosemary Radford Ruether, "An Unrealized Revolution: Searching Scripture for a Model of the Family," *Christianity and Crisis* (October 31, 1983): 399–404, esp. 403.

4. William H. Lazareth, *Luther on the Christian Home* (Philadelphia: Muhlenberg Press, 1960), 220.

5. Rosemary Radford Ruether, "Church and Family II: Church and Family in the Medieval and Reformation Periods," *New Blackfriars* (February 1984): 77–86, esp. 84.

6. See Barbara Hargrove, "Family in the White American Protestant Experience," in *Families and Religions: Conflict and Change in Modern Society*, eds. William Y. D'Antonio and Joan Aldores (Beverly Hills: Sage, 1983), 113–16.

7. Janet Fishburn, *Confronting the Idolatry of Family: A New Vision for the Household of God* (Nashville: Abingdon Press, 1991), 50.

8. See Hargrove, "Family in the White American Protestant Experience," 120–33.

9. James Davison Hunter, *Culture Wars: The Struggle to Define America* (New York: Basic Books, 1991), 42; his emphasis above.

10. Judith Stacey, *Brave New Families: Stories of Domestic Upheaveal in Late Twentieth Century America* (New York: Basic Books, 1990), 18, emphasis added.

11. Most of the material in this section is based on selections from chapters 1, 5, and 8 of my book *Also a Mother: Work and Family as Theological Dilemma* (Nashville: Abingdon Press, 1994). Reprinted by permission.

12. Cynthia Fuchs Epstein, *Deceptive Distinctions: Sex, Gender, and the Social Order* (New Haven, Conn.: Yale University Press, 1988), 13.

13. William Countryman, *Dirt, Greed and Sex: Sexual Ethics in the New Testament and Their Implications for Today* (Minneapolis: Fortress Press, 1990), 260.

14. David Heller, *The Children's God* (Chicago: University of Chicago Press, 1986).

15. Robert G. Kemper, "Where Have All the Assumptions Gone?" *Chicago Theological Seminary Register* 77, 1 (1987): 5–6.

16. Sharon Watkins, "Disciples Women in 1993: Serving Potlucks and Pulpits," *The Disciple: Journal of the Christian Church (Disciples of Christ)* 131, 5 (May 1993): 8–11.

17. Mary Guerrera Congo, "The Truth Will Set You Free, but First It Will Make You Crazy," in *Sacred Dimensions of Women's Experience*, ed. Elizabeth Dodson Gray (Wellesley, Mass.: Roundtable, 1988), 76–84, esp. 78.

18. Elisabeth Schüssler Fiorenza, *In Memory of Her: A Feminist Theological Reconstruction of Christian Origins* (New York: Crossroad, 1983), 347–48.

19. Fishburn, *Confronting the Idolatry of Family*, 141.

20. Ibid., 30.

21. Lenore E. Walker, *The Battered Woman* (New York: Harper & Row, 1979); Marie H. Fortune, *Sexual Violence: The Unmentionable Sin* (New York: Pilgrim Press, 1983).

## STUDY QUESTIONS

1. What are the two diverging forces in Protestant Christianity? What are the implications of such forces for the family? Be specific.
2. What New Testament teachings shift Christianity's emphasis from family ties to personal relations? Is a similar emphasis at work in Protestant Christianity today? Is Protestant Christianity a New Testament church? Explain your answer. Use examples.
3. What does the author mean when she describes the family as "an ecclesiola in ecclesia"? Do you agree? Why? Why not?
4. Describe the diminishing role of women in the Protestant Reformation. What are two reasons for this negative evaluation of women during the Protestant Reformation? Can you think of other reasons for the decline of women's power that occurred as a result of the Protestant Reformation?
5. From the author's personal experiences, what are four premises that show her understanding of the Protestant heritage and notions of family? List and describe.

# 12

## PETER J. HAAS

# Religion and Ethics

As we go through life, we are constantly confronted with situations and challenges that require some moral judgment. Often these are problems we have not faced before. One of the most important things a religion does is give us a way of thinking about such new problems. It does this by providing an intellectual framework within which moral decisions can be made. Through the stories, lessons, and rules of the religious tradition, we are able to cast our current moral conflicts into frameworks and terms that are already familiar. Further, in most cases religions also tell us what kind of reaction or solution to the problem would be most appropriate or most like what God would want. Religious beliefs and convictions, then, can have a tremendous influence on how we, as individuals and as a nation, react to new situations, new ideas, and new technologies.

This is, in fact, one of the major functions of religious literature, whether that literature is the Christian Bible, the Jewish Tanakh, the Islamic Qur'an, or the Hindu Upanishads. All of these literatures contain stories that tell the reader what the world is like, what constitutes good and evil, and what it takes to be a good and ethical person. We read stories of people who have done the right things and seen good flow from that, and of people who have made the wrong decisions and have had to suffer the consequences. When we read these books, we constantly are moved to ask ourselves how we fit in, what God would want for us, which characters we are most like, and how we might act in similar situations.

Of course, there is no single book or collection in any religion that will prepare us for every one of the possible situations that we will face in our lives. Especially in this age of new technology, we are more and more likely to find ourselves facing difficult moral issues in unprecedented situations or those that are not explicitly described in any ancient religious book. For this reason, every religion has established ways of interpreting its ancient texts so that they can be used to address new situations. Usually, some kind of authority structure is set into place in which certain people act as normative interpreters, as teachers or judges: the *qadi* in Islam, the bishop or pastor in Christianity, the rabbi in Judaism. Such people may claim authority on the basis of special selection or ordination, special training, or even prophecy. In all cases, their job is to translate the meaning of the ancient religious texts into normative rules for the community of believers. In this way, believers are not forced to think through each new moral dilemma on their own but can fall back on the collected wisdom and experience of their faith community.

In what follows, I want to show how this process works in one religion, namely, Judaism. Judaism is a good example because its process of applying religious texts to moral problems is so systematically developed. This is due in large part to the historical situation in which Jews have found themselves. Since Roman times, Jews have lived as a tiny minority among large non-Jewish populations: Christians in the West, and Muslims in North Africa and the Middle East. In many cases, Jews lived in small towns or villages, often without rabbis or other religious leaders. When a conflict or question arose, the solution was found by writing to a well-known rabbi in a large town or city. This authority would then write back a "rescript" (like a modern legal brief), telling the community what it should do and offering reasons and explanations. Literally hundreds of thousands of such letters, called "responsa," have been preserved from as early as the eighth century until today. They come from communities all across Europe, North Africa, and the Middle East. As new problems arose, rabbis consulted not only the Bible and the Talmud and other sacred books but also past responsa that treated similar situations. The result is that today we have a remarkably complete record of how the Jewish attitude toward moral problems developed over the last two millennia.

The responsum I examine here has to do with when it is permissible to let a suffering person die. It was written by Hayyim Palaggi, a very prominent rabbi in Turkey, in the first half of the nineteenth century. I have chosen it because it deals with a medical problem with which we still are struggling today, even though our medical technology is much more sophisticated than our author could have ever imagined. This example shows how traditional religious writings and thought can help us make moral decisions, even though our technology is so different.

Below is the actual question and part of the answer composed by Palaggi. It is number 50 in a collection of his rabbinic answers titled *Hikkeke Lev*.[1] You will notice that the people involved here lived in an age when traditional religion was taken very seriously; everyone was thoroughly convinced that whether you pray or not and what you pray will really make a difference. The point is that, for them, stopping a prayer is the moral equivalent of our "pulling the plug."

As you read the responsum, there are a few things to keep in mind. First, even though this is a Jewish text, remember that the process it demonstrates is true of nearly all other religions in one way or another. It is one example of how ancient religious texts are studied and applied to new problems. Second, notice the steps the author goes through: (1) he identifies and defines the moral issues involved; (2) he cites a variety of religious authorities to establish the moral rules involved; and (3) he tells the family what all this means for them. You will also notice that the family cites one traditional religious text, the late talmudic tractate *Semakhot*.

## THE ETHICAL ISSUE:
## LETTING A SUFFERING PERSON DIE

QUESTION: A God-fearing scholar has a pious wife. Because of our many sins this woman has been afflicted with a long-term disease. For more than twenty years she has been crushed and burdened with pain. Her arms and legs have shriveled up, forcing her to be confined to a corner of her house. This woman suffers greatly from these afflictions. Her husband, however, accepts the suffering of his wife with patience, never troubling her even for a moment. On the contrary, he shows her special affection and love so that she may have no worry on this account. Because of her unbearable pain, the aforementioned woman has already prayed that God take her. She prefers death to life because in death she will find rest from her pain. Her husband and children, however, may God bless them, comfort her and continually bring her physicians and medicines in the hope that a remission might occur. They have even hired a maid to wait on her so that she should have no worries.

Now, as if the continual pain and bitter suffering she has had up to now were not enough, her condition has worsened, bringing with it terrible agony, such as accompanies dreadful diseases, leaving her totally stricken and disabled. Even the physicians have given up hope, especially since the disease has affected her internal organs, an event that occurs twenty days before death, as written in Tractate *Semakhot* 3:11: "For this is the death of the righteous as opposed to the other kinds of plagues, wounds, afflictions, and diseases." Recently, she began to ask others as well to pray for her death. She especially pleads with her husband and children to intercede on her behalf. But her husband and children, though they are worn out with her suffering, do not listen to her because of their love and affection, she being a righteous and pious woman. On the contrary, they seek scholars who would teach on her behalf so as to bring healing, and they increase their giving of charity and paying redemption and atonement money and buying oil for the lamps—all in order to obtain healing for her.

Let our master in righteousness now instruct us as to whether or not there are any grounds for prohibiting prayers that she find rest in death. If there is no prohibition—what if her husband and sons are so concerned with her life that they do not want to see her die? May they pray that she not die, ignoring her own wishes; or, since according to the physicians there is no way she will live and there is no longer hope that she will recover naturally, would this be against her well-being (such that they must not pray for her to live longer and may even pray for her speedy death)? May the master instruct us, and may his portion in heaven be doubled.

We can easily see here the moral dilemma facing the family. On the one hand, they know from their religious upbringing that they must always pray for God to help and heal people. It is always wrong to hope for, let alone pray for, the death of another. On the other hand, their wife and mother is suffering deeply and is begging for relief. Certainly, they want to help the poor woman and relieve her of her agony. In this case, they are not thinking of doing anything as drastic as actively killing her. Nonetheless, they want to do something. Even just stopping their prayers for her life might help hasten her death. But can they do even this much? Our modern analogy might be to withhold extraordinary means from a patient who is being kept alive artificially.

Let us now look at how Hayyim Palaggi advises the family on what to do.

I. ANSWER: First of all, it is clearly forbidden in all cases to pray that another person die. This is so even if one is praying only that some misfortune befall an enemy. Torah commands, for example, that if you see the mule of one who hates you collapse under its burden and you refuse to help, you will be abandoned just as you abandoned the animal (Deut. 22:4). Torah is concerned here that you not cause the animal's owner any material loss. How much the more is Torah concerned that you not cause your enemy to lose his life. Thank God no Jew is suspected of doing this!

II. There is another prohibition involved, namely, that this kind of curse, in fact any curse on one's fellow, is forbidden. This is so even if done without explicitly naming the intended victim. In fact, if one pronounces a curse on another by name, the curser [deserves to be] flogged, as it is written in BT [the Babylonian Talmud] Temurah 4b. See also MT [i.e., the *Mishneh Torah* of Maimonides] Sanhedrin 27:1 and the *Arbaah Turim* and the *Shulkhan Arukh* Hoshen Mishpat 27:1.

III. We turn now specifically to wishing harm to one's spouse. Our masters, may their memories be a blessing, say in BT Qiddushin 83a, "It is forbidden for one to marry a woman before he sees her lest when he sees her he find something detestable in her and she be disgraced by him—for the Merciful One said, 'You should love your neighbor as yourself.'" This verse, a central rule in the Torah, applies also to one's husband or wife. [The point is that you should not get yourself in a position in which you might wish harm to your spouse.]. . . .

IV. [All the above speak about wishing harm to one's spouse. But the law also speaks specifically about wishing for the spouse's death.] Our masters report in the beginning of chapter 3 of *Avot de Rabbi Nathan*, for example, "He used to say, 'As for one who wishes his wife to die that he may marry her sister, or anyone who wishes his brother to die that he may marry his wife, his end will be that they [i.e., the intended victims] will bury him during their lifetimes.' As regards such a person, Scripture says (Eccles. 10:8), 'The one who digs the pit will fall into it; and a serpent will bite the one who breaks through the wall.'" This is to say that if one hopes his wife will die so that he might marry another woman, heaven will arrange for the opposite to occur.

V. [Can a mere thought be the concern of the law, however?] R. Hayyim Yosef David Azulai writes in *Kise Rahamim*, "If one merely has an evil thought, the Holy One, Blessed be He, does not consider it to be an evil deed, and so does not punish that person on its account." . . . However, on the other hand, BT Sota 9a (bottom) says, "Whoever looks greedily upon what is not his—that which he wants will not be given to him and that which he has will be taken away." [Here Talmud implies that, in fact, the mere thought is subject to divine punishment].

VI. Now, in my humble opinion, [the cases assumed by the above rulings] are different from the case before us. All of the aforementioned rulings are based on a particular prohibition from the tradition. The rabbis take the command "Do not devise evil against your fellow" (Prov. 3:29) to apply to one thinking about divorcing his wife; all the more so to one hoping that she will die. There is also the positive command, "Love your neighbor as yourself," which our rabbis, may their memories be a blessing, apply especially to one's wife. Besides these there is the prohibition of "not hating your brother in your heart" (Lev. 19:17). This applies not only to brothers, for it is clear that one must love one's wife also and show affection for her—as written in BT Yebamot 72b (bottom), "One who loves his wife as himself . . . [is blessed]." She also what our master and teacher Meir b. Baruch of Rothenburg wrote in his collected responsa 81:30, "As for one who beats his wife, I have learned that we deal with him more harshly than with one who beats his neighbor. For he is not obligated to honor the neighbor, but he is obligated to honor his wife." There is also the prohibition against casting the evil eye on his wife, especially so as to cause her to die. There is also the prohibition recorded in BT Baba Mezia 107a and in BT Baba Bathra 2b: "It is forbidden for one to cast the evil eye on his neighbor's field when it is full of standing grain." . . .

IX. They also said in Tractate Derekh Erets Rabbah 11:13, "Ben Azzai says, 'One who hates his wife is a murderer, as it is said: He will falsely accuse her and will finally hire witnesses against her and bring her to the execution place.'" They also say (Ibid., 2:12), "One who lives in an obscene manner with his wife or one who tells false tales about her in the neighborhood in order to divorce her, about such a one Scripture says, 'I the Lord investigate the heart and examine the innermost parts' (Jer. 17:10)." It turns out that from all that has been said it is forbidden to wish that one's wife die because of hatred. This being so, we deduce [further] that it is absolutely forbidden to pray that anyone die, especially as regards a wife, who is like one's own self.

X. However, all this appears to apply only if the wish comes from hatred and without the wife's knowledge and consent. But when, to the contrary, she acquiesces to this wish because she no longer can bear the suffering of the body, then we can say that such a wish is permitted. I say this with BT Ketubot 104a in mind:

On the day that Rabbi [Judah] died, the sages declared a public fast and they prayed saying, "If anyone says, 'Let Rabbi die'—let that one be run through with a sword." The maidservant of Rabbi went up on the roof and said, "The angels seek Rabbi and the creatures seek Rabbi. Let it be Thy will that the angels give way to the creatures." When she reflected on how often Rabbi had entered the privy and taken off his tefillin [as an act of piety, not to be wearing them in such a place] and [then had to] put them on [again] and how he was now suffering [she had a change of heart]. She prayed, "Let the angels have way over the creatures." But the rabbis did not stop praying [and so Rabbi still did not die]. She finally took a jug and threw it among [the praying disciples] from the roof. They stopped praying and Rabbi [immediately] died.

It is clear from this passage that the maidservant of Rabbi, when she saw how he was suffering, prayed for his death. Furthermore, we find in BT Moed Katan 17a and also in some of the pertinent commentaries in *Rosh, Arbaah Turim,* and *Shulkhan Arukh* Hoshen Mishpat 40:34 that the ancient authorities adduced legal rulings from what Rabbi's maidservant did because she was his servant [and so would surely conduct herself as he instructed her] and also because they deemed her to be a scholar in her own right, being filled with wisdom and the fear of heaven. This being so, we may adduce from this story the following: that it is permitted to pray that a sick person who is suffering greatly might die, thereby finding rest. Were this not so, the Talmud would not have cited this story. Or, had the Talmud meant only to report the event [but with the understanding] that the maidservant acted wrongly, it would have had to say so explicitly.

Now you might want to argue that, on the contrary, the fact that the masters prayed for Rabbi's life without regard for his suffering ought to be the legal precedent [and not what the maidservant did]. In response, I would argue that they at first did not pay any attention to this sufferings, while his maidservant did. Later, when they realized how much he was suffering, they in fact did stop praying. Further, it is clear that the rabbis did not disagree with what Rabbi's maidservant did, for had they disagreed they would have rebuked her straightway, especially since they had just decreed that anyone who said, "Let Rabbi die," was to be run through with a sword. Surely this should include one who prayed that he should die. Further, had her act been wrong, you would think that the Talmud would not remain silent but would protest that what she did was improper. But since the Talmud does remain silent and since the rabbis appear in fact to agree with the maidservant's actions, the inevitable conclusion is that in the case of the affiliated woman who is ill and suffering much pain and who is begging others to pray that she die, it is certainly entirely permitted to do so. This is now clear.

I also saw in the writings of Rabbenu Nissim to BT Nedarim 40a: "that we do not need to pray for him at all neither that he live nor that he die." It seems to me that this means that at times one may pray that a sick person die, for instance, when the sick person is suffering greatly from his disease and cannot go on living much longer anyway, as we have read in BT Ketubot 104a that when Rabbi's maidservant considered how he entered the privy regularly and always took of his phylacteries and was now suffering, [she] said, "May it be Thy will that the angels hold sway over the creatures," that is, that Rabbi be allowed to die. Thus it is that the prayers of one who visits the sick are efficacious [whether they be for life or for death]. . . .

It appears, in my humblest of opinions, that because of all this it makes sense to do as [follows]: if she is suffering very much from her many bitter afflictions, and if the physicians all say that there is no hope that she will live and they have given up in despair, then as regards even her husband and children and relatives, if they do not want to pray that she live, let them not pray explicitly that she die, either. Rather, let them sit and do nothing. For if they pray that she die, there is the chance that, heaven forbid, one out of a thousand will see this and come to the unlikely conclusion that he is praying for her death so that he might be free from her and from her demands. That is, someone might assume that he has an interest in her death. This is especially so as regards the husband, for there is always room for the suspicion, heaven forbid, that he desires her death for his own benefit, even if he is pious and a proper scholar. For Scripture says, "I am the Lord who searches the heart and investigates the innermost parts." [That is, only God can know what one really is thinking.] This is referred to several times in *Avot de Rabbi Nathan*. In all events, the best, in God's eyes, is to make no prayer or petition that she die, even if by refusing to pray for her death he does not show proper respect or compassion for her or the family. He should refrain from praying that she die even if he has her best interests in mind.

Now there is something to be said for this view. One surely can make a distinction between what Rabbi's maidservant did in openly praying for his death and what we today may do. If the Talmudic masters already could say (in BT Shabbat 112b), "If the earlier sages were sons of men, we are like donkeys, and not even like the donkey of R. Pinhas b. Yair [which knew Jewish law and was careful never to break it—cf. BT Hullin 7ab], but like ordinary asses," then surely one can say, "We are not like Rabbi's maidservant and so cannot do what she could do." Now to pray that she live is hard because of the pain she must suffer and the bitter agonies she must endure. If you reflect on the matter you will see that it is not always preferable that she continue to live. On the other hand, as we noted, it is really not proper for them openly to pray that she die, either. However, as for others, who are strangers and not under any of the aforementioned suspicions—if they pray that she die so that her soul might find rest, they may do so. All is according to what is written, "God searches the heart and the innermost parts, the Lord is righteous." Our rabbis, may their memories be a blessing, have said that all that is in the heart is to God as if it were spoken. Therefore fear the Lord. . . .

Now all this applies when the sick person is not actually in the throes of death. However, if that person is in the throes of death, there is no way that one may pray [for continued life]. It is written in *The Book of the Pious* #234 that one ought not cry out at the time when the soul leaves the body. The reason for not doing so is that the soul not be induced to return to the body and cause the patient more suffering. Why did Ecclesiastes say there is a time to die? Because when a person dies—when the soul is leaving the body—they ought not cry out loud that the soul return, because the patient cannot live but a few more days anyway and during those days would suffer nothing but agonies. [This line of reasoning is not negated by the fact that Ecclesiastes] also says "a time to live," because human beings have no control over the time of death. We may conclude, then, that according to *The Book of the Pious*, one is not to pray for a person who is in the throes of death. See also what Isserles writes in his gloss to *Shulkhan Arukh* Yore Dea #339. That is what, in my humble opinion, I must write, although in haste because the strength of the sufferer is weak. May Almighty God say "enough" to our troubles and save us from error and show us wonders from the Torah. May this be God's will. Amen.

## HOW THE RELIGIOUS TRADITION
## PROVIDED GUIDANCE

It is easy to see from this question and its answer that the Jewish religion has played a major role in the way the people involved talk about the problem in front of them. First, we see the high regard ascribed to life as sacred, regardless of circumstances. This is why the family takes it for granted that they must pray for the woman's recovery every day. In contrast, of course, is the basic religious principle to alleviate suffering. So the family is caught between two apparently conflicting religious principles: to preserve life and to prevent suffering. The problem is that whatever they do will appear to violate some religious principle.

Palaggi's answer shows us very clearly how religious traditions not only create moral dilemmas but also guide us in solving them. First, the religious tradition here helps us understand the problem better by defining the various principles at stake. Second, it shapes a response by considering similar situations and what other holy and religious people have done or not done.

With this in mind, let's look at Palaggi's answer. He begins by defining the problem and the exact principles at stake. First of all, we know that one may not pray for another person to die (paragraph I) or even for another person to come to harm (II). It is especially wrong to do so if the intended victim is one's husband or wife (III), and even more so if the prayer is for that person to die (IV). This leads to a brief excursus in V about whether a mere thought, as opposed to an actual prayer, is equally wrong. This is the first horn of the dilemma.

But now Palaggi makes a very important move. He clarifies this principle for us by showing that the prohibition against praying for the spouse's death assumes that death would be for the benefit of the one who is praying. That is, it is wrong to pray for someone's death if you have something to gain by that death (paragraphs VI–IX; I have left out a lot of the argument). This is not the problem in front of us, however. Palaggi concludes, therefore, that there is no real moral problem in the family's hoping for the woman's quick death in a case such as this, in which both they and the patient simply want a quick end to her suffering.

In fact, in X, Palaggi finds a story about a pious rabbi that is a precedent for precisely the situation at hand. Rabbi Judah's handmaiden caused his disciples to stop praying for his life and so allowed the angels to take his soul. Everybody understood this was the right thing to do. Palaggi ends his answer by saying, first, that while the family *may* pray for her death, they should not do so out of concern for appearances, and second, that given the fact that she is already in the process of dying, withholding further prayer for her life is certainly valid. So, in the end, Palaggi has shown the family how to act in a morally responsible way that is fully in accord with the sacred path of Judaism.

This responsum, then, makes the point with which I began, namely, that religion helps us learn from ancient wisdom and revelation how to respond to moral crises, even if these crises involve modern technology. It is important to keep in mind that Palaggi does not just announce a decision. Rather, he leads us through a careful discussion to adduce what is right.

I think he did this for two reasons. First, he wanted to make sure he understood all sides of the problem and what the religion had to say to each of them. In a sense, Palaggi is "thinking out loud" on paper. Once he is sure we understand all parts of the problem and what scripture has to say on each, he turns to the second task, to counsel the family and show them that what he is suggesting is proper. This is why, I think, Palaggi tells the story about the death of Rabbi Judah. This story is important because Rabbi Judah is considered to be one of the greatest of holy men in Judaism after the people in the Bible. Surely what happened to him is God's will and is what God would have us do for our beloved. By telling this story, Palaggi is assuring the family that they are not acting in a strange and heartless manner but doing what even the holiest men of history did.

## HOW RELIGIOUS TRADITIONS
## CAN GUIDE US TODAY

When I introduced the responsum, I mentioned that its problem was similar to ours today of when to disconnect a dying patient from life-support systems. Like the family addressed in the responsum, we do not want to kill the patient (pray for her death), but we want to end the agony of dying. Of course, Palaggi could never have dreamed of the kinds of medical treatments and machines that we have today. Yet his thinking through the situation of his time and place can help us understand better the questions of our own time.

We live in a world in which technology is changing faster and faster, and in which it seems to be getting harder and harder to know what is the right thing to do. And the questions facing us are not just individual decisions anymore. As a whole society, we are faced with decisions that are full of moral significance and about which we are confused. What is the moral thing to do about allowing the sale of assault rifles? Should we screen people for genetic defects? Should we keep nuclear weapons as a deterrent against war? Should we perform heart transplants? To be sure, none of these problems was specifically discussed in ancient religious writings. They are all relatively recent problems.

But as in the case of "pulling the plug," the basic moral ideas and values are ancient ones, concepts that have been thought about and talked about for ages. By looking back at what religious traditions can teach us, we can get a better idea of how to understand and think about these problems. That doesn't always mean we will find easy answers. But religion can help us identify the moral issues and so help us discuss the problems in a more sophisticated and informed way.

In a way, then, religion helps us see that we are not alone in the world, forced to fall back on our own resources. The "new" dilemmas we are facing turn out not to be new at all, but rather old problems that have taken on a new form. We have guidance through our religions on how to deal sensitively and intelligently with these problems, if only we listen to the wisdom of God, as carried to us across time and space by our religions.

### NOTE

1. Hayyim Palaggi, *Hikkeke Lev* (Salonika, 1840), 90a.

## STUDY QUESTIONS

1. List three reasons that make the author believe that Judaism is a good example for applying religious texts to moral problems. Can you see other traditions that might function similarly? Explain your answer.

2. What are two ways that religious traditions not only create moral dilemmas but also guide in solving them? How does the tradition of storytelling relate to the notion of moral dilemma and religious solution? Be specific.

3. Have you ever told a religious story from your tradition in order to address a moral dilemma in real life? Explain your answer and give specific examples.

4. Do you agree that religious storytelling helps us to see that we are not alone in the world? What do you find important about facing moral dilemma as a community? Be specific. Give examples.

# 13

## STEPHEN G. POST

---

# Religion and Medicine

Religion does many things in the medical world. It shapes actions with regard to contraception, prenatal genetic testing, elective and selective abortion, utilization of blood products, treatment termination, organ procurement and transplantation, caregiving, human and animal research, and many other areas of health care. Religious communities negotiate with the medical world and modernity in their own ways. For example, the Amish will not use cars or refrigerators, but they will hire vans and drivers to bring them to urban hospitals where high-tech treatments are available.

This chapter considers two topics in depth, dementia of the Alzheimer's type and AIDS, both in relation to the function of religion. Many other topics might have been selected, but space is limited. Alzheimer's disease and AIDS are linked because they are both leading public health concerns that in the 1980s came into the limelight of public attention. The stories in this chapter show that religion provides meaning even in the midst of decline, bestows dignity on those who are so forgetful as to lose all self-identity, sustains often burdensome long-term caregiving, and asserts high definitions of love that have nearly disappeared in modern culture but that must be recovered.

## MEANING IN CARING FOR
## THE ILL AND DISABLED

Alzheimer's disease is an irreversible dementia, or mental decline, that results in death after a period of gradual deterioration, usually lasting for seven or eight years. All elements of self-identity eventually fade away until, in the severe stages, the patient lacks any discernible sense of connection between past, present, and future. Memory, the temporal glue that makes self-identity possible, is eroded by such deep forgetfulness. Neurons die, the brain erodes, the self seems absent. Unrecognized family members use various metaphors to describe this absence—Grandpa is "gone," Grandma is a "shell" or a "husk."

What has become of the glorious being created in the very image of God and just "a little lower than the angels"? The critic of religion can easily see an argument for atheism: if a terrible natural evil such as neurodegeneration can occur, then God better not exist, because if God does exist, He or She or It has absolutely no excuse!

Your ancestors were lucky in a way; they did not generally live long enough to manifest Alzheimer's disease, and adult children therefore were spared the sometimes burdensome duties of caregiving. Ironically, the very technology that, according to myth, frees us from responsibilities has added to them greatly, for we now live, on average, well into our seventies. At the time the American Declaration of Independence was signed, few people lived into their forties. The average undergraduate student today will have filial duties greater than those of any earlier generation in world history.

The following two stories are actual cases of Alzheimer's disease patients. How could these stories in any way be connected with religious life? The first story is taken verbatim—though lightly edited—from a forty-three-year-old woman named Jan who has Alzheimer's disease, which rarely strikes people this young. The second story is about an old man's lament.

### Jan's Diagnosis

It was just about this time three years ago that I recall laughing with my sister while in dance class at my turning the big four-0. "Don't worry, Jan, life begins at forty," she exclaimed, and then sweetly advised her younger sister of all the wonders in life still to be found. Little did either of us realize what a cruel twist life was proceeding to take. It was a fate neither she nor I ever imagined someone in our age group could encounter.

Things began to happen that I just couldn't understand. There were times I addressed friends by the wrong name. Comprehending conversations seemed almost impossible. My attention span became quite short. Notes were needed to remind me of things to be done and how to do them. I would slur my speech, use inappropriate words, or simply eliminate one from a sentence. This caused not only frustration for me but also a great deal of embarrassment. Then came the times I honestly could not remember how to plan a meal or shop for groceries.

One day, while out for a walk on my usual path in a city in which I had resided for eleven years, nothing looked familiar. It was as if I was lost in a foreign land, yet I had the sense to ask for directions home.

There were more days than not when I was perfectly fine; but to me, they did not make up for the ones that weren't. I knew there was something terribly wrong, and after eighteen months of undergoing a tremendous number of tests and countless visits to various doctors, I was proven right.

Dementia is the disease, they say—cause unknown. At this point it no longer mattered to me just what that cause was, because the tests now had eliminated the reversible ones, my hospital coverage was gone, and my spirit was too worn even to care about the name of something irreversible. I was so confused and felt so alone, and I didn't want to hear their advice that the support I so badly needed was available at the Alzheimer's Association.

I was angry. I was broken, and this was something I could not fix; nor, to date, can anyone fix it for me. How was I to live without myself? I wanted Jan back!

She was a strong and independent woman. She always tried so hard to be a loving wife, a good mother, a caring friend, and a dedicated employee. She had self-confidence and enjoyed life. She never imagined that by the age of forty-one she should be forced into retirement. She had not yet observed even one of her sons graduating from college, or known the pleasures of a daughter-in-law, or held a grandchild in her arms.

Needless to say, the future did not look bright. The leader must now learn to follow. Adversities in life were once looked on as a challenge; now they're just confusing situations that someone else must handle. Control of *my life* will slowly be relinquished to others. I must learn to trust—completely.

An intense fear enveloped my entire being as I mourned the loss of what was and the hopes and dreams that might never be. How could this be happening to me? What exactly will become of me? These questions occupied much of my time for far too many days.

Then, one day, as I fumbled around the kitchen to prepare a pot of coffee, something caught by eye through the window. It had snowed, and I had *truly* forgotten what a beautiful sight a soft, gentle snowfall could be. I eagerly but so slowly dressed and went outside to join my son, who was shoveling our driveway. As I bent down to gather a mass of those radiantly white flakes on my shovel, it seemed as though I could do nothing but marvel at their beauty. Needless to say, he did not share in my enthusiasm. To him, it was a job; but to me, it was an experience.

Later I realized that for a short period of time, God granted me the ability to see a snowfall through the same innocent eyes of the child I once was, so many years ago. Jan is still here, I thought, and there will be wonders to be held in each new day. They are just different now.

## A Last Tango in Paris

There is a second story to be told about dementia, this one about Mrs. G. and Mr. R (I follow the medical tradition of confidentiality in disclosing only partial names in case presentations), although I do not have access to Mr. R.'s words, and Mrs. G was severely demented before I ever met her.

Mrs. G came from an old Episcopal family of distinction, out in the eastern Cleveland suburbs. I am visiting her in the Alzheimer's wing of a fancy nursing home. She carries an old book under one arm as she walks slowly down the corridor. She shows it to me and smiles. It is a James Audubon print book. They tell me she always has it open to the same page and points gleefully to the same picture of a bluebird, as though that picture were forever new. (I think, a bit sardonic for a moment, that at least, with dementia, novelty requires only one book and only one picture, so there need be no more monthly bills from the bookstore.) I guide Mrs. G. to a table and we sit. I ask her how her children are. She responds after my repetition. She seems to mutter the word *sky*, but it is hard to tell. Her communication system is badly broken. I wonder if, under this chaos, there is still a self there, trying to get through but hidden, scientifically unverifiable and unfalsifiable. Or is the temporal glue between past, present, and future experience that would allow for self-identity really gone? Is Mrs. G. no longer here, a shell of her former self, a husk? Is the glass of her self half full or half empty?

She still as a certain graceful charm, a smile. She seems to have adjusted emotionally. Not all Alzheimer's patients do. It has been said that habitual mannerisms and demeanor are so ingrained that they are the last things to go. Slowly, Mrs. G. arises and walks away, a little tear in her eye. She seems to have emotions left, anyway.

I ask around about Mrs. G. She is now beyond the stage of dementia where behavioral abnormalities such as delusion and hallucination are commonplace in many patients. A nurse's aide tells me about her. A year back, when Mrs. G. was hallucinating and more difficult to care for, she projected her long-since deceased but very much beloved husband's image upon another resident in the Alzheimer's unit, Mr. R. She managed to convey her love to this gentleman, who was mildly to moderately demented himself and therefore capable of some insight. Mrs. G. would bring him any object she could reach for and make of it a gift. The old gentlemen was thrilled.

On one of his better days—and patients do fluctuate in the moderate stages—Mr. R. managed to ask the doctor if he might cohabitate with Mrs. G. This was to be an old man's "last tango in Paris," his final and ultimate hope. The doctor took the request to the administration, which in turn took it to Mrs. G's adult daughter. The daughter was appalled at the request. Had not her mother and father loved each other for decades? Had they not been utterly faithful and devoted to their marriage? Cohabitation makes a mockery of fidelity, nursing-home ombudsman be damned! No, Mrs. G. would be demeaned by intimacy with another man, himself demented and loved only on the basis of being mistaken for a dead spouse. So the nursing-home administrator broke the bad news to the old man. No last tango; she thinks you're someone you're not. She mistook you for her husband. She sometimes mistakes people for coatracks.

The old man did not understand. He became increasingly depressed as the days wore on. He stopped talking and eating. He no longer wandered about. The staff put a feeding tube down his throat, all very uncomfortable. After two months, the old man was moved to another nursing home. Several months later, with a feeding bag surgically implanted in his abdomen, he died of pneumonia. His family said it would be wise to let him die. No antibiotics were given. The nurses said this was one case where an old man died of despair.

### What Religion Does

In Jan's case, religion provides subjective hope where, objectively considered, there is almost none. Even in the worst of circumstances, Jan is able to maintain composure and character through a religious interpretation of events. Behind her dementia she finds a God who is returning her to the simple freshness of a child. Snow can again be seen for the first time.

Have you ever noticed that people tend to get prayerful when they are in trouble and out of solutions? When they can no longer control events, when they are threatened by circumstances over which they have no power, God enters in. People find peace of a sort through the belief that no matter how dim things might look, they are still in the hands of a loving God. I very recently heard that Jan now forgets that she forgets, and this is a blessing, for she no longer can feel the anxiety and fear that coincide with the earlier stages of self-loss.

Because despair is so painful and so frequently part of the dementing or dying process, it falls within the scope of religion to minister to it. Each small step in the loss of self causes a certain amount of despair, and when disintegration slips beyond medical help, as is the case with Alzheimer's disease, despair may be severe. Despair is so painful because it is the nature of human beings to hope.

For some cultural groups, dismissal of hope is always contrary to truthfulness. For example, among Arab Muslims, "hope helps a patient mobilize his own resources to cope with the illness, even if such hope is false by Western standards. As long as the patient has faith in Allah and his power, hope is never false."[1] For the Arab Muslim, "only Allah" knows the prognosis; it is therefore unacceptable for the physician to disclose a bleak prognosis with any certitude. God, hope, and truthfulness are intertwined; only hopelessness is false.

Theologian Paul Tillich wrote that "the ontological side of courage is taken into faith (including hope)."[2] Trust and hope are linked. The opposite of hope is despair—from the French *désespoir*, which is literally "without hope." Tillich describes despair: "No way out into the future appears. Nonbeing is felt as absolutely victorious."

Hope is a thin veneer over the seething cauldron of despair. (I follow William James in my suspicion of simple-minded happiness.) The veneer is sufficiently thin that human beings at their creative best construct symbols and narratives to strengthen it. The human "will to hope" is certainly as basic to being human as Nietzsche's "will to power" or William James's "will to believe." Religion is the major way in which most people preserve hope, for despair in this world can be transposed into hope for the world to come. This is the juncture at which pastoral care is as important as medical.

When a person no longer recognizes loved ones, is incontinent of bowel and urine, and appears to have no relational capacities or self-identity, why should we take the time and energy to care for that person? Demented people in such a state have little or no quality of life or anything to contribute to the lives of others. They are so far "gone" that one of my students refers to them as "cell cultures." Why treat them with dignity when they appear to have none? If we lived our lives appraising the value of others only in terms of specific positive properties, severely demented people would score a zero. However, the property-based life, that is, "I care about Mrs. G. *only* because she has property $x$," is contrary to religion.

Many of us have an understandable pessimism about the lives of demented people. The Episcopal *Book of Common Prayer* speaks of human beings as made "in the image of God," just "a little lower than the angels"; but here there is no discernible image left. Is this the handiwork of God?

But religion *does* help us better care for the demented. It bestows dignity even on lost selves, a dignity that cannot be established on the basis of an appraisal of intrinsic positive properties in a Mrs. G. In its monotheistic form, religion offers a center of evaluation that bestows dignity from above, regardless of properties. True, Mrs. G. has no social-utilitarian contributions to make. She is utterly unproductive in a production-oriented society; she is utterly irrational in a culture that values cognition over all else, in the spirit of the Enlightenment and self-control and independence.

Religion is radical because it requires us to value all human beings as the children of God and therefore as worthy of respect. They may be so devastated that they have no intrinsic value, for they lack all the essentials of personhood, from rationality and relational capacity to memory and self-identity. Yet they retain an inviolability because they are the creatures of God, for whom we are stewards. This notion of stewardship is what religion gives us.

Of course, there is a tendency to abuse and even kill the demented elderly for their lack of productive value, as was the case in Adolf Hitler's euthanasia program. Judaism, in its wisdom, makes "Honor your father and your mother" the very first moral commandment in its Ten Commandments, or Decalogue. The power of religion is to assert the dignity of human lives unconditionally, and to resist strictly social evaluations. The sanctity of life thus maintains a healthy tension with assertions that the quality of a particular life is unworthy of life.

We have innumerable nursing homes based in the Christian and Jewish traditions. The Jewish *chesed,* or "steadfast love," and the Christian *agape,* or "love of bestowal," assure that caregiving has a cosmic meaning in the imitation of God. Caregivers in both families and nursing homes are often religiously motivated. Nurse's aides working for the minimum wage often do nothing all day but clean human excrement from dementia patients. These aides frequently mention the place of religion in their sense of vocation. Religious congregations frequently play a crucial role in supporting family caregivers by providing respite services, adult day-care centers, and pastoral counseling. It has been said that it takes a village to raise a child; it can be said that it takes a religious community to care.

Theologian Gilbert Meilaender has written an article titled "I Want to Burden My Loved Ones."[3] Our laissez-faire society is rooted in philosopher John Locke's myth of an individual in a state of nature prior to society, rather than in the Greek myths of care or the religious narratives of love. Many of us know of lives that have been profoundly altered by care of ill elderly parents, children with serious impairments, or spouses with chronic illnesses, both physical and mental, who will never again regain independence. More and more, obligations arise that family members never seriously imagined as real possibilities. Although the difficult requirements of caretaking must be acknowledged, what religion does is ensure an attitude of dignity and care, without which civilization would probably be lost. No love based in appraisal, with its property-based core, can last in the face of severe dementia, serious mental illness, major retardation, and innumerable other debilitating conditions.

I define *religion* etymologically from the Latin. It means, literally, "to rebind," and following Augustine, to rebind the fallen soul with God, the source of all true internal peace. To love God means that we must also love the children of God, and this is the basis of all dignity. Religion does something vital: it instills a readiness to serve others at inconvenience to one's own interests, out of loyalty to God.

## YOUNG WOMEN AND AIDS PREVENTION

Now we turn to the dementia of the young, AIDS (acquired immune deficiency syndrome). A majority of AIDS patients suffer from a form of dementia related to HIV (human immunodeficiency virus) itself or to other brain viruses associated with the syndrome. I begin with the story of an epidemic focused on adolescent women.

### The Cutting Edge of an Epidemic

In August 1993, the United Nations Development Program issued a major report titled *Young Women: Silence, Susceptibility and the HIV Epidemic.*[4] This report draws on the clear epidemiological evidence (i.e., evidence drawn from the study of all factors of the disease) that adolescent women are particularly vulnerable to HIV infection. This is because the genital tract of a young woman is a less efficient barrier to virus penetration than that of an older woman. Mucous membrane transition from a single layer of cells to a thick, multilayered wall is not complete until the late teens or early twenties.[5] Furthermore, mucus serves an immune function that is less proficient in young women because of lower production levels. These facts are consistent with knowledge that the incidence of cervical cancer due to human papillomavirus is higher in young women who began sexual activity before age seventeen.

The exact biological basis for HIV susceptibility remains to be more precisely clarified. The United Nations report covers Thailand, Myanmar (Burma), Uganda, and elsewhere, demonstrating that between the ages of fifteen and nineteen, rates of HIV infection are two to three times greater in females than in males. The report indicates that in one geographic area, as many as half of the women between ages fifteen and nineteen are infected, while in other areas, the figure is one-third or one-fourth. The report asks, "When will the agony of these young infected women press upon us?" and asserts that the "silence" must be broken if young girls are to avoid the fate of their mothers and sisters. It encourages efforts to lengthen the time before the onset of sexual intercourse in young women, to allow them more control over situations of sexual intimacy, and to create safe havens such as Casa de Passagen (Passage House) in Brazil, where peer pressures and gender oppression can be set aside. Cultural change must be created by "influential community leaders, older women, the elders, as well as by those who are now demanding such change, young women and their parents."[6]

These hard facts about young women are relevant to the United States. As the AIDS epidemic in our heterosexual population grows, young women will increasingly be at the cutting edge. In 1993, for the first time in the United States, heterosexual sex surpassed intravenous drug use as the primary cause of HIV transmission for women. The Centers for Disease Control and Prevention indicate that in Florida's Palm Beach County, for example, 32 percent of AIDS cases are due to heterosexual contact and 24 percent of AIDS cases occur in poor African-American and Hispanic women. The pattern of the disease in our nation's urban minority communities may gradually match that of the heterosexual epidemic worldwide. Moreover, a study indicates that 40 percent of students at the University of California at Berkeley have had a sexually transmitted disease.

As psychiatrist Willard Gaylin, cofounder of the Hastings Center, states, "The only empirical results of that illegitimate offspring of Freudian philosophy, the sexual revolution, seem to be the spread of two sexually transmitted diseases, genital herpes and AIDS; an extraordinary rise in the incidence of cancer of the cervix; and a disastrous epidemic of teenage pregnancies."[7]

## What Religion Does

One of the classic roles of religion is to impose healthful order on sexual intimacy, often through a powerful emphasis on the theological significance of marriage. Uncommitted sex is a false substitute for real love. On some existential level most people understand this falseness, so intelligent conversation is possible regardless of religious background.

Our culture needs to recover the religiously shaped link between sex and love and the insight that love, to be worthy of the word, does not require sexual expression. Love is manifest in a deep caring for the welfare of the other; it is a rejection of the self-centered tendency and a transfer of interests to another for his or her own sake. Myriad partial definitions can be combined to suggest that love includes joy, compassion, commitment, and respect: love rejoices in the health, existence, growth, and presence of the other; love never harms; love responds to the suffering of the other; love is committed and patient; love honors the other's freedom, integrity, and individuality, including the freedom to refuse sexual intimacy. Love generally exists without any sexual expression, for example, in parental love, love of children for parents, friendship, or compassion for the suffering. One necessary response to AIDS lies in a religious rejection of the assumption that happiness is achieved as a matter of course through liberation from the boundaries of love and commitment within the context of mutual and creative fidelity.

Religion worthy of the word asserts sexual morality. I wonder if, after our society has deconstructed every tradition of sexual restraint in the often-valid revolt against repression and oppression, we can construct a culture of idealism that looks forward rather than backward. Otherwise we may as well leave the future of our society to the Spur Posse, that gang of male high school athletes who made a competitive sport of tallying sexual conquests. For them, sex was linked not with love but with its opposites, including victimization of girls as young as age ten.

While we should avoid all prejudice against the human body, the modern cultural assumption that happiness is achieved as a matter of course through sexual liberation from the order of loyal marriage has proved unfounded. Although Christianity has, at times, been unduly morbid in its attitude toward sex, its excesses seem a useful counterpoint to the extreme preeminence of sex in modern secular culture. It has been observed that modern secular culture "envisages man the external phenomenon, his sensual well-being. And increasingly it envisages this well-being in isolation from the objective hierarchy of real and spiritual goods."[8]

Psychiatrist and theologian Paul R. Fleischman writes that if sexual repression dominated the psychological landscape in Sigmund Freud's Vienna, the current problem is quite the reverse. On a point of minor correction, Fleischman might have written that sexual repression dominated the landscape for the *haute bourgeoisie*, or upper middle class, of Vienna but not for the aristocracy or the peasants and working class. But it is Fleischman's assessment of current clinical psychiatric practice that is central to my concerns:

> Among the hurt and pained in need of help, who may suffer from broken marriages, fluctuating or fallen self-esteem, obsessive constrictions, panicky

attachments to parents, bewildering isolation, uncontrolled rages, and haunting depressions, the common denominator is an inability to transcend themselves with care and delight, to reach over and touch another heart.[9]

Fleischman's patients report that they suffer emotionally because they have assumed that genuine love requires sexual intimacy. They then pursue such relations, even when inappropriate, and suffer the consequences. Their experience may be summed up thus: "The binding together, the touch of person to person, is sought concretely, rather than spiritually, and dyadically rather than communally. The substitution of sexuality for religious life constitutes one of the most prominent and pervasive elements of cultural pathology that a psychotherapist encounters."[10]

Many people seek to touch physically for the sake of sexual intimacy alone, failing to see physical touch as at all expressive of a deeper spiritual meaning. They make sexual intimacy rather than spiritual values the center of their lives. It was in the 1950s that philosopher C. S. Lewis, for one, rightly warned against the loss of any serious moral caution regarding sexual intimacy: "Poster after poster, film after film, novel after novel, associate the idea of sexual indulgence with the ideas of health, normality, youth, frankness, and good humour. Now this association is a lie."[11] It is a lie, wrote Lewis, because sexual indulgence without commitment and steadfast love has always been associated with disease, deception, jealousies, and emotional pain.

Lewis claimed that our society had lost sight of definitions of love that do not place sexual intimacy at their center, that it had illusory expectations of this intimacy, and that the result was oppressive. He rejected the practice of sexual union when it is isolated "from all the other kinds of union which were intended to go along with it and make up the total union."[12] He complained against the "contemporary propaganda for lust" that makes it appear perverse to resist sexual union out of respect for a lasting and total union. Lewis considered it urgent to articulate nonsexual manifestations of love, such as friendships, parental love, and charity.

Popular culture has wrongly abstracted the sexual area from the wider aspects of human personality and made a mockery of the notion that there are positive physical and emotional advantages in adopting a philosophy of life that places the sexual experience within a committed and trusting relationship. Insofar as religion acquiesces to the popular culture, it fails a generation and leaves death in its wake. The ultimate response to AIDS and other sexually transmitted diseases is a recovery of the religious ethic of sex that takes love and commitment seriously. This is because there is a sacredness and profound religious meaning in conjugal love that deserves affirmation. The traditional Christian notion of the sanctity of the human body has roots in Judaism. Jesus' view of the body as God's temple is not without value. We have lost a sense of the sanctity of the body.

Our culture allows little room for youthful innocence or for refusal of physical intimacy. An ethical theory may help to reverse our flight. It can be a necessary condition of such healing, but a theory alone is likely to be insufficient. Religious transformation is required, and that no theory can give.

## NOTES

1. A. I. Meleis and Albert R. Jonsen, "Ethical Crises and Cultural Differences," *Western Journal of Medicine* 138 (1983): 889–93.

2. Paul Tillich, *The Courage to Be* (New Haven, Conn.: Yale University Press, 1952), 8.

3. Gilbert Meilaender, "I Want to Burden My Loved Ones," *First Things* 16 (October 1991): 12–16.

4. Copies of the report *Young Women: Silences, Susceptibility and the HIV Epidemic* (New York: United Nations Development Programme, 1993) are available at the following address: The Director, HIV and Development Program, United Nations Development Programme, 304 East 45th Street, Room FF 1094, New York, New York 10017 (telephone: 212-906-6976).

5. B. Forrest, "Women, HIV and Mucosal Immunity," *Lancet* 335 (1990): 835–36.

6. UN Development Program, *Young Women*, 6.

7. Willard Gaylin, *Rediscovering Love* (New York: Penguin Books, 1986), 11.

8. Max Scheler, *On the Eternal in Man*, trans. B. Noble (1921; reprint, London: SCM Press, 1960), 367.

9. Paul R. Fleischman, *The Healing Zone: Religious Issues in Psychotherapy* (New York: Paragon, 1989), 173.

10. Ibid., 174.

11. C. S. Lewis, *Mere Christianity* (New York: Macmillan Co., 1952), 78.

12. Ibid., 81.

## STUDY QUESTIONS

1. What were four functions of religion in the medieval world?
2. What are three ways religion provides meaning in periods of physical/mental decline? Can you give example from your own religious tradition of religion's "comforting" dimensions?
3. Cite one reason that technology has become both a blessing and a curse in the contemporary medical field. Can you think of other reasons?
4. What are three ways religion helps Jan in even the worst of her circumstances? Have you seen similar circumstances in your own lives, where religion functions positively in the life of a sick family member or friend?
5. What are two ways religion helps us to better care for the demented? Do you believe that "religion is radical" because it does require us to value all human beings? Why? Why not? Be specific.
6. What is one of the classic roles of religion in relation to sexual intimacy? Do you believe uncommitted sex is a false substitute for love? Explain your answer.
7. What are three ways in which physical touch can be not only for the sake of sexual intimacy but also an expression of spiritual meaning. Do you believe that both dimensions are necessary for the healthiest types of existence? Why? Why not?

# PART 4

---

# RELIGION AND THE IMAGINATION

# 14

## DIANE APOSTOLOS-CAPPADONA

# Religion and Sacred Space

Before you begin reading this chapter on the relationship between religion and sacred space, take a few moments to consider how you feel when you are outside of a building as opposed to inside a building. Try to create a mental picture of your favorite interior space (this could be a particular building or a specific room), noting the way you feel when you are inside this space and the specific details of the space, such as the height of the ceiling, the number of windows and doors, the color of the walls, and the objects within the space. Then make a mental picture of your favorite "outside" place, taking into consideration the shape of the place (e.g., mountainous or flat) and its characteristics (e.g., if it is near water, such as a lake or the ocean). As you read this chapter, have these mental pictures of your favorite space and place handy, and also consider how you feel when you come into a space or place you know as opposed to when you enter a space or a place for the first time.

The experiences of encountering interior space as opposed to exterior place, of entering a space for the first time as opposed to reentering a known space, and of the way a space is created by height, color, and shape are common human experiences that would be recognized by the medieval Christians written about in this chapter, as well as by you, the living reader. If you remember both this generalization about being human and your mental pictures of favorite space and place as you read this chapter, you will find the text more meaningful and also may participate in it as a modern pilgrim who seeks to understand the role of religion in human history.

## THE RELIGIOUS IMAGINATION AND
## THE EXPERIENCE OF THE SACRED

One of the fundamental characteristics of being human is the gift of imagination. Much more than the ability to dream or to pretend, the imagination responds to varied stimuli, such as religion or faith experiences. In those talented persons we identify as artists, the engaged imagination results in works of art. For the rest of us, these inspired works of art bring about religious responses, thereby allowing us the opportunity to experience fully an encounter with the sacred.

Through narrative stories and visual images, religion provides the ways in which we as believers can become connected to/with the sacred. In myths or stories of origin, a particular religious tradition presents an explanation of how and why human beings came to be, of the establishment of society, and of the foundation of the tradition. Myths as religious stories explain the passage of life and death and provide moral and ethical courses for human action in the world. In other words, myths as religious stories tell us who we are, why we are, and how to act—all in relation to the sacred or the holy.

In religions such as Christianity that have a history of the visual arts, religious images and symbols play roles similar to those of myths as religious stories. Thus religious images help us shape our sense of individual self, community, and the sacred. Stories and images bring about an aesthetic response in the audience through the mind, body, and spirit of the individual believer, who, through hearing and seeing them, is integrated into a unified experience of self, world, and sacred. Engaged by symbols and images, the Christian imagination brings about emotional and bodily responses, resulting in an integrated human response through gestures, bodily postures, patterns of breathing, physical sense of size, and silence.

One of the ways in which religion evokes such a response in the believer is through the arts, in particular through the delineation and experience of space, especially in the creation of sacred space. All religious traditions have a "sense" of sacred space—that geographical site at which the human is closest to encountering the sacred, whether the sacred be identified as God, Allah, or Śiva. In most religious traditions, sacred space is distinguished from ordinary space by the construction of a religious building, such as a temple or a church. The site of the religious building is predicated on the experience(s) of a miracle, a healing, or a vision by a holy person or religious believer on that exact spot of ground. Thereby the site becomes identified as a sacred place at which the sacred and human beings can interact in a unique but identifiable manner. This place then becomes the "site of the sacred," on which a temple or church will be built and where religious worship, such as the Christian liturgy, will be celebrated.

The church or temple that is built on this sacred site helps to define by its size, shape, and decoration (or lack thereof) the immediate and physical response of those entering it for worship, personal prayer, or religious ceremony. The spatial environment created by both the exterior and the interior of the church or temple shapes our experience of the sacred, of religion, and of ourselves. Such variables as the size of the room, the colors of walls, the amount of natural light, and the height of the ceiling affect our way of being in this world. In its best possible presentations, religious architecture coordinates with the teachings and beliefs of religious faith to bring about the bodily and spiritual engagement of the believer according to that tradition's interpretation of the God–human relationship. For example, high-ceilinged rooms precipitate one type of bodily response and interpretation of God, whereas low-ceilinged rooms cause a different experience of space, self, and God.

## THE MEDIEVAL CATHEDRAL AND THE EXPERIENCES OF THE SACRED

Consider, for example, the situation of a Christian believer living in that historical time known as the Middle Ages. In medieval Europe, there was one dominant religion—Christianity—that was interpreted as the source of human existence, from the political to the social to the economic and, of course, to the religious sphere. Contemporary medieval theologians argued and medieval Christians believed that all things, all persons, the world, and life as they knew it began and ended with the sacred source they identified as God. Both as a sign of this belief in God and as an expression of their respect for God's power and authority, medieval Christians sought to create religious edifices of great beauty, which signified both a temporary experience of the glory of heaven and an adoration of God. By the High Middle Ages, these religious edifices were identified as cathedrals and had become elaborate expressions of Christian faith.

The word *cathedral* is derived from the Latin word *cathedra*, meaning "chair" or "seat of authority." In this medieval Christian use of the term, the cathedral was identified as the religious building that contained the bishop's chair, or cathedra.

Fig. 1. Panoramic view of the city of Chartres, showing the cathedral. Chartres, France. Cathedral, Chartres, France.

## The Cathedral Site

In France, as in other parts of medieval Europe, the cathedral was built on a sacred site that usually translated into the highest physical site in the city, thereby one visible throughout the city. The city or town would radiate outward from this sacred site, symbolizing the centrality of religious belief and of God for the medieval Christian world. The cathedral, then, was the most visible building in the town.

Think of what it must have been like for the medieval religious pilgrim, who walked for days, if not weeks, to come to the city of Chartres, for example, to participate in a special religious ceremony honoring the Virgin Mary; or for the peasant farmer, who worked his master's fields all day long. A simple upward glance relieved the pilgrim and the peasant of their physical pain of living in this world and reminded them that the true goal of human existence was to be a member of the Kingdom of Heaven in the next—eternal life, which was the reward of Christian believers. (See Figure 1.)

Further, the placement of the cathedral at the town's center indicated not only the centrality of Christian faith to everyday life but also that religion permeated all aspects of human existence. The plaza or piazza in the front of the cathedral created an exterior and public place that had multiple functions. The primary function of the plaza was to signify the transition from the secular world outside to the sacred realm inside the cathedral. For Christian believers, be they local residents or visiting pilgrims, the plaza supplied a place for reflection and preparation before entering into the sacred realm that the cathedral's interior space symbolized.

This public plaza, however, became more than an open place for spiritual reflection, just as religion was more than simply the performance of rituals and practice of traditions. The plaza became the site for local trade fairs, which were usually held in conjunction with the feast days of the city's patron saints, thereby bringing financial resources into the city. On a more mundane economic level, the plaza was often the site of the local market. And as the medieval practice of pilgrimage became more and more popular, and thereby brought larger and larger numbers of visitors into the city, the liturgical dramas were performed on a stage erected on the front steps of the cathedral, allowing all present the opportunity to see the players and transforming the plaza into an open-air sacred space.

During the High Middle Ages, the cathedral was directly connected to a monastery, thereby heightening the religious nature of the city center but also noting the total intersection of religion and life, for the cathedral-monastery was the place the medieval Christian identified as a hospice, a legal court, a school, and a source of food during times of famine or war. The cathedral was a building that signified the passage of human existence, as the individual Christian came here for a lifetime of religious and social rites: to be baptized (thereby entering into the community), to be catechized, to receive First Communion, to participate in liturgical services, to be married, to watch the baptism of children (and perhaps grandchildren), and to be anointed before burial, as well as to be heard at legal trial, to receive sanctuary, to buy and sell goods at the weekly market, to participate in liturgical dramas, to be treated at the hospice, to be educated at the school, and to be a citizen of the town.

The cathedral, then, was the geographic center of the town and the physical center of the major and minor activities of a Christian's daily life.

## Cathedral Architecture

Medieval cathedrals like that of Chartres were more than the geographic centers of their towns. By their architectural style and presentation, medieval cathedrals characterized medieval Christianity through the creation of sacred space and spiritual environment. Remember the medieval pilgrim and peasant farmer who were able to see the cathedral from wherever they stood. For the pilgrim, this was a dual reminder of his earthly goal and his spiritual goal; and for the peasant, a reminder that this life was only transitory and that the next life in heaven would be his reward for all he suffered. Individual cathedrals, such as the cathedral at Chartres, signified these meanings by their size, decoration, and style of architecture.

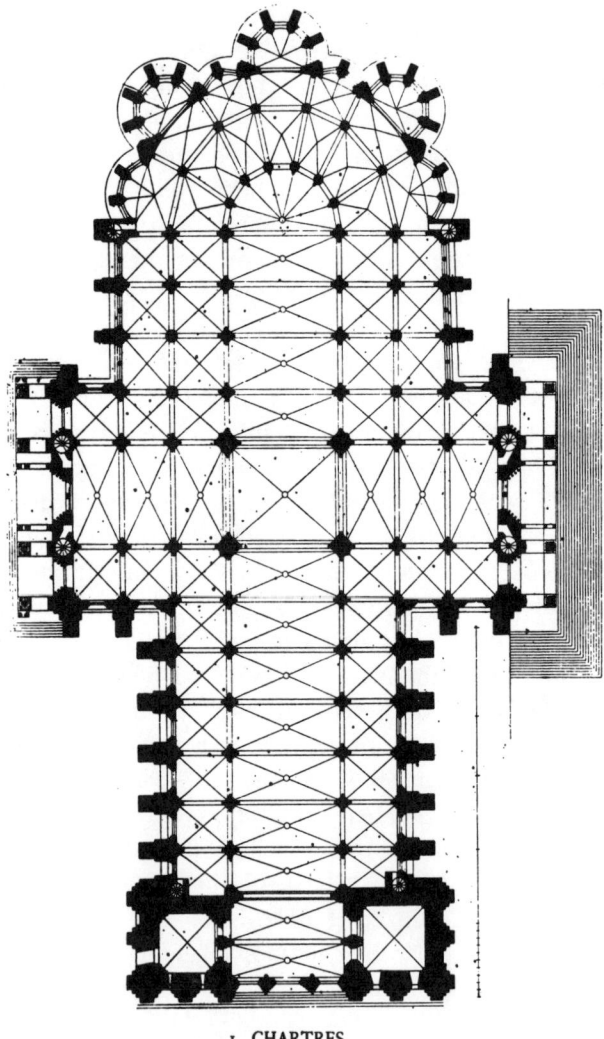

1. **CHARTRES.**

Fig. 2. Floor plan. Cathedral, Chartres, France.

The architectural style of medieval cathedrals is usually identified as either romanesque or gothic. The earlier style is romanesque, which imitates, by the use of thick walls, Roman arches, minimal natural light, and decorated capitals, the architecture of Imperial Rome. Cathedrals constructed in the High Middle Ages, such as that of Chartres, are identified as gothic. Although the term *gothic* was coined in the eighteenth century to describe the barbaric overdecoration and aesthetic lightness of this medieval style of art and architecture, since the nineteenth century, we have come to identify gothic as the high point of medieval art and architecture and as a tangible expression of the medieval synthesis.

In terms of architectural style and size, the gothic cathedral moved beyond the romanesque cathedral by extending the physical size of the building as well as the interior height of the ceiling. The gothic cathedral continued its romanesque predecessor's use of the Latin cross for its floor plan (see Figure 2) and thus had an elongated nave leading toward the high altar and a foreshortened apse behind the high altar.

The development of the gothic style of cathedral architecture was in part the practical result of the growth of pilgrimage routes and the number of pilgrims who made these religious journeys. To accommodate both these spiritual pilgrims (and the moneys they brought to a town) and the daily needs of the religious community who attended liturgy at a cathedral, the internal side aisles that circumambulated (circled) the building were expanded both in size and number. In the romanesque cathedral plan, only one side aisle had circumambulated the interior space of the cathedral and had separated, by means of thick pillars, those who made a pilgrimage to see and pray before the cathedral's relics from those who came for daily liturgy or performance of a sacrament, such as baptism. By the time of the gothic cathedral, both the number of pilgrims and the demands of local communities had so expanded that two aisles were required: one for the pilgrims circumambulating the cathedral and one for those who wished to attend liturgy or some religious service in one of the many side chapels of the cathedral building.

The architectural advance known as "flying buttresses" made possible the development of the elongated nave and the expanded side aisles, as did the thinner walls, pillars, and expanded window areas that provide the gothic cathedral with its characteristic airiness, at least in comparison to the heavier dark space inside a romanesque cathedral. The weight of the building's roof was now placed on the flying buttresses, not on the walls and pillars of the cathedral, thereby allowing for the thinner walls and pillars. Thinner walls, of course, permitted the use of larger window areas, and the more area given over to window space, the better the sense of natural light in the interior space. The development of stained-glass windows reached its peak during the gothic era, and these brilliant, colorful illuminators also distinguished the gothic cathedral from its romanesque counterpart.

Fig. 3. West Facade. Portail Royal, ca.
1145–50. Cathedral, Chartres, France.

## First Impression:
## The Cathedral Facade

As the Christian pilgrims approached a cathedral like that at Chartres, their first encounter with the front, or facade, of the building revealed a symbolic and spiritual vision (See Figure 3.) The facade of a gothic cathedral was decorated with ornate carvings around and above the doors and with embellished steeples that rose upward toward the heavens. These carved images visually affirmed the stories and teachings of the Christian faith, such as the events in the life of Jesus Christ, the prophets of the Hebrew Scriptures, and the Last Judgment.

As the pilgrims came closer to the cathedral and began to see these religious images in more careful detail, they were confronted by the three front doors, with a carved tympanum placed above each of the doors. (See Figure 4.) For the Christian pilgrim, these three doors signified the Trinity, that is, the Christian belief in God the Father, God the Son, and God the Holy Spirit. The central door, or Royal Portal, was reserved for use by the archbishop, cardinal, pope, or king and queen and was also used during those special times identified by the pope as Holy Years. (Pilgrimages made during Holy Years had a heightened spiritual significance, and those pilgrims who came to Rome during a Holy Year were absolved of all their sins.) The theme of the carving in the tympanum over the Royal Portal was that of the Last Judgment.

The doors to the left and right of the Royal Portal were the ones by which pilgrims and members of the congregation entered the cathedral. Usually, as a pilgrim, one approached the cathedral at the right portal and noted that the tympanum carving displayed an image of the Virgin Mary or episodes from her life. Then the pilgrim entered the cathedral, circumambulated the interior space by the side aisle, and exited through the left portal, whose tympanum displayed an image of the patron saint or religious feast of the cathedral. In the case of Chartres, the cathedral was dedicated to the Virgin Mary and honored her feast day of 15 August (the Day of Assumption, on which Mary was said to have ascended to heaven).

Fig. 4. West Portals. Cathedral, Chartres, France.

## Interior Sacred Space

Returning to the pilgrims' journey inside the cathedral space, the immediate experience was one of darkness, as the pilgrims adjusted their eyes from the daylight outside the cathedral to the lack of daylight initially experienced inside the building. Then the pilgrims began their journey through the interior sacred space of the cathedral, noting with prayers or devotions the different saints and holy events brought to memory by the images on the carved capitals and stained-glass windows and by the holy relics displayed in the side chapels. This journey took on the pattern of the cathedral's floor plan—that is, a Latin cross—and thereby brought to the pilgrims a heightened awareness of the journey of Jesus of Nazareth on the Via Dolorosa, or Road of Sorrows, on the way to his crucifixion on Calvary. The varied shimmering colors of the stained-glass windows and their patterned reflections on the floor of the cathedral heightened the pilgrims' sense of sacred space, an experience of the heavenly realm.

Fig. 5. Interior, Chartres, choir. Cathedral, Chartres, France.

In a similar manner, the believer who entered the cathedral's sacred space to participate in the liturgy or a sacrament experienced this internal space as different from the secular world of everyday existence. These believers also entered by the right portal and had to adjust their eyes to the difference in light inside the cathedral. However, instead of walking through the cathedral's aisles, they came to the central nave and walked toward the area reserved for those participating in the liturgical service. (See Figure 5.) As the believers walked toward this area, they, like the pilgrims, saw the images on the carved capitols and stained-glass windows, but they had a different line of vision and had the high altar as a focal point.

For believers who came to attend the liturgy and partake of the sacrament of Eucharist, this physical experience of entering the cathedral and walking toward the high altar took on added significance. As a spiritual journey, this path toward the high altar was a final preparation for the believer's meditation on the meaning of the Eucharist as the sacrifice of Jesus Christ and the spiritual gift of new life. The believers walked slowly toward the altar with the visual sense that the carved image over the Royal Portal was directly behind them. The Last Judgment was, of course, a vision of the reckoning of one's life before the Resurrected Christ as Judge. The believers then reached the high altar and received the sacrament of Eucharist, thereby experiencing a form of spiritual rebirth.

As they turned away from the high altar, these renewed believers walked into the light streaming through the rose window, which was placed above the Royal Portal and its tympanum of the Last Judgment. (See Figure 6.) A medieval symbol for the Virgin Mary, the pattern of the rose window signified the grace and love of the Virgin as Mother Church for all Christians. Thus, having received the sacrament of the Eucharist and experiencing spiritual renewal, the believers who had entered the cathedral with a recognition of human sinfulness and finitude began their exit under the sign and light of Mary's grace.

This constant play of light and dark, like the images throughout the interior of the cathedral, was a significant element in the experience of sacred space as distinct from any other space. The initial darkness, experienced by believers and pilgrims alike on entering the cathedral, signified the passage from the secular to the sacred realm. In a gothic cathedral such as that in Chartres, there was an intentional manipulation of light through the colors of the stained-glass windows. The darker colors were placed on the lower registers of the windows, while the lighter colors, especially white, were employed in the uppermost registers of the windows. Given the medieval Christian affirmation of God as light—it was maintained that an experience of God was, in fact, one of blazing, white light—and of God as *the* resident of the heavens, this artistic placement of white and clear glass at only the uppermost registers of the windows was not an artistic choice but a symbolic one. As the human eye always seeks the light rather than the shadows or the darkness, the arrangement of colors within the stained-glass windows directed the pattern of vision of those entering the cathedral. The lower levels of "darkness" created by the dark colors caused the human eye to move upward toward the "light" of the white and clear glass.

Fig. 6. View of nave toward west end. Cathedral, Chartres, France.

As one's vision was drawn toward the light, the believer or pilgrim experienced a physical sensation of moving upward that simultaneously provided an awareness of God being up in heaven (the transcendent God of medieval Christian theology) and a recognition of the smallness of the human body. This recognition of the insignificant stature of the human in comparison to the divine was echoed in the high-ceilinged spaces inside gothic cathedrals, especially when these ceilings were flooded with light. Thus the spiritual experience of the immense power and sacred authority of the transcendent God was made clear by the believers' and pilgrims' bodily experiences of being inside the sacred space of a gothic cathedral like Chartres.

## CONCLUSION

In a manner similar to the medieval cathedral, other spaces can affirm the religious experience of the sacred or the holy. For example, the Quaker belief in an immanent and personal God is reflected in the simplicity of the architectural design of the Quaker meeting house, with its low-ceilinged space, clear glass windows that open onto natural vistas, and sparsity of decoration. The classical Greek recognition of the omnipresence of the sacred in nature was symbolized by the special sitings and open-air walls of their temples. Similar analogies can be found between the belief systems and sacred spaces of other religions of the world.

Religion, then, can be seen as more than a code of beliefs or a code of moral actions in the world. Through an examination of its aesthetic expression, such as architecture and the visual arts, we can see that religion provides a recognition of the relationship between the human and the sacred. The bodily experiences of believers in encountering sacred spaces and sacred images permit personal recognition of what it means to be human, to be an individual, and to be a believer. Religion, then, is a path toward self-definition, and by defining oneself, the believer is able to recognize the other—the sacred.

## STUDY QUESTIONS

1. List two ways in which narrative stories and visual images connect us to/with the sacred. Can you imagine other ways in which this connection might take place? Be specific.
2. Define sacred space? Name two geographical sites that are sacred to you and/or your tradition. Why are they sacred?
3. In what ways did the cathedral in medieval Europe function as a sacred site and as sacred architecture? Be specific in your description of the cathedral.
4. What is the relationship between the gothic cathedral and the growth of pilgrimage routes during the High Middle Ages? Speculate on how the pilgrim might feel as s/he approached the cathedral at Chartres.
5. Compare and contrast the sacred space of the cathedral of medieval Europe with the architectural design of the Quaker meetinghouse. How does each function to affirm the religious experience of the sacred? Be specific with your descriptions.

# 15

## JOHN UPDIKE

---

# Religion and Literature

By "religion" I mean humankind's transactions with what it believes to be the supernatural. The relation between religion and literature is ancient and far from incidental. To keep track of goods shipped and received, accountants invented writing, but priests soon took it in hand. The earliest written language, Sumerian, appears around 3100 B.C. in the form of business and administrative texts and school exercises; lists of gods and kings, however, occur early. Sumerian texts from the second millennium before Christ include the range of religious literature to be found also in the Jewish Old Testament—creation myths, epics about early kings, lamentations, hymns, and proverbs.

## A BRIEF HISTORY
## OF THE RELIGIOUS EPIC

### Gilgamesh

The best-known Sumerian epic, and the world's most ancient work of enduring literature, is the story of Gilgamesh. Gilgamesh was, in Sumerian tradition, an early ruler of the city-state of Uruk, the builder of the city's mighty walls. Not only to the Sumerians but to the Assyrians and Babylonians, who absorbed the language and civilization of Sumer, Gilgamesh was both a hero-king and a god, worshipped as a deity of the underworld. Figurines in his image have been found in the tombs of the Sumerian dead. His story existed in a number of versions; though some fragments go back to the late third millennium B.C., the epic has descended to posterity primarily in the form of twelve broken tablets in the Akkadian language of Babylonia, from the seventh century B.C.

The story, in its emphasis on male love and the fear of death, seems surprisingly modern and secular. It deals with, in order, the taming of a wild man, Enkidu, by a temple prostitute, Shamhat; the intense love that springs up between Enkidu and King Gilgamesh after a combat between the two, which Gilgamesh wins; their journey together to slay a forest monster, Huwawa; Gilgamesh's rejection of an offer of marriage from Ishtar, the goddess of love; Enkidu's death; Gilgamesh's inconsolable mourning and his journey to visit Utnapishtim, the sole survivor of the Babylonian flood, who tells Gilgamesh how to avoid death with a magic plant, which a serpent steals from him. The Babylonian tablets end with a grim report from Enkidu on conditions in the underworld.

The tale is unclear at many points and certainly disjointed. What we may observe about it, as typical of early literature, is (1) the inclusion of fabulous elements from a credulous cosmology that populated the world with spirits and divine emissaries; (2) the ambiguous nature of the hero, whose elevation to the status of king falls well short of the tranquil well-being of the deathless gods; (3) the metaphysical nature of the hero's quest, as he explores a hostile, inhuman, and confusing world. His is the poignance of being "two-thirds a god, one-third a man, the king."[1] A hero, it could be generalized, is a mortal on the way to becoming a god; outside the bounds of the story, in Sumerian religion, Gilgamesh has become a god, but within the story he suffers doubt, fear, and loss. He seeks an answer to the appalling mystery of personal death. His anguish and vulnerability arouse empathy in us still, but to the teller's audience and to the scribes who committed the tale to writing, his significance derived from his legendary kingship, his divine antecedents (his father was a mortal but his mother was the goddess Ninsun), and his larger-than-human status.

The fortunes of royalty primarily concern the bard, for, by a basic term of the archaic social contract, the king's vitality determines that of the tribe or state. The monarch's health includes our own. In a number of societies studied by anthropology, the king must die, as the year dies, so that the world can be renewed; a sickly king is put to death, rather than being allowed to drag his kingdom down into unhealth with him. A trace of such magical thinking remains in the morbid fascination the British public expresses toward its royalty, especially the morally suspect Prince Charles, and in the relatively recent withholding from the American public the extent of President Roosevelt's and President Kennedy's physical infirmities. The tales of kings, even their mere names in a chronological list, deliver vital information to the present moment. Literature, in its first oral forms, acquaints the listeners with their collective case history.

What, we might wonder, about Gilgamesh made him the most popular of his culture's heroes? The surviving literature holds no more than clues. He built the protective walls of Uruk and attempted to solve the problem of death; though he failed to retain the magic herb of immortality, this attempt was also, construably, protective. Like the suffering King of the Jews centuries later, he shouldered death on mankind's behalf. More murkily, in the fragments that remain, the hero on several occasions spurned seduction by the feminine principle, manifested by Ishtar and Siduri: he held fast to the ideal of masculine comradeship and patriarchal purity against, it may be, representatives of an older matriarchal order. He enacted the warrior's necessary desertion of the nurturing mother to join the father's perilous world. Gilgamesh is seen, in our glimpse of him, as a rebel against nature, a seeker after the supernatural.

### Middle Eastern and Eastern Literature

As civilizations arose on the planet, they generated writings of pervasively religious character. The *Egyptian Book of the Dead,* the collective name given to a fund of charms, spells, and formulas to be used by the deceased in their passage to the afterworld, contains items as old as the earliest anecdotes of Gilgamesh. Although—as visitors to the Nile know—images and inscriptions devoted to the deities are omnipresent on the walls of temples, tombs, and funerary stelae, few complete mythic narratives emerge from the Egyptian ritual texts and devotional poems; the Greek historian Plutarch is the source of the famous legend of Isis and Osiris.

In India, Sanskrit literature begins, in about 1500 B.C., with the Vedas—hymns to the gods of the invading Aryan peoples, employed in the liturgy of these invaders' religious ceremonies. As Sanskrit over the next millennium became a purely literary language employed by an educated elite, two immense national epics were spawned: the *Mahabharata* and the *Ramayana.* These sprawling accounts of dynastic struggles abound in fantastic and religious elements. The fraternal heroes of the *Ramayana* collectively compose the seventh avatar of the Hindu god Vishnu, and the *Mahabharata* contains one of the world's great religious texts, known as the Bhagavad Gita (The Song of God), preached on the eve of battle by Vishnu's divine incarnation, Lord Krishna.

In China, the *I Ching* dates from the twelfth century before Christ, and the published sayings of Lao-tzu and the *Analects* of Confucius from the sixth.

## Homerian Epics
### The Iliad *and* The Odyssey

The point needs no belaboring: creation myths, hymns to divinity, liturgical formulas, spells, charms, and essays in theosophic wisdom compose much of each culture's early literature. What can easily be overlooked or minimized, however, is the supernatural ingredient in the two Homeric epics, the *Iliad* and the *Odyssey*, which form the fountainhead of Western humanism. The events around which accumulated the legends of the Trojan War occurred in the vicinity of 1200 B.C.; the Homeric telling of them was written down four to five centuries later. Homer—to give the authors of the epics a single name—was dealing with a world that was, to him, archaic. His treatment of the gods is sometimes lighthearted, and he was criticized by Renaissance critics as—compared to the Roman Virgil—irreverent.

Yet we are not allowed to forget that the Trojan War was an event determined in the sky. Eris, the goddess of discord, was excluded from the nuptials of Peleus and Thetis and takes her revenge by throwing into the festivities a golden apple inscribed, "For the fairest." Hera, Aphrodite, and Athena all claim the prize and ask Zeus to adjudicate. He throws the decision to a mortal, Paris, son of Priam, king of Troy, who awards the prize to Aphrodite on her promise of giving him for his wife the fairest woman on earth. This is Helen, the wife of King Menelaus of Sparta; Paris, as a guest in Menelaus's palace, persuades Helen to elope with him. Menelaus and his brother Agamemnon, king of Mycenae, organize a vast Greek invasion fleet to reclaim Helen, and the Trojan War has begun.

The launch of the fleet is delayed by another affront to a female divinity. Agamemnon has slain a stag sacred to Artemis, and she denies a favoring wind and inflicts pestilence on the lingering troops until Agamemnon sacrifices to her his daughter Iphigenia. The subsequent fortunes of war are repeatedly influenced by the sympathies of the gods: Poseidon, the god of the sea, and the slighted goddesses Hera and Athena favor the Greeks; Aphrodite and her lover Ares, the god of war, favor the Trojans; Zeus and Apollo are uneasily neutral.

Homer assumes his audience to be acquainted with this theological context. The *Iliad* opens by relating how Agamemnon, in taking as a spoil of war the daughter of Chryses, the priest of Apollo, has offended this god. Yielding up his fair captive, Agamemnon replaces her with another, Briseis, who had belonged to Achilles. Achilles, furious, withdraws from the war and remains in his tents. Achilles's anger and his final triumphant reënlistment in the Greek cause, which brings about the death of Hector, the son of King Priam and the leader of the Trojan forces, form the basic curve of action—occupying a mere forty days—of this saga of Bronze Age war. *The Iliad* ends when the semidivine Achilles (the son of King Peleus and the sea nymph Thetis), in bowing to Priam's plea that he give decent burial to Hector's corpse, restores himself to the sacralized order of noble civility. As if to a kind of father, Achilles tells the aged Priam:

> I myself am minded
> to give Hector back to you. A messenger came to me from Zeus, my
> mother, she who bore me, the daughter of the sea's ancient. I know you,
> Priam, in my heart, and it does not escape me that some god led you to the
> running ships of the Achaians.[2]

The *Odyssey* more marvellously makes us feel the enveloping religious pressures. Odysseus wanders through a Mediterranean populated by gods and the offspring of gods: Scylla, Charybdis, Aeolus, Polyphemus, Calypso, and Circe all have their divine pedigrees and prerogatives. Aeolus controls the winds, and Circe is a sorceress who turns men into swine and directs Odysseus to Hades, the underworld, where he interviews a host of specters, including his own mother and a number of his companions-at-arms at the seige of Troy, now among the dead. The animosity of the sea god, Poseidon, repeatedly delays Odysseus's return home, which is achieved only with the help of his patroness, the goddess Athena. When he at last arrives in Ithaca after his ten years of tortuous travel, she greets him in the disguise of a young shepherd; when he tells her a string of lies about how he came to these shores, she at last laughs in affectionate delight and, revealing herself in the form of a tall and radiant woman, caresses him and fondly exclaims. "What a wonderful liar you are, indeed!"[3] She goes on:

> Any man, or even any God, who would keep pace with your all-round
> craftiness must needs be a canny dealer and sharp-practised. O plausible,
> various, cozening wretch, can you not even in your native place let be these
> crooked and shifty words which so delight the recesses of your mind?
> Enough of such speaking in character between us two past-masters of these
> tricks of trade—you, the cunningest mortal to wheedle or blandish, and me,
> famed above other Gods for knavish wiles. And yet you failed to recognize
> in me the daughter of Zeus, Pallas Athene, your stand-by and protection
> throughout your toils![4]

Such tender teasing and gleeful collusion approach love between a goddess and her pet mortal. Swathing him in mist, coaching his wife, Penelope, and darting here and there in disguise, Athena engineers the hero's slaughter of his wife's suitors and his final return to the connubial bed. For all the fearful carnage that accompanies his return and the loss of all his shipmates on the way, the *Odyssey* is, in its happy outcome, a comedy, demonstrating how a man's native wits and courage, reinforced by a supernatural guardian who is like a shadow-self, can win out against all peril. Civil and domestic order are restored.

The *Odyssey*'s mingled world of gods and men is a benign vision wherein nature's harsh imperatives and men's fragile aspirations achieve a pact; the gods personify and humanize the natural forces amid which we are otherwise helpless and negligible. Nature is a live field of latent supernature. The *Odyssey*'s hero, placed in this ambiguous field, achieves not merely the transient triumphs of a Gilgamesh but a basis for personal happiness.

## GREEK TRAGEDY AND THE
## COURSE OF RELIGION IN DRAMA

The three great tragic dramatists of Athens in the fifth century B.C.—Aeschylus, Sophocles, and Europides—together trace a decline in the reality of the gods. Greek drama began as ritual devoted to a latecomer among the gods, Dionysus, god of fertility and wine. A god of the poor, he consoled them with violent and ecstatic rites. As part of the god's festivals, dithyrambic (irregular and rapturous) hymns were sung by a chorus, with improvisations by a leader from the chorus.

### Aeschylus

Aeschylus is credited by Aristotle with adding a second actor and thereby inventing drama. His dramas remain simple in structure, with the chorus still prominent and the action close to theological debate. *Prometheus Bound*, for instance, portrays the stationary sufferings of the Titan who, amid Zeus's successful overthrow of the Titans, the previous gods, gave mankind fire; for his punishment, he is nailed and shackled to a rock in the Caucasus Mountains, where eagles tear at his liver. This punitive Zeus is not the beneficent, if lecherous and distractable, god of Homer, but a cruel tyrant. "The mind of Zeus is hard to soften with prayer, and every ruler is harsh whose rule is new," Prometheus is told, and "only Zeus is free."[5] Yet Zeus is himself subject to the rulings of the Fates, and Prometheus foresees his own eventual release.

The question of justice, in a universe ruled by a pantheon seemingly arbitrary and ruthless in its dispensations, bears upon such legendary situations as that of the family of Agamemnon, who was murdered on his return from Troy by his wife, Clytemnestra, and her lover, Aegisthus. Plays on the topic were written by Sophocles and Euripides, and by Aeschylus in his trilogy called the *Oresteia*. As the trilogy proceeds, Orestes, Agamemnon's son, returns from the safety of exile and, with his sister Electra's connivance and encouragement, kills his mother and her lover in revenge for his father's murder.

But matricide is a heinous crime, and a sequence of wrongs reaching into the past makes simple moral judgments impossible. Clytemnestra argues in her own defense that Agamemnon sacrificed their daughter, Iphigenia, to further the invasion of Troy, and furthermore he brought a concubine, Priam's daughter Cassandra, home from Troy. Aegisthus for justification can look back to the unspeakable crime committed against his father, Thyestes, by Thyestes's brother Atreus, who, in the guise of hospitality, fed him his own slaughtered children. Agamemnon and Menelaus are the sons of Atreus, whose royal house is rightfully cursed: "A house that God hates," Cassandra says, "guilty within of kindred bloodshed."[6]

Aeschylus's chorus, contemplating this tangle of atrocity and suffering, offers the consolation that "Zeus . . . has laid it down that wisdom comes along through suffering. . . . From the gods who sit in grandeur, grace comes somehow violent." The triology as a whole concludes the matter within the framework of belief, as Athena persuades the Furies to give up their pursuit of the guilt-haunted Orestes and to accept, in return, shrines and worship within Athens. Thus the darkest and most nebulous of the gods are brought within a religious system; Athena assures the Furies, "No household shall be prosperous without your will."[7] The bloody workings of taboo and revenge morality achieve a precarious truce with civic light and reason.

### Sophocles

Sophocles, perhaps thirty years younger than Aeschylus, introduced a third actor into drama and diminished choral expostulation to make room for more interplay among characters. In recasting the myths of the heroic age, he retained the supernatural framework with an appearance of conviction. His *Antigone* concludes, "There is no happiness where there is no wisdom; no wisdom but in submission to the gods."[8] Indeed, of the three great Attic playwrights, he provides the most vivid sense of workaday Greek religion—its dank and gloomy oracular caves, its decaying rustic shrines, its bloody sacrifices and desperate auguries, its ghosts and prophetic dreams, its sense of purity and pollution, its ritualized libations and lavations, its intensely localized sacred spaces rimmed with uncertainty and terror.

The gods in Sophocles, however, come in for some severe indictments. The hero of *Philoctetes* asks, "How can I praise, when praising Heaven I find the Gods are bad?"[9] *The Women of Trachis* ends this way:

> You see how little compassion the Gods
> have shown in all that's happened; they
> who are called our fathers, who begot us,
> can look upon such suffering. . . .
> You have seen a terrible death
> and agonies, many and strange, and there is
> nothing here which is not Zeus.[10]

Yet Sophocles does not condemn the divine dispensations. Two of his last plays, *Oedipus at Colonus* and *Philoctotes,* show the redemption of cursed social outcasts and imply a benign Providence. His version of the Orestes story, *Electra*—even though a character in it perceives that "there are times when even justice brings harm with it"[11]—proceeds inexorably to its merciless denouement. Neither Electra nor Orestes has any second thoughts or reservations; they force Aegisthus to look upon the face of his slain mistress, and Orestes marches him off, vowing,

> I must take care that death
> is bitter for you. Justice shall be taken
> directly on all who act above the law—
> justice by killing. So we would have less villains.

The chorus appears to agree, proclaiming that the house of Atreus has come at last "to freedom, perfected by this day's deed."

### Euripides

If Sophocles accepts the creaking divine framework as the necessary adjunct to human heroism, Euripides, a mere ten years younger, rebels and presents religion as a nightmare. In his nineteen surviving plays, a roiling mass of barbaric violence borrowed from the old legends is intensified and warped by human psychology, portrayed with an insight and depth that remain strikingly modern. Two of his best plays, *Hippolytus* and *The Bacchae,* show gods—Aphrodite, Dionysus—ruthlessly destroying mortals—Hippolytus, Pentheus—who fail to honor them. "O, if only men might be a curse to Gods!"[12] the dying Hippolytus exclaims. The chorus bewails the loss of faith bred by "the inflexible hearts of the Gods":

> The care of God for us is a great thing,
> if a man believe it at heart:
> it plucks the burden of sorrow from him.
> So I have a secret hope

> of someone, a God, who is wise and plans;
> but my hopes grow dim when I see
> the deeds of men and their destinies.

The religious impulse is poignantly analyzed:

> The life of man entire is misery:
> he finds no resting place, no haven from calamity.
> But something other dearer still than life
> the darkness hides and mist encompasses;
> we are proved luckless lovers of this thing
> that glitters in the underworld.

Or, as the love-crazed queen Phaedra observes, "I think that our lives are worse than the mind's quality would warrant." In the drama of Euripides, internal demons have replaced deified Furies.

Insofar as the gods of Greek religion personify natural forces, they cannot be exonerated from these forces' cruelty. The tender collusion between Odysseus and Athena is not, as it were, a repeatable experiment. As often as not, the gods destroy us. Euripides's retelling of the Orestes story in the two plays *Orestes* and *Electra* feverishly ripples and ramps through the permutations of a vengeful matricide demanded by Apollo and furiously urged by a sexually deprived princess kept in rags by a wicked stepfather. "I accuse Apollo. The god is the guilty one,"[13] Orestes cries in the wake of his murder of his mother. In a wryer mood, when Menelaus asks why Apollo has not helped him in his misery, Orestes blasphemously jests, "Oh, he will. In his own good time, of course. Gods are slow by nature." The whole stately "matter of Troy" comes close to parody in its enactment by earthbound neurotics; Menelaus and Helen are serenely selfish and diffident in the wake of the vast slaughter on their behalf. The majestically fraught tower of revenge murders, descending to tormented Orestes from Atreus and even Atreus's grandfather Tantalus, loses its barbaric seriousness with the anachronistic announcement that judicial courts exist: "Legal action, not murder. That was the course to take."

Relieved of reverence, the author achieves all sorts of startling and lurid turns. For the first time in the evolution of Greek drama, we become aware of the playwright as a personality—devastating in his insights, careless in his construction, rather cynically sensational in his effects. While he has no use for the gods as moral guides, Euripides has much theatrical use for them; the device of the *deus ex machina,* wherein a god is lowered by machinery to terminate an otherwise unresolvable plot, is frequently and shamelessly exploited. In two plays, *Helen* and *Iphigenia in Tauris,* heroines of the Trojan tragedy are implausibly rescued from their old roles to star in a newly invented genre, romantic comedy. In winning through to the purely human, with the old religious figurations shrunk to private devils, Europides enters into the problematical freedom of modern authorship.

For, without the gods, what significance, what direction, do human adventures have? The cowering, wavering, haunted, brutal, frantically scheming Orestes of Euripides is no hero in the old sense, no king on his way to becoming a god. There is no longer an upward arrow in human affairs, only the lateral arrows between lovers and haters, mates and rivals, hunters and the hunted. Orestes displays a vivid variety of characteristics but not the God-sent grandeur of an ancestor, a prototype. In *Electra*, he states the muddled case:

> Alas,
> we look for good on earth and cannot recognize it
> when met, since all our human heritage runs mongrel. . . .
> How then can man distinguish man, what test can he use?[14]

Religion created Greek literature and died within its embrace. In the wide regions, now Christian and Islamic, where Zeus/Jupiter and his fellow gods were for two thousand years the objects of joyful celebration and fervent prayer, the temples are empty ruins, their incomparable beauty testifying to an idealism paradoxically sponsored by an erratic, immoral, dimly seen pantheon. The gods and heroes live only in literature, where they continue to inspire retellings of their stories as various as Eugene O'Neill's *Mourning Becomes Electra*, James Joyce's *Ulysses*, and the recent remarkable, synoptic *Marriage of Cadmus and Harmony* by the Italian Roberto Calasso. They haunt us in paintings and children's books, in manufacturer's trademarks and Freudian terminology.

## BIBLICAL LITERATURE AND HEROES

The literature of the Judeo-Christian religion still speaks for itself, though intimate familiarity with the Bible diminishes from generation to generation. In my childhood home, which was of average Protestant piety, biblical characters were as familiar, and as frequently mentioned, as relatives on a distant farm. Elijah's chariot of fire and Joseph's coat of many colors brightened our stock of mental imagery; adjurations such as Christ's parable of the talents and Paul's advice on the position of women stimulated our thoughts and familial conversation, in a household that included my maternal grandparents.

The biblical hero is typically a stalwart of faith: Abraham, Moses, Daniel, David, Job, Jesus Christ, Peter, and Paul keep faith with God. At the heart of the Judaic and Christian religions, respectively, Abraham's willingness to sacrifice his son Isaac at God's behest and God's willingness to let God's Son Jesus be crucified echo the sinister familial murders of Greek legend, but, in both cases, with a redemptive intercession from above. In the thousand years between the emperor Constantine's public conversion and Dante's composition of *The Divine Comedy*, the Christian faith ruled the mind of Europe, and the hero of faith took forms as various as El Cid and Saint Francis.

## FAITH AND SKEPTICISM IN LITERATURE

When a hero was created whose faith was perceived as excessive and misplaced, however lovably and entertainingly so, a new era, if not an absolutely post-Christian era, began. Such a hero was the protagonist of Miguel de Cervantes's *Don Quixote*, published in two parts in 1605 and 1615 and commonly considered the first modern novel. For the deluded don, as he acts out the visions of knightly romances, his faith wins only a series of beatings, though it also enables him, one would say, to sustain the beatings buoyantly.

A contemporary of Cervantes, William Shakespeare, born a generation later but arrived at greatness somewhat earlier than the Spanish author, is a playwright who reminds us of Euripides in his wealth of invention and psychological insight, in the sense he gives of a near-chaotic, feverish overflow, and in his apparent skeptical removal from the religious creed of his time. God is invoked, ghosts appear, and curses are laid, but the events in Shakespeare seem purely human, in all the contradictory richness of which human nature is capable—a torrential spillage of self-importance beneath an enigmatic heaven. At times, as with Euripides, Shakespeare seems overwhelmed by disgust at the human spectacle, so the drama becomes ineffective: for example, *Timon of Athens*, *Troilus and Cressida*, and the immense *King Lear*, have an almost unbearable piling on of calamities. The first two have Greek milieus, and the third contains these Euripidean lines:

> As flies to wanton boys, are we to the gods;
> They kill us for their sport.

Not that skepticism and pessimism are Shakespeare's only notes, or that he necessarily expressed them in his personal life. In an age when atheism was punishable by death, he was probably conventionally observant,[15] just as he was, from the little we know about him, a property-acquiring bourgeois and a good team member of the Globe theatrical company. A writer's professed religious convictions do not necessarily control the religious content of his writing. Jonathan Swift's being an Anglican priest did not mute the savage indignation of his satire, nor did Alexander Pope's being a Roman Catholic prevent him from being, in his poetry, the proponent of a bloodless and melioristic Deism. Milton's announced determination in *Paradise Lost*, "to assert eternal Providence, and justify the ways of God to Men" did not prevent him from glorifying God's enemy Lucifer, this religious epic's most vivid and eloquent character.

## MODERN WRITERS AND BELIEF

The twentieth-century reader will find little orthodox comfort in the fiction of such professedly Christian novelists as Graham Greene, Muriel Spark, Evelyn Waugh, Flannery O'Connor, François Mauriac, and Georges Bernanos. It is a bleak world they display, often comic in its desolation and inconsequence—not the world of arrived faith and its consolations but the fallen world whose emptiness, perhaps, led them to make the leap of faith. And given the limits of hagiography (biography of saints) and the ineffability of God, isn't that all a novelist can be expected to deliver—*this* world, in its pain and mangled glory?

Graham Greene, writing as a critic, detected a divide between this century and the preceding one:

> After the death of Henry James a disaster overtook the English novel. . . . For with the death of James the religious sense was lost to the English novel, and with the religious sense went the sense of the importance of the human act. . . . Even in one of the most materialist of our great novelists—in Trollope— we are aware of another world against which the actions of the characters are thrown into relief.[16]

James was not himself a believer, but he retained an instinctive religiosity that gave his society novels the weight and interest of moral drama. The English Victorians, speaking broadly, wrote out of a consensual Christian sensibility that supports not only Charles Dickens's extremes of good and evil characters and his sentimentally providential endings but George Eliot's more agnostic investigations of human motive and fulfillment.

The modernists, confronted with the rubble left when Darwin, Marx, Freud, and the higher criticism[17] shook Victorian Christianity to its foundations, proposed to make a religion of art itself. The Jesuit-trained James Joyce created, on the outline of the *Odyssey*, a giant novel of the formless quotidian, as packed with arcane references and rigorous schematics as any ancient book of spells. Marcel Proust, isolated and enfeebled, poured his life into a verbal cathedral of remembrance. The excesses and sufferings of Proust and Franz Kafka and Arthur Rimbaud resembled the self-mortifications of saints. The idea of the writer as priest—performer of marvels and supplier of values—went back to Flaubert and perhaps, in essence, to Wordsworth, who presented his religious perceptions in a secular context of personal sensation. The American poet Wallace Stevens expressed it bluntly: "In an age of disbelief, or, what is the same thing, in a time that is largely humanistic, in one sense or another, it is for the poet to supply the satisfactions of belief, in his measure and in his style."[18]

The satisfactions of belief, however, stem from assertions about the nature of reality rather than matters of measure and style. "To see the gods dispelled in midair and dissolve like clouds is one of the great human experiences," Stevens goes on to say, and, with passionate subtlety, "It is important to believe that the visible is the equivalent of the invisible."[19] It is important, but difficult. Such an equivalence is like that expressed in the Hindu *yuganaddha*—"a state of unity obtained by perceiving the identity of the phenomenal world and the absolute."[20] This is metaphysical sleight of hand, equating the natural with the supernatural.

Yet it remains curiously true that the literary artist, to achieve full effectiveness, must assume a religious state of mind—a state that looks beyond worldly standards of success and failure. A mood of exaltation should possess the language, a vatic tension and rapture. Even grimly tragic views, like those of *King Lear,* Samuel Beckett, Céline, and Herman Melville, must be expounded with an air of celebration. The work of literary art springs from the world and adheres to it but is distinctly different in substance. We enter it, as readers, expecting an intensity and shapeliness absent in our lives. A realm above nature is posed—a supernatural, in short. Aesthetic pleasure, like religious ecstasy, is a matter of inwardness, elevation, and escape.

## NOTES

1. David Ferry, trans. *The Epic of Gilgamesh* (New York: Farrar, Straus & Giroux, 1992).

2. Homer, *The Iliad,* trans. Richmond Lattimore (Chicago: University of Chicago Press, 1951).

3. Robert Graves, *The Greek Myths,* vol. 2 (Baltimore: Penguin Books, 1955).

4. Homer, *The Odyssey,* prose translation by T. E. Lawrence (New York: Galaxy, 1956).

5. "Prometheus Bound," trans. David Grene, in *Aeschylus,* vol. 1 of *The Complete Greek Tragedies,* ed. David Grene and Richmond Lattimore (Chicago: University of Chicago Press, 1959).

6. "Agamemnon," trans. Richmond Lattimore, in vol. 1 of *The Complete Greek Tragedies.*

7. Aeschylus, "The Eumenides," trans. Richmond Lattimore, in vol. 1 of *The Complete Greek Tragedies.*

8. Sophocles, "Antigone," trans. Dudley Fitts and Robert Fitzgerald, in *Sophocles,* vol. 2 of *The Complete Greek Tragedies,* ed. David Grene and Richmond Lattimore (Chicago: University of Chicago Press, 1959).

9. Sophocles, "Philocletes," trans. David Grene, in vol. 2 of *The Complete Greek Tragedies.*

10. Sophocles, "The Women of Trachis," trans. Michael Jameson, in vol. 2 of *The Complete Greek Tragedies.*

11. Sophocles, "Electra," trans. David Grene, in vol. 2 of *The Complete Greek Tragedies.*

12. Euripides, "Hippolytus," trans. David Grene, in *Euripides,* vol. 3 of *The Complete Greek Tragedies,* eds. David Grene and Richmond Lattimore (Chicago: University of Chicago Press, 1959).

13. Euripides, "Orestes," trans. William Arrowsmith, in *Euripides,* vol. 4 of *The Complete Greek Tragedies,* eds. David Grene and Richmond Lattimore (Chicago: University of Chicago Press, 1959).

14. Euripides, "Electra," trans. Emily Townsend Vermeule, in vol. 4 of *The Complete Greek Tragedies.*

15. As an Anglican, presumably—though G. K. Chesterton expressed the fond belief that Shakespeare was a Roman Catholic.

16. Graham Green, "François Mauriac," in *Collected Essays* (New York: Viking Press, 1983).

17. As opposed to the lower criticism, which sought to establish merely correct biblical texts through comparison of manuscripts, the higher criticism investigated the Bible with the same methods used on secular texts, seeking to establish authenticity, time of authorship, chronology, and sources, using relevant data from linguistics and archaeology. The scholars, French and Ger-

man, scandalized many Christians by taking such a scientific approach to writings long thought to have been literally dictated by God.

18. Wallace Stevens, "Two or Three Ideas," from *Opus Posthumous* (New York: Alfred A. Knopf, 1969).

19. Ibid.

20. Mircea Eliade, *A History of Religious Ideas*, vol. 2, trans. Willard R. Trask (Chicago: University of Chicago Press, 1982).

## STUDY QUESTIONS

1. What are three characteristics of the Sumerian story of Gilgamesh that reflect typical early literature? Does contemporary literature reflect similar characteristics? If not, how do you perceive it to be "different"?

2. Take three of the ancient texts described by the author and list two religious dimensions of each. Do you see a commonality of interests and questions found in each text? Be specific.

3. Is literature universally religious, according to Updike? Explain your answer and give examples.

4. What characteristic(s) tend to identify the biblical hero from the Jewish and Christian traditions? Is it faith? redemption? both? Explain your answers.

5. What two religious dimensions of human existence is the novelist expected "to deliver" in his or her work, according to Updike? Do you agree? Why? Why not?

6. Why, according to Updike, must the literary artist assume a "religious state of mind" to be effective? Do you agree with his observation? Explain your answer.

# 16

## MALCOLM DAVID ECKEL

# Buddhist Approaches to Death

I could begin by saying that one of the most important things Buddhists do is die, but that simple fact hardly sets them apart from anyone else. It is better to say that Buddhists have a tradition in which they deliberately and thoughtfully *prepare* to die, and that they turn to the resources of their faith not only to understand and deal with the approach of their own death but to understand and deal with the death of someone who is close to them. How, then, do Buddhists prepare for the experience of death?

The answer to this question takes us back to the very beginning of the Buddhist tradition, to the story of Siddhartha Gautama, the man whom Buddhists revere as the Buddha, or "Awakened One," and the founder of the tradition. Siddhartha Gautama was born in the sixth century B.C. to a princely family, in a region of India that is now located in the foothills of southern Nepal. According to the stories Buddhists tell about the Buddha, the young Siddhartha Gautama was raised in luxury and insulated from the ordinary sufferings of life. He was married, had a child, and then, in his early thirties, saw four troubling sights: a sick man, an old man, a corpse, and a wandering monk. The sights left him shaken. He realized that life was fleeting and full of pain, and he decided to become a wandering monk to find a solution to the problems of suffering, old age, and death. In an event that is reenacted today whenever a Buddhist man or woman becomes a monk or a nun, Siddhartha Gautama left the palace, gave up his possessions, and began a life of strict self-discipline and meditation. The solution he was looking for came to him in a moment that is called his "awakening" (*bodhi*)—the event that made him Buddha—and he spent the rest of his life teaching, consoling, and presiding over a growing band of disciples who had chosen to follow his example.

What kind of solution did the Buddha discover? To answer this question in the style of the Buddha requires a look at the traditional Indian understanding of death. For several centuries before the time of the Buddha, Indian people had come to think that death was not something that happened once and for all. It was something that happened again and again, as a person died and was reborn in a process known as *samsara*, or the "wandering" of a soul from one life to the next. In the West we are accustomed to calling this process "reincarnation" or "rebirth," but it is more faithful to the Indian tradition to call it "redeath." The challenge for a sage such as the Buddha was to find a way through the forest of *samsara* so that a person could die in peace and never be reborn. The "way" that the Buddha found is called the Noble Eightfold Path (consisting of right understanding, right thought, right speech, right action, right livelihood, right effort, right mindfulness, and right concentration), and the goal of the path is Nirvana, the cessation of suffering and desire and the blissful termination of the process of rebirth.

These formulaic phrases, however, do little justice to the depth and significance of Buddhist approaches to death. Like other religious traditions, Buddhism brings these concepts to life through the art of storytelling. One of the most beloved stories about death is the story of an encounter between the Buddha and a woman who had lost her only son. The woman was deeply distraught and came to the Buddha, convinced that he had extraordinary power, to ask that he bring her son back to life. The Buddha told her that he would agree to do what she asked if she could bring him a seed from a household in her village that had not suffered a similar loss. She went from house to house, heard one story after another of family members who had died, and came back to the Buddha to tell him that all had suffered losses similar to hers. She said something else as well: she realized in her sad journey from house to house that death was part of life and that even her grievous loss was something that could be accepted and allowed to pass away. She thanked the Buddha for his lesson and went on her way.

This attitude of wise acceptance has been a crucial part of the Buddhist approach to death from ancient times and has colored the way Buddhists look not just at the final moments of their lives but at the flow of life itself. I once made the mistake (fairly common among beginning students of Buddhism) of asking a Buddhist monk, who was said to be the reincarnation of an important Tibetan lama, whether he could tell me about his previous lives. He laughed and said that he could hardly remember what he had eaten for breakfast, let alone what he had experienced in a previous life. I took his comment to be more than a graceful exit from an embarrassing question. It typified for me a deep-seated Buddhist respect for the flow and changeableness of life. Buddhists sometimes say that it is no more difficult to believe that a person can die and be reborn in another body than to believe that I can wake up in the morning and think I am the "same" person who went to sleep the night before. The process of life—the evolution of each personality—is a process of constant change. What I was yesterday is gone. What I am now is just a flickering moment in the process of becoming something new. Life itself is a process of death and rebirth. And a wise, attentive attitude toward life involves a graceful acceptance of the death in the midst of each passing moment that allows everything to become new.

## THE TIBETAN BOOK OF THE DEAD

One of the most striking Buddhist examples of a response to death that is also a meditation for the living is the text known as *The Tibetan Book of the Dead*. The text is used by Buddhists in Tibet and in the border areas of the Himalayas as a ritual guidebook, to be recited to a person who has recently died in order to help the dead person's consciousness navigate successfully through the experiences of the afterlife. To start the funeral, the family of the dead person lays out the corpse in a room that functions as the household shrine. The household altar is decorated with objects of worship that traditionally are offered before images of the Buddha. These include sacrificial cakes, bowls of water, flowers, incense, fruit, and ceremonial lamps. The monks who are commissioned to perform the funeral ceremony come to the home and set up a table with an array of ritual objects, including a bell and a symbolic thunderbolt (representing the female and male aspects of consciousness), a drum, cymbals, a bowl of rice, and a jug of water. The offerings are made to invoke the compassionate power of a variety of Buddhas, associated with different directions and forces in the cosmos, and the ritual objects are meant to serve as props in a symbolic drama that leads the consciousness of the dead person through the hazards of the afterlife and either brings it to a better rebirth or allows it to escape the process of rebirth altogether.

At the start of the funeral, which can last as long as forty-nine days, the text is recited in the presence of the corpse of the dead person. After several days, when the corpse has been removed and buried or cremated, the consciousness of the dead person is invoked and enshrined in a small diagram or picture. The rest of the ritual, with its teachings about the terrors and opportunities of the afterlife, is directed to the consciousness that is enshrined in the picture. At the end of the ritual the picture is burned to symbolize, as one interpreter explains, "a second death on a higher, ritual plane, whereby the earthly death of physical decay is overcome."[1]

What kind of instruction does the text provide? It describes the intermediate state (or *bar-do*) between one life and the next as a three-stage process. Each stage presents the consciousness of the dead person with a new set of challenges and opportunities. At each stage, the consciousness runs the risk of being bewildered and falling back into a painful birth in this world, but it also has the opportunity of hearing and attending to the teaching of the text in such a way that it can avoid being reborn. (For this reason, the text is known in Tibetan as the *Bar-do Thos-grol*, or "Liberation through Hearing in the Intermediate State.") Even if consciousness fails to escape the process of rebirth completely, it can use the teaching of the text to control the location of its next birth and give itself a greater opportunity for liberation in the next life.

In the first stage, known as the *'Chi-ka'i Bar-do* (the *bar-do* of the moment of death), the consciousness of the dead person merges into a state of pure, nondualistic awareness. Consciousness is aware of no object apart from itself and glows in the fullness of its own luminosity. The text says that its instructions about this stage should begin, if possible, even before the actual moment of death:

> O son of noble family, [name], listen. . . . This mind of yours is inseparable luminosity and emptiness in the form of a great mass of light; it has no birth or death, therefore it is the buddha of Immortal Light. To recognize this is all that is necessary. When you recognize this pure nature of your mind as the buddha, looking into your own mind is resting in the buddha-mind.[2]

This instruction about the nature of the mind is supposed to be spoken to the dying person by name and should be repeated three or seven times in a clear and distinct voice. If the consciousness of the dying person recognizes this state of luminous awareness as its own nature, it becomes inseparably united with it and is freed from the necessity of rebirth.

Behind these words about the luminosity of consciousness lies a long tradition of Buddhist reflection and meditation about the nature of the mind. In one of the most basic practices of Buddhist meditation, a person sits down in a quiet place, concentrates on the movement of the breath, and allows the mind to become as still as a placid pool. When the mind has been stilled, it can recognize its own nature and free itself from desires and distractions—the desires and distractions that fill life with suffering and lead a person to be born again in this world. It was this deep sense of understanding about the nature of the mind that made Siddhartha Gautama a Buddha. *The Tibetan Book of the Dead* thus begins by speaking to the consciousness of the dying person and telling it that it is entering a state of awareness in which it, too, can become a Buddha. If it can recognize the stillness and luminosity of the mind as its own and can merge with it, it can rest in a state of "Buddha-mind" and allow the sufferings of life to pass away.

For experienced practitioners of meditation, who have learned to calm the mind, to sense its stillness, and to scrutinize its nature, these words recall a familiar experience. The text tells us that these practitioners pass beyond this experience very slowly, if they pass beyond it at all. For others, who know little about the nature of the mind and are distracted by fear and desire, consciousness quickly loses its luminosity and begins to manifest itself in forms that are both seductive and terrifying.

In the next stage of the text (known as the *Chos-nyid Bar-do*, the intermediate state that is identified with the nature of reality), the consciousness of the dead person confronts the projection of its own fears and desires in a series of Buddha images. These Buddha images appear first in a peaceful form and then in a form that is angry and threatening. The forms themselves are similar to the paintings that Tibetans use as guides for meditation and are painted on small cards to be shown to the consciousness of the dead person while the descriptions of the images are being recited from the text. At each step in the process, the recitation of the text is meant to calm the consciousness of the dead person and teach it to recognize the images as projections of itself (as if it were flashing images of itself on an invisible screen). If consciousness is able to recognize the images as manifestations of itself, it can merge with them and escape the cycle of rebirth.

The first images are of "peaceful" Buddhas, but even these peaceful images terrify the unsuspecting mind with their brightness and intensity. The text warns that each image will be accompanied by a great roar of thunder, like a thousand thunderclaps sounding simultaneously, and it says that the dead person's consciousness should remember that it has lost its physical body and the images will do it no harm.

The first image in the sequence is of the Buddha Vairocana (the Buddha who is associated with the sun). His body is white, he sits on a lion throne, he holds an eight-spoked wheel in his hand, and he embraces his female counterpart, the queen of the realm of space. From the heart of Vairocana comes a blue light, representing consciousness itself. The light is so intense that consciousness is hardly able to bear it. At the same time, consciousness becomes aware of a softer and more inviting light that comes from the realm of the gods. The text explains that consciousness will be distracted by the residues of its previous actions and will try to escape from the intense light of Vairocana. At the same time, it will be attracted toward the soft light of the gods. The text warns that this attraction has to be resisted if the consciousness wants to escape rebirth:

> Do not take pleasure in the soft white light of the gods, do not be attracted to it or yearn for it. If you are attracted to it you will wander into the realm of the gods and circle among the six kinds of existence. It is an obstacle blocking the path of liberation, so do not look at it, but feel longing for the bright blue light, and repeat this inspiration-prayer after me with intense concentration on Blessed Vairocana:
>
>> When through intense ignorance I wander in samsara,
>> on the luminous light-path of the dharmadhatu wisdom,
>> may Blessed Vairocana go before me,
>> his consort the Queen of Vajra Space behind me;
>> help me to cross the bardo's dangerous pathway
>> and bring me to the perfect buddha state.
>
> By saying this inspiration-prayer with deep devotion, he will dissolve into the rainbow light in the heart of Vairocana and his consort.[3]

If consciousness misses the opportunity to merge with Vairocana, another Buddha appears, and the process continues until all the peaceful images of the Buddha have been exhausted. Then the Buddhas begin to manifest their wrathful forms. The first of these images, the Buddha Heruka (the wrathful form of the Buddha Vairocana), has a dark red body, three heads, nine eyes, six arms, and four legs. His eyebrows are like flashes of lightning, his teeth are like copper, he laughs out loud with sounds of "a-la-la" and "ha-ha," and he sends out a loud, whistling noise that sounds like "shoo-oo." His red hair sticks straight up from his head; he wears a crown that is decorated with dried skulls and the sun and the moon; his body is wrapped in snakes; and his hands bristle with weapons. Like Vairocana, he embraces his female counterpart, the Buddha who is called "Queen of Wrath." With one of her arms she holds onto his body, and with the other she holds a skull cup full of blood to his lips. As he drinks, loud gurgling sounds come from his mouth, and flames of wisdom come from the hairs on his body. This is not a pleasant sight, and it is easy to see why consciousness would flee from a wrathful Buddha even more quickly than from the intense image of Vairocana. But each image still provides an opportunity to recognize the Buddhas as projections of consciousness, to merge with them, and to escape the cycle of rebirth.

If consciousness lets even these opportunities slip by, it enters the *Srid-pa'i Bar-do*, the state of "becoming." Here consciousness slowly turns from the challenge of escaping the cycle to the challenge of controlling and manipulating the place where it is to be reborn. Escape is still a possibility if consciousness can fix itself in a state of pure awareness and not be blown around by the winds of fear and desire, but the storms become even more intense, and the lure of reentry into the world becomes even more difficult to resist. The text says that consciousness first will try to go back into its old body and will find that the old body can no longer sustain life. Winter will have frozen it or summer will have made it rot, and relatives and friends will have buried it, burned it, or fed it to animals and birds. When it realizes it cannot go back, it will visualize new possibilities for rebirth, depending on the lingering effects of its previous actions. If it still hungers for the possessions it has left behind, it may be reborn in hell or as a hungry ghost. The text gives instructions about visualizing different locations in the physical world that will bring it back in a pleasant human birth. If it fails to follow any of the directions in the text, it may visualize a dung heap, be overwhelmed by the sweetness of its smell, and be reborn as a worm.

To understand the impact of *The Tibetan Book of the Dead,* it is important to recognize that its audience is not just the dead person's consciousness. The text also belongs to the living, to the religious specialists who recite it and to friends and relatives who listen to its recitation—to all those, in other words, who use it to ease the dead person's passage into the next life and, in the process, to ease thoughts and fears about death. The days of mourning and all the solemn rituals that accompany them give the dead person's friends and family a chance to express their grief and heal the wound that death creates in their community and their world. It is no accident that the recitation of the text ends with the burning of the picture that represents the personality of the deceased. At the end, even the image of the dead person has to be let go so that he or she can move on beyond this world and the mourners can return to their own lives.

But the connection between the ritual for the dead and the lives of the living is even more direct than this. The text does not just map the stages of the afterlife; it charts the evolution of consciousness itself, for the living as well as for the dead. The friends, family members, and ritual specialists who sit through the ceremony come face to face with their own images of the terrifying brightness of consciousness, the shadowy images of wrath and destruction that lurk beneath the bright surface of consciousness, and the alluring images of life in the world of rebirth. They have the opportunity to contemplate their fears and let them go as they learn to relax their grip on the consciousness of the person who has died. When they do this, they also come face to face with an aspect of Buddhist teaching that goes back, it seems, to the Buddha himself. For Buddhists, death is a part of life. And it is a part of life not just at the moment when the body ceases to function and consciousness begins its journey into the afterlife but in the flow of life itself. To allow each moment to "die" while it makes itself new is to experience some of the stillness and luminosity that *The Tibetan Book of the Dead* directs to the living as well as the dead.

## THE PURE LAND TRADITION

While it may be one of the most elaborate, the ritual associated with *The Tibetan Book of the Dead* is by no means the only way Buddhists have attempted to contemplate and guide the process of death and rebirth. Chinese and Japanese Buddhists have developed a lively tradition of meditation on the figure of Amitabha Buddha (called Amida Buddha in Japan) at the moment of death. According to this tradition, any person who hears the name of Buddha Amitabha (Infinite Light) or Amitayus (Infinite Life) and meditates on it at the moment of death will be visited by Amitabha and carried away to a heavenly realm that is referred to in the texts as "the Pleasurable" (*Sukhavati*) and is commonly known as "the Pure Land." This tradition stems from a group of Indian Buddhist texts that describe the process that led to Amitabha Buddha's awakening. Before his awakening, Amitabha (or, more literally, the figure who was to become Amitabha at the moment of his awakening) made the following promise:

> If those beings who have directed their thoughts toward the highest perfect knowledge in other worlds, and who, after having heard my name, when I have reached awakening, have meditated on me with serene thoughts; if at the moment of their death, after having approached them, surrounded by an assembly of monks, I should not stand before them, worshipped by them, so their thoughts may not be troubled, then may I not obtain the highest perfect knowledge.[4]

Another text specifies that the visit of Amitabha to the dying person's bedside will result in rebirth in the Pure Land.

It seems that this Buddhist practice of invoking a deity at the moment of death was widespread in India in the first few centuries A.D. We read, for example, in the Bhagavad Gita (a Hindu text that was compiled in this period) of similar promises that are attributed to the Hindu god Krishna. Krishna says that all who remember him at the moment of death will certainly come to him as they make their passage into the afterlife. In both the Hindu and Buddhist traditions, the word *remember (smrti* or *anusmrti)* came to refer to a meditation practice that might best be called an act of visualization. Unlike the meditation that seeks to calm the mind and empty it of all images, this act of remembrance is meant to fill the mind with an intense and absorbing image of the heavenly being with whom the believer hopes to be united after death. And it is not necessary in the Indian tradition even to wait for the moment of death. There are accounts of Buddhist monks and devotees who fasted and prayed in the midst of this life in the hope of being giving a vision of the heavenly world. We even hear of travelers who fell into the hands of pirates and robbers and managed to escape from danger by visualizing a journey into the heavenly world.

The practice of meditating on the figure of Amitabha at the moment of death took on new life when the Buddhist tradition was transmitted from India into China. A Chinese monk by the name of Shan-tao, who played an important role in the development of Pure Land Buddhism in Asia, told his monks to attend carefully to reports of visions at the moment of death. Accounts of these visions sometimes had to do with the believers' evil deeds and the punishment they expected in a future life. (In such cases, Shan-tao advised his monks to listen to the dying believers' confessions so that they could be freed from the consequences of their sins.) Some visions had to do with the scene believers hoped to see in the throne room of Amitabha when they were transported to the Pure Land. The Japanese tradition that grew from these Pure Land beliefs in China contains stories of what we would call "near-death" experiences, in which someone appears to die and then returns miraculously to life. Often these travelers spoke of a strange journey into the afterlife, where they crossed a river, then visited a golden palace, only to turn back, retrace their journey, and return to this world.

One of the most important components in Pure Land Buddhism as it is practiced today in Japan and America (notably by the Buddhist Churches of America) is the chanting of Amitabha Buddha's name. This practice is called the *nembutsu* and consists of repeating the phrase *Namu Amida Butsu* (Homage to Amitabha Buddha). The scriptural accounts of Amitabha's vows stress the need to hear Amitabha's name and chant it with faith. So the remembrance of the Buddha that lies at the heart of Pure Land Buddhism does not need to be thought of as visualization in an elaborate or technical sense. It can simply be the act of calling on the Buddha's name with a pure heart. With this act, a person invokes the power of Amitabha Buddha's compassion and connects to the promise of the Pure Land.

While the recitation of the *nembutsu* grows out of the ancient Indian practice of meditation at the moment of death, it also, like *The Tibetan Book of the Dead*, has a strong connection with meditation that focuses the mind in moments of danger or discouragement in the midst of life. I have heard a modern priest in one of the Buddhist Churches of America say that the most important thing young members of his community should take with them as they head out into the world is the *nembutsu*. He was thinking of the *nembutsu* not simply as a way to call on Amitabha's compassion in order to die in peace but as a way of being sustained by Amitabha's compassion in this life. The shift of focus from the moment of death to the process of life has deep roots in Japanese tradition and carries with it a shift in the understanding of the Pure Land itself. The priest Ryoyo in 1385 said that

> the ordinary conception of the soul's being transported to Paradise and born there was merely a figure of speech . . . the fact being that neither Amida, nor the sainted beings, nor the "nine ranks" are to be conceived as existing "over there" at all, because the Pure Land is the ultimate and absolute reality, and that is everywhere, so that we may be identified with it right here where we are.[5]

This shift of attention from the Pure Land as a reality that exists after life to an experience that can be found within life can also be found in the work of Shinran, one of the most authoritative and radical of Pure Land thinkers. Shinran understood the traditional concept of Amitabha's appearance by the bed at the moment of death as another way of saying that Amitabha welcomes us home in this life. Here we once again find ourselves in the presence of a teaching about death that becomes a vehicle for strengthening and enriching a person's experience of this world.

## ZEN POEMS ABOUT
## THE MOMENT OF DEATH

Another fascinating Buddhist tradition associated with the moment of death is the Japanese Zen practice of composing a verse to express one's state of mind at the moment when one is taking leave from this world. Some of the poems grew out of the violent world of the samurai, where death could often come quite swiftly and a warrior could be compelled by his sense of honor to die at his own hand rather than accept the defeat of the lord he was pledged to defend.

One such poem, written just as the warrior was about to commit suicide, speaks eloquently of the Buddhist ideal of wisdom and calm in the midst of suffering:

> The sharp-edged sword, unsheathed,
> Cuts through the void—
> Within the raging fire
> A cool wind blows.[6]

Here the sword that is about to bring the samurai's death is taken as a reflection of the ancient Buddhist symbol of the sword of wisdom, which cuts through the illusions of this world. The image of the raging fire is an ancient Buddhist image of the sufferings of life, which are cooled by the Buddha's wisdom.

Other poems speak of the experiences of this world as if they were a dream and of death as a moment of awakening:

> Throughout the frosty night
> I lay awake. When morning bells
> rang out, my heart grew clear—
> upon this fleeting dream-world
> dawn is waking.[7]

The movement of thought in these poems seems almost the reverse of the movement that characterized the tradition of death meditation in the *Tibetan Book of the Dead* and the texts of the Pure Land. There the focus on death and the meditations that accompanied it came first and were then appropriated as guides for the living. Here we see the entire discipline of detachment and concentration that characterizes a person's life being focused in a few short, poetic lines on the moment of death.

It is not surprising that there was a movement within the tradition of "death poems" that attempted to reverse the process and see all of a person's life (and all of a person's poetry) as expressing an awareness of death. Sometimes this was done by writing satirical poems that mocked conventional concerns for death. The poet Sengai, for example, was once visited by a man who told the poet that he had lost his will to live. Sengai wrote:

> If your time to die has come
> and you die—very well!
> If your time to die has come
> and you don't—
> all the better.[8]

Perhaps the most telling response, however, was not to mock a person's concern for death but simply to refuse to draw a line between the poems that were intended for the moment of death and the poems that were intended to express attitudes toward life itself. When the great poet Basho lay on his deathbed and his pupils hinted that he ought to leave a death poem, he said that any of his poems could be considered an appropriate meditation on death. Basho was a great traveler and had a remarkable ability to capture his experience of melancholy when he took leave from a place that he loved, as in the poem that starts his famous *Narrow Road to the Deep North*:

> Behind this door
> Now buried in deep grass,
> A different generation will celebrate
> The Festival of the Dolls.[9]

The remnants of the armor of a long-dead warrior could elicit in Basho the same sense of melancholy:

> I am awe-struck
> To hear a cricket singing
> Underneath the dark cavity
> Of an old helmet.[10]

It is easy to understand why Basho would have deferred the request for a special poem at the moment of his death when so much of his poetic life had been a celebration and commemoration of the fleeting quality of life and the presence of life in the midst of death.

## CONCLUSION

Basho's poetic insight shared a deep kinship with the traditions of *The Tibetan Book of the Dead* and Pure Land Buddhism, and this was a kinship that all three shared with the story of Siddhartha Gautama himself. Like Siddhartha Gautama, all three were concerned with death. In one way or another, they taught people to face death squarely, to be freed from its terrors, and to accept its presence as part of life. They refused to separate themselves from the experience of death or to treat death as something that lay only at the end of life.

I said earlier that Buddhists insist that a wise attitude toward life involves a graceful acceptance of the death that comes in the midst of each passing moment and allows each moment to become new. I also said that one of the most important things Buddhists do is prepare for death. That is true, but it is only part of the truth. It is just as true to say that Buddhists prepare to live, and their meditation on death is a crucial part of their preparation to be fully alive.

## NOTES

1. Detlef Ingo Lauf, *Secret Doctrines of The Tibetan Book of the Dead,* trans. Graham Parkes (Boulder, Colo.: Shambhala, 1977), 82.

2. Francesca Fremantle and Chogyam Trungpa, trans., *The Tibetan Book of the Dead: The Great Liberation through Hearing in the Bardo* (Boulder, Colo.: Shambhala, 1975), 37.

3. Ibid., 42.

4. Carl B. Becker, *Breaking the Circle: Death and the Afterlife in Buddhism* (Carbondale: Southern Illinois University Press, 1993), 70.

5. Cited in ibid., 72.

6. In Yoel Hoffman, *Japanese Death Poems Written by Zen Monks and Haiku Poets on the Verge of Death* (Rutland, Vt.: Charles E. Tuttle Co., 1986), 51.

7. Ibid., 67.

8. Sengai, in ibid., 74.

9. Basho, *The Narrow Road to the Deep North and Other Travel Sketches* (Harmondsworth, Middlesex: Penguin Books, 1966), 98.

10. Ibid., 134.

## STUDY QUESTIONS

1. What is the definition of *samsara?* What is the goal of the Buddhist in relation to samsara?
2. What is *The Tibetan Book of the Dead?* What is the book's function as a ritual guide book? Be specific.
3. What are the stages of the journey of the dead as described by *The Tibetan Book of the Dead?*
4. What are three ways in which *The Tibetan Book of the Dead* functions as a text for the living? Speculate—Do you think that all religious ritual that concerns the dead may also concern the living? Explain your answer.
5. What is the Pure Land? To what religious idea from your own tradition might you relate the Buddhist idea of the Pure Land? List their similarities. How does the Buddhist concept of the afterlife differ from your tradition's?
6. What are three functions of the Buddhists' poems about death? Do you sense fear or courage in these poems? Explain your answer.

## REFERENCES

Basho. *The Narrow Road to the Deep North and Other Travel Sketches.* Harmondsworth, Middlesex: Penguin Books, 1966.

Becker, Carl B. *Breaking the Circle: Death and the Afterlife in Buddhism.* Carbondale: Southern Illinois University Press, 1993.

Evans-Wentz, W. Y. *The Tibetan Book of the Dead.* 1927; 3d ed., London: Oxford University Press, 1957.

Fremantle, Francesca, and Chogyam Trungpa, trans. *The Tibetan Book of the Dead: The Great Liberation through Hearing in the Bardo.* Boulder, Colo.: Shambhala, 1975.

Hoffmann, Yoel. *Japanese Death Poems Written by Zen Monks and Haiku Poets on the Verge of Death.* Rutland, Vt.: Charles E. Tuttle Co., 1986.

Lauf, Detlef Ingo. *Secret Doctrines of the Tibetan Book of the Dead.* Translated by Graham Parkes. Boulder, Colo.: Shambhala, 1977.

# Conclusion

## WILLIAM SCOTT GREEN

---

# Diversity and Tolerance: Religion and American Pluralism

### "YOU DEMONIZE US ... "

In midwinter 1995, a large and active Muslim community in the American midwest gathered at its local mosque for a daylong conference on the image of Islam in the American media. The meeting was filled with presentations by a panel of visiting scholars, educators, and journalists. Each presentation was followed by a vigorous group discussion. The audience's comments and questions revealed the community's anxiety about the status of Muslims as minority newcomers in American society. Their intensity showed that they understood that much is at stake in how they and their religion are perceived by the larger American public. In particular, the group expressed alarm about the impact of Christian television evangelism on the public perception of Muslims and Islam.

In the discussion that followed the third presentation, a man in the audience rose. He spoke with courtesy and firmness. "I am an evangelical Christian," he declared, "and I have many Muslim friends, people I admire and like very much. But I am here to tell you that we Christians have a right to preach our religion, to declare what we believe to be the truth, and we can do it in airports, on television, on the radio, and in other public places. We have a right to seek converts and to tell people our belief that their salvation depends on their believing in Jesus as their savior, on their becoming Christians."

The room fell silent. The audience and the panelists turned to the *imam*, a sophisticated Egyptian who is the community's religious leader and teacher. With grace, generosity, and a smile, he replied, "We do not require such teaching, for we are already Christians." With this remark, the *imam* was asserting the Muslim belief that Muhammad is the last, or "seal," of God's prophets in a chain of prophecy that includes Abraham, Moses, and Jesus. Islam teaches that Muhammad came to correct the Jewish and Christian misunderstandings of the true prophetic teaching that was transmitted in this chain. Because Islam lays claim to prophets before Muhammad, Abraham, Moses, and Jesus are part of the Islamic tradition.

A woman wearing a traditional Muslim headcover, an accomplished and experienced physician, rose to speak. Her remarks to her Christian neighbor were passionate and pointed. "You do not realize the impact of your teachings," she said. "Your words have real consequences. Many patients who come to my office tell me what they have learned about Islam from Christian evangelists. They say that the Qur'an has no teaching about love, that Islam has no belief in charity. These things are wrong." She looked across the room at her Christian conversation partner. "You demonize us with these teachings," she said.

I witnessed this encounter and participated in the conversations that followed. Even if I have missed some of the exact words, I believe I have captured the vigor and the point of what was said and what was meant. These exchanges exhibit both the problems and the promise of America's great experiment in religious freedom and religious pluralism. They show how religion can divide American society and how dealing with religious difference is increasingly a part of everyday life.

## RELIGION AND DIVERSITY

One of the most important features of modern American life in the 1980s and 1990s is the politics of diversity. The intense debates on such issues as affirmative action, the Equal Rights Amendment to the Constitution, and bilingual education—among many others—show that extending equality and fairness to all of American society remains a serious challenge. During the eighties and nineties various cultural and national groups found their voices and asserted the value of their distinctive heritages in American society. People use many terms to describe these developments: political correctness, multiculturalism, identity politics, or the politics of recognition. But whichever label we select, learning how to live with—and therefore to make sense of—people who in fundamental ways are not like us (whoever we are!) is a central concern of American life.

The political struggles over cultural diversity have centered primarily in the arenas of gender, ethnicity, sexual orientation, and national origin.

Religion has been an inconsistent player in most of these debates. Some religious groups have been vocal on issues of sexual orientation and abortion, but religion has been relatively quiet on other questions concerning gender equity, ethnicity, and national origin. Religion's role in America's politics of diversity is uncertain partly because the First Amendment to the Constitution gives Americans the freedom to practice their religion. The separation of church and state also leads most Americans to regard religion as essentially a private matter and therefore as something that falls outside our public debates about dealing with difference. But this view may be mistaken. Alexis de Tocqueville, a nineteenth-century French intellectual who visited America and wrote insightfully about American society, asserted that, "In the United States, religion exercises but little influence upon the laws and upon the details of public opinion; but it directs the customs of the community, and by regulating domestic life, it regulates the state."[1] He thus points to a connection between our private lives and our public policy and claims that the latter cannot—and does not—ignore the former. I would like to apply that insight in a particular way and offer two reasons that religion should be an important component of America's national debate about difference.

First, religion shapes American pluralism in distinctive ways. Second, religion, particularly Western religion, has supplied some of the most durable models of difference our society uses. Let us take these up in turn.

## RELIGION AND AMERICAN PLURALISM

The American doctrine of freedom of religion grounds and in many ways justifies American pluralism. The First Amendment guarantees that individual Americans have the right to believe what they want to believe, and it allows communities, within some limits, to live out those beliefs. Therefore, religious liberty implies the freedom, and perhaps the right, of communities to work to survive, to preserve their distinction. Whatever its initial intent (which may have been limited to Protestant denominations) the First Amendment's restriction of government control over religion places difference—both individual and collective—at the heart of America's character.

The First Amendment guarantees that America will have more than one religion. It affirms that religion is a legitimate, legally protected form of difference in American society. Americans are supposed to differ from one another religiously. We do not all have to be the same. The First Amendment assumes that difference is a plus rather than a minus for our national life. It is no exaggeration to suggest that America's ability to see difference as a social benefit comes from our Constitution's commitment to religious freedom. To be sure, Americans were different from one another before there was a Constitution. But the First Amendment shapes a distinctive American attitude toward diversity by depicting difference as a cultural good, as something to be appreciated, defended, and maintained. Because of our belief in the worth of religious difference, pluralism—particularly on questions of value—has come to characterize our national life. In important ways, America's diversity is justified by the freedom of religion. In America, whatever else religion is about, it is about the freedom to be different.

## RELIGION AS A MODEL
## FOR DIFFERENCE

Broadly speaking, our attitudes about people who are unlike us come from culture rather than nature. The way we react to those who are different from us is more something we learn and get used to than something we are born with. Religion should play a leading part in America's national discussion about difference because many of our most persistent mental habits and social practices for dealing with difference come from religion. In the West—in Europe and the United States—religion has been one of the major sources of teaching about how we should think of and behave toward those who are unlike us or who disagree with us.

Let us look at one of the most enduring Western patterns of otherness: the relationship between Judaism and Christianity. These two religions—in very different ways, to be sure—are defining components of Western civilization. In its various forms, Christianity has dominated Western culture; since the fourth century it has been the religion of the majority and the mainstream. By contrast, Judaism, from which Christianity emerged, has been the quintessential religion of the minority and the periphery. Since ancient times, these two religions have been in almost constant disagreement over basic ideas, and the relationship between them has been at best uneasy and usually hostile. Although there are exceptions, for most of Western history, Jews have been cast as the quintessential outsiders of Western culture because of their non-acceptance of Christianity. Christian-Jewish relations thus constitute a longstanding Western pattern of how the majority treats a dissenting minority. This is one way religion supplies models of otherness that shape our society in serious ways.

A very influential model of difference that emerges from Jewish-Christian relations is one we can call "otherness by exclusion." This is a model in which otherness is conceived not in terms of mutuality and reciprocity, but in terms of singularity. It is a model in which difference is cast in terms of negation and denial of the other. It is a model that says, "me, not you," or "us, not them." In its most extreme form, it says, "For me to live, you must die." As it is manifest historically in the encounter of Judaism and Christianity, the model of "otherness by exclusion" is one of the most painful elements in the Jewish-Christian encounter. It has been a foundation stone—some might say a stumbling block—in religious exchanges between Jews and Christians since the first century.

The model of "otherness by exclusion" is a familiar part of biblical and other ancient Jewish and Christian writings. Some forms of the idea of Israel as God's chosen people—the idea that God has spoken only to a single people—can be said to illustrate the model. The Christian doctrine of supersession represents it as well. That doctrine holds that Christianity has replaced or superseded Judaism because Christianity is right and Judaism is wrong. The depiction of difference in the model of "otherness by exclusion" has become so basic a part of Western consciousness that many of us have adjusted to it, absorbed it, and can hear it without flinching. The price of our accommodation to the model of otherness by exclusion is evident in a range of historical and contemporary settings. Because we are used to this model, we can apply it unwittingly and unawares. As the novelist David Grossman writes, in a somewhat different context, "We are social creatures . . . and even when we are alone we create internal relationships with different parts of ourselves. And when we accustom ourselves to relations like those between master and slave, that division is stamped within us as well. It suddenly becomes a possible model for our relations with our friends."[2] Likewise, when we accustom ourselves to the model of "otherness by exclusion," it becomes a model for our relations to others in a variety of circumstances, not merely in religion. This model of difference is a longstanding part of the Western religious and cultural heritage, and it is a major influence on the form—indeed, the possibility—of Western pluralism. To understand the nature and limitations of our pluralism, we need to understand how the model works. How shall we make sense of it?

To begin, we have an intellectual responsibility neither to condemn this model nor apologize for it. Dismissing it will not help us to understand it. If religion really is at the heart of American pluralism, then the study of religion will expose the stark barriers of irreconcilable difference—in belief, behavior, values, and worldviews—that make pluralism both necessary and difficult. Religious difference is a particular challenge because religion is a powerful force in peoples' lives. The appeal and persistence of religions lie partially, if not principally, in their conviction of the fundamental correctness of their vision of reality, which both shapes and is generated by their adherents' experience in the world. Religions are compelling because of their affirmations of certitude and truth, because of their refusal to compromise on basic convictions, and because of the extent of their claims on the human person. Unlike other aspects of culture—politics, philosophy, economics, gender identity, or ethnicity, for example—religion tends to extend its reach, to be comprehensive in scope. Religion exhibits enormous range of expression. It attacks all the senses—not only in speech and writing but also in art, music, and dance, in smell and taste, in ethics, sexuality, and intellect. Most religions have cosmologies and eschatologies, theories of nature, birth, gender, marriage, suffering, and death. Political systems, social ideologies, or philosophies rarely have such a reach or exhibit religion's capacity to make definitive demands on the total human being. Americans usually prefer to focus on the agreements between religions rather than on disputes. But attention to the nature of religion teaches us that the differences among them matter very much and will not dissolve or disappear. That is why understanding religious models of difference is important to understanding pluralism.

What, then, is at stake in the model of "otherness by exclusion"? Which factors brought it about and sustain it? To begin to answer these questions, we need to take a brief historical trip back into time. In the year 586 B.C.E., the Babylonian Empire defeated the Kingdom of Judah in the land of Israel and destroyed the holy Temple in Jerusalem, the central place of Israel's worship of God. The Babylonian conquerors took substantial portions of the Israelite population—including the priests of the Temple, the religious elite—into exile. Some years later, in 540 B.C.E., the Persian emperor Cyrus conquered Babylon, and in 538 B.C.E. Cyrus issued an edict that allowed the exiled Jews to return to their native land.

The years 538–333 B.C.E., known as the Persian period, were decisive in the development of Western religion. The model of otherness by exclusion emerges with clarity in the Persian period. The Babylonian exile, which began with the destruction of the Jerusalem Temple in 587–86 B.C.E. and forced the upper echelons of Israelite society to migrate from the land of Israel to Babylon, was a time of decisive transition in which the exiles' social organization, type of leadership, and religious practice underwent significant alteration. Living in a land and a culture of a foreign power forced the Israelites to change their way of living to adapt to a dramatic new circumstance. The exile was a frightening and traumatic experience. The parts of the Bible that were written during the exile are preoccupied with the theme of suffering. The Israelites faced cultural death and had to devise strategies to survive. They had three options for resistance: military, political, and cultural. Counseled by their prophets, particularly by Jeremiah, the exiles chose to resist culturally but to forge useful political relations with the ruling powers. They built strong cultural boundaries between themselves and their non-Israelite neighbors and transformed elements of their pre-exilic heritage into symbols of their identity. In this period, the concept of Israel's holiness increasingly became identified with group distinctiveness and separation. During this era, observance of the Sabbath appears to have become freshly important. Likewise, prohibitions against intermarriage and concern with purity rules and food taboos loom large.[3]

The identification of separation with holiness has self-evident and far-reaching consequences for our model. The strategy of survival devised by the exiles was successful—the Bible is proof of its effectiveness[4]—and it assumes and responds to a circumstance of nearly total political powerlessness. The Israelites' strategy makes resistance to oppression internal rather than external and tries to make the ruling powers work to the advantage of the internal culture.

In exile, the Israelites adapted their religion to keep from disappearing, to prevent cultural death. But later on the context changed, and the strategies for survival were applied in a new setting and took on a new meaning. As already noted, in 538 B.C.E., nearly a half century after the exile began, the Persian emperor Cyrus, who had conquered Babylon the year before, issued an edict allowing the Jews to return to their native land to rebuild their destroyed Temple. Under a sequence of leaders—Zerubbabel, Nehemiah, and Ezra—and as clients of the Persian emperor, some Jews returned home to a land in which most of them had never lived, and they imported the religion of separation and holiness they had so brilliantly crafted during an exile of powerlessness. But now the context was different, both for them and their religion.

First, there was a new cast of characters. After the return to the land of Israel, the returnees' ideology of protection and cultural maintenance—developed to protect them from real aliens in Babylonia—was not applied to the Israelites' cousins, so to speak, people who did not share their experience of exile and deprivation, who remained at home. Those people, whom the Bible calls "the people of the Land," claimed to be Israel just as the returnees did.

Second, the returnees' political situation had changed. They had more power at home than they did in exile. More power, but not real power. The returning exiles, as well as "the people of the Land," were still colonized, still dependent on the Persians. In effect, there were now two different Israels, each claiming to be the true Israel. Each Israel had to rely on the colonial power to legitimate the group's status and authenticity as Israel. The Persians apparently practiced "ethnic collectivization," and membership in "ethnically distinct groups" may have determined possession of land and property.[5] If so, then getting the Persians' endorsement carried material benefits, as well as social and political legitimacy.

This context establishes a new setting for the application of the model of "otherness by exclusion," a setting very different from the exile itself. The following passage from Ezra 4:1–3, whatever the historicity of its specifics, illustrates the changes clearly:

> When the adversaries of Judah and Benjamin heard that the returned exiles were building a temple to the LORD, the God of Israel, they approached Zerubbabel and the heads of the families and said to them, "Let us build with you, for we worship your God as you do, and we have been sacrificing to him ever since the days of King Esarhaddon of Assyria, who brought us here. But Zerubbabel, Jeshua, and the rest of the heads of families in Israel said to them, "You shall have no part with us in building a house to our God; but we alone will build to the LORD, the God of Israel, as King Cyrus of Persia has commanded us."[6]

All the elements of the model of "otherness by exclusion" are here. The colonial backdrop is explicit. The returnees alone will build God's temple, which they do with the authority of the pagan king. Indeed, the passage suggests a direct connection between legitimacy in the Lord's house and the emperor's support.[7] We can learn from this passage that "otherness by exclusion" is a response to imperial domination, to uncertain legitimacy, to lack of power. In the Bible, the model is aimed internally, not externally, at or against others who claim to be Israel. Away from home, the religion of holiness and separation protected Israel's exiles from becoming culturally similar to those who were different. At home, in the land of Israel, the same religion allowed them to declare themselves different from those who were culturally similar to them.

The Persian period—and its contexts of exile and imperialism—is pivotal for understanding basic patterns of thought and action in the model of "otherness by exclusion." But the imperialism did not end with the Persians. Far from it. We often fail to appreciate—though we frequently acknowledge—the depth and persistence of a colonial situation and the way it has shaped the basic texts of Western religion. Both Judaism and Christianity are religions invented and developed in contexts of political weakness, if not outright powerlessness. With the exception of the brief period of the Maccabees (164–63 B.C.E.), the land of Israel was colonized continuously from 587–86 B.C.E. through the production of the Palestinian Talmud in the fourth century—first by the Babylonians, then by the Persians, then by the successors to Alexander the Great, then by the Romans. This means that the scriptures of Judaism and Christianity (the Hebrew Bible and the New Testament) and other important postbiblical Jewish and Christian writings were produced, and made sense, in a context in which their authors had circumscribed and limited control over their own destiny and significant portions of their lives. Thus, the model of "otherness by exclusion" was a major force that shaped intragroup relations among Jews and among Christians and that defined relations between Jews and Christians under imperial rule. In the early centuries of Judaism and Christianity within a context of political weakness—or perceived weakness—when Jews and Christians disagreed among themselves or with one another religiously, perhaps the strongest tendency, though not the only one, was mutual exclusion rather than negotiation.

"Otherness by exclusion" is evident, for example, in the way some Dead Sea scrolls denouce their authors' enemies, the "defiled" priests of the Jerusalem Temple. We also encounter it in an early rabbinic document, the Tosefta, Tractate Hullin 2:20–21, in a savage rabbinic condemnation of the so-called *minim*, a term translated as "sectarians," which some take to be Christians:

> The sacrifice of a *min* is idolatry. Their bread is the bread of a Samaritan, and their wine is deemed the wine of idolatry, and their produce is deemed wholly untithed, and their books are deemed magical books, and their children are *mamzerim* [illegitimate]. People should not sell anything to them or buy anything from them. And they should not take wives from them nor give children in marriage to them. And they should not teach their sons a craft. And they should not seek either financial or medical assistance from them.

Whether or not the *minim* were Christians is less important than the fact that rabbinic literature describes them as wearing phylacteries, offering sacrifices, and reading and writing Torah.[8] Early rabbis, like the returned exiles, had to prove their legitimacy now to Roman imperial power, and they drew sharp, exclusionary boundaries around those who resembled them too closely.

Likewise, the model of "otherness by exclusion" characterizes much of early Christian as well as Jewish literature. It is apparent, for instance, in the undeserved scorn the Gospel of Matthew heaps on its hated "scribes and Pharisees." It can also be seen in the writings of Paul, the Letter to the Hebrews, and other New Testament books. The pattern is applied with special vigor in the writings of early Church Fathers, particularly of Melito of Sardis (d. 190 C.E.), who accused the Jews of deicide, that is, of killing God, and of John Chrysostom (347–407 C.E.), a preacher in Antioch and later Bishop of Constantinople. In these two cases in particular, the heat of the polemic is a function of too much political weakness and too much similarity. In Sardis, where Melito wrote, the Jews were politically powerful, the owners of a massive urban synagogue and members of the town council. Melito was a figure, so far as we can tell, of no import at all. Perhaps his very insignificance inflamed his rhetoric. Likewise Chrysostom—his sermons reached a feverish and unhealthy pitch largely because he feared the influence of the synagogue on his congregants. To be sure, once the Roman Empire became Christian, the words of Matthew, Melito, and Chrysostom acquired a power their authors perhaps never intended, with ugly consequences for the Jews.

All these examples suggest that to understand the conflict between these two religions, the similarities between them are of more consequence than the differences. As religion scholar Jonathan Smith has recently written:

> The issue of difference as a mode of both culturally encoding and decoding, of maintaining and relativizing internal as well as external distinctions, raises . . . the observation that, rather than the remote "other" being perceived as problematic and/or dangerous, it is the proximate "other," the near neighbor, who is most troublesome. That is to say, while difference or "otherness" may be perceived as being LIKE-US or NOT-LIKE-US, it becomes most problematic when it is TOO-MUCH-LIKE-US or when it claims to BE-US. It is here that the urgency of theories of the "other" emerges, called forth not so much by a requirement to place difference, but rather by an effort to situate ourselves. This, then, is not a matter of the "far," but preeminently of the "near." The deepest intellectual issues are not based upon perceptions of alterity, but, rather, of similarity, at times, even, of identity.[9]

To proximity—whether cultural or geographic—we must also add the variable of political power, the power of self-control, because the model of "otherness by exclusion" began in weakness and ended in unequal power relations. This model has been so successful that its patterns of perception and discourse of exclusion have persisted even when the circumstances of origination have changed drastically. "Otherness by exclusion" is deeply embedded in—and perhaps in some basic way characteristic of—the religions of the West, and it is not likely to go away. By understanding the kinds of forces that brought the model about and that keep it going, we can get a better picture of the kind of pluralism we need to develop and to nurture the Constitution's vision of religious freedom in America.

## EPILOGUE

Pluralism is not simply a matter of the acceptance of mere difference; it requires the tolerance of irreconcilable difference. What makes pluralism plural is the brute fact that, in the end, we are not going to change one another very much. American culture long ago renounced the possibility that irreconcilable differences would lead to social and political divorce. The Muslim–Christian exchange with which this article began is but one example of the kinds of conversations that increasingly will mark American life in the future. The multiplicity of religions in a context of freedom poses fresh challenges for all religions and creates new realities that traditional religious sources may not have contemplated. The religions of America will have to learn more about one another—and be committed to knowing and telling the truth about one another—for religious pluralism to allow all religions to flourish as they will.

American democratic pluralism requires a public that can respect difference. But we cannot respect what we cannot understand, and, more important, we destroy our common bonds as Americans if we judge one another without understanding. And invariably we do judge one another. Respect for difference does not come naturally; it has to be taught, and it has to be learned. Genuine tolerance is not only an acquired skill; it is also an acquired taste. Religion is at the core of American pluralism and must support and protect a rich American heritage of toleration.[10]

## NOTES

1. Cited in Isaac Kramnick and R. Laurence Moore, "Is the U.S. Constitution Godless," *Chronicle of Higher Education,* March 29, 1996, A68.

2. David Grossman, *The Yellow Wind* (New York: Delta, 1988), 40.

3. For a full account of the religious importance of the exile, see Daniel L. Smith, *The Religion of the Landless* (Bloomington: Meyer-Stone Books, 1989).

4. Smith, ibid, makes this point very effectively.

5. Kenneth Hoglund, "The Achaemenid Context," in Philip R. Davies, ed., *Second Temple Studies: 1. The Persian Period* (Sheffield: Sheffield Academic Press, 1991), 54–72.

6. For a discussion of the translation of this verse, see Joseph Blenkinsopp, "Temple and Society in Achaemenid Judah, in Philip R. Davies, ed., *Second Temple Studies: 1. The Persian Period* (Sheffield: Sheffield Academic Press, 1991), 22–52.

7. See Blenkinsopp, ibid, 39–40, and Robert P. Carroll, "Israel, History of (Post Monarchic Period)," *Anchor Bible Dictionary*, vol. 3 (New York: Doubleday, 1993), 567–76.

8. W. S. Green, "Otherness Within: Toward a Theory of Difference in Rabbinic Judaism," in J. Neusner, ed., *To See Ourselves as Others See Us* (Chico: Scholars Press, 1985), 49–70.

9. Jonathan Z. Smith, "Differential Equations: On Constructing the Other," The University Lecture in Religion, Arizona State University, 1992.

10. My thanks go to Douglas R. Brooks, Th. Emil Homerin, Ray L. Hart, Charles Winquist, Gerald Gamm, Dana Rittenhouse, and Julie Nowak for help and stimulation. I am also grateful to Stephanie Egnotovich for both editorial acumen and patience. Substantial portions of this chapter appeared in a somewhat different form in W. S. Green, "The Difference Religion Makes," *Journal of the American Academy of Religion*, 62/4 (winter 1994): 1191–1207.

## STUDY QUESTIONS

1. What does the First Amendment say about religious belief?
2. What are the author's two reasons for suggesting that religion should be a part of America's debate about difference? Do you agree? Do you think that the author's view conflicts with the First Amendment? Why? Why not?
3. What does the author mean by "otherness by exclusion"? Give concrete examples of this idea at work?
4. What is the Christian doctrine of "supersession?" Is this depiction of difference conducive to tolerance? Why? Why not? Explain your answer.
5. What three options of resistance were available to the Israelites during the Persian exile? Are these options viable today when different religious communities clash? Explain your answer.
6. In talking about excluding because of difference, why is it equally important to talk about the similarities between two religions? Develop your answer with specific examples.
7. What are the factors that can lead to hostility between religions?

# Index